SURVIVAL

OF THE

PRETTIEST:

the gender, mental health, & sexualization crisis as told by a teenager

Thank you SO much!! :)

ASHLEY OLAFSEN

This Book Belongs To:

_____

If Lost, Please Contact:

_____

Dedication
Mom and Dad -
Thank you for your selflessness.
I am forever grateful and so, so blessed that you are my parents.
Love, Ashley

Table of Contents

INTRODUCTION

****

Opening Quote:

"It is my thesis that the core of the problem for young women today is not sexual but a problem of identity - a stunting or evasion of growth that is perpetuated by the feminine mystique. It is my thesis that as the Victorian culture did not permit women to accept or gratify their basic sexual needs, our culture does not permit women to accept or gratify their basic need to grow and fulfill their potentialities as human beings, a need which is not solely defined by their sexual role."

- The Feminine Mystique, 1963

****

Introduction & Why I'm Writing This Book

My story is similar to many kids and teenagers growing up today - perhaps even yours. I've struggled with self-esteem, body image, expectations, media, popularity, friendships, pressure, and unhealthy relationships. I have been down on myself and afraid to get help, I've been whole heartedly confused on sex and sexualization before, and I have gossiped as well as been gossiped about.

I used to be an insecure, miserable, ashamed mess who wouldn't speak up in class for fear of judgment. One time, I sat next to a 'popular' boy and *apologized to him,* because I really believed that I was not worthy of sitting next to him. My potential was being wasted - my energy was spent on hating myself, my focus was spent on rearranging my body so no one would see my thighs, and my concentration was used on being invisible. I was holding myself back.

And so were my friends. I have watched every single one of my smart and amazing friends suffer thanks to poor body image and low self-esteem. I have watched tons of my friends refuse to get help, despite needing it badly. I have watched girls get asked for nudes time after time, and I see them get called names like 'slut' and 'whore' when they **refuse**. I have seen friends affected by racial stereotypes and slurs. I have seen friends go through abusive relationships, and I know girls who have been raped and sexually assaulted. I have watched bright, bubbly, amazing people lose their voices and give into the pressure that comes with growing up today. Myself included.

It may have taken me a while, but I have rediscovered my voice. And I would like to share it with you.

When I was 15, I decided to do something about all of the problems my friends and I were facing. So on May 17th, 2013 I gave my first ever self-confidence workshop, alongside three of my best friends. Our goal was to help eighth grade girls by sharing our own personal stories about body image, popularity, media, and so much more. During the workshop, we watched videos, did activities, and had a small group discussion.

Despite the fact that I was supposed to be the one inspiring others, I ended up being moved to tears by the whole thing. I literally could not believe how much energy, passion, and emotion I was filled with!

My name is Ashley Olafsen, and on June 4th 2013, God let me know my purpose. I knew in my heart that I had to keep giving self-confidence workshops, and I had to stay on this path - whatever the path was going to end up being. In my soul, I *knew that this was God's plan for me, and that He would be on my side*.

So, over the past two years, I have become a self-confident, self-actualized, driven and capable individual. As I edit this part, I am eighteen years old and I have given fifteen self-confidence/empowerment workshops to middle and high school students all across Massachusetts (my home state), I have given six major speeches - including one TEDx and one in Atlanta (!), I am my class Vice President, I send out a weekly online newsletter with hundreds of subscribers, I won 'most likely to succeed', I was the only student who had the honor of winning the 'Principal's Leadership Award', I am writing a book, I am a cofounder of a company, AND I'm co running a summer program this year all on body image, media, empowerment, and more!!

I did a complete flip and went from being a scared, insecure little girl to a courageous female who is speaking up about important issues. **Part of the reason why I am able to live up to my full potential is because I have self-confidence. And THAT'S why I am writing this book.**

I am writing this book because I know that <u>self-confidence unlocks potential.</u> Self-confidence played a role in transforming me into the person that I am today.

<u>Sadly, there is a lot of potential being wasted.</u> There are many roadblocks getting in the way of reaching our full potentials. Personally, I was held back by a limiting beauty standard, insecurities, a need to be liked by boys, and a fear of what would happen if I was truly myself. The roadblocks are different for everyone, and depend greatly on your social identities.

What are some things that are holding you back from reaching your full potential?

_____

_____

_____

This book is my attempt to tackle those roadblocks, and to empower you to reach your full potentials. **All of you have potential to do great and big things.** For a lot of you though, I'm assuming your potential is a little bit hidden. My potential was always hidden - no one except for me, barely, knew that I was capable of doing things like I'm doing. My grades were always average, I sucked at sports, and I didn't come off as this really remarkable student who was going to change the world. But when I became confident, my pent up potential became unlocked. Because that's what self-confidence does. **I know that every single one of you has potential to do amazing things and I will do my best to help you become a confident individual. After all, confidence unlocks potential.**

So let's talk a little bit about how this book is going to work...

****

How the Book Works

This book will be unlike anything you've ever read before. I hope that you will become more aware, more confident, and more vocal after reading Survival of the Prettiest.

I'm going to write this book by discussing some of the current problems teenagers and children are facing today, and after I'll propose solutions. I'll also share my own stories, and back them up with studies and references to add validity! I'll end each chapter by giving you a couple of reflection questions.

As for social media, if you like the book or a line of the book or anything about Survival of the Prettiest, join the conversation by tweeting, instagraming, tumblring (does that even work??), facebooking (again a stretch, I know), etc. pictures and quotes from the book. Make sure to hashtag it #SurvivalOfThePrettiest so that way I can see it and like or favorite it. Additionally, share your own story, your own thoughts, pictures, videos, etc. under those hashtags to create a large conversation & we will have a wonderful place for ideas to be fostered! You can also tag it #jointheMOVEment, because my best friend Lexie and I have started a MOVEment (Motivate. Overcome. Value. Empower.) that you're all invited to join!

Also, I want this book to essentially be like an empowerment workshop, where you get to be part of the experience! So, I'm writing this in a sort of 'workbook form'. I'm going to ask you a bunch of questions and leave spaces for you to fill in your thoughts and opinions. **Read this book with a pen in hand and mark down your thoughts! Underline what is important to you, and write your own personal notes on the sides of this book. That is super, super important, so if you haven't already, go grab a pen!**

****

What This Book is Even About

The book is split into five main sections. Here is a little bit of what you should expect from each:

Section One - Introduction: This is what you're reading now! I'm basically introducing myself, my motivation, the book, why this book matters, and a few other notes.

Section Two - Femininity, Competition & Masculinity: I discuss how gendered expectations, perpetuated by the media, are having destructive implications on the lives of children, teenagers, and more. As a result of these dangerous and foolish expectations, we are being held back from reaching our full potentials. This is the longest section, and it's split up into three subsections: Femininity, Competition, and Masculinity.

Section Three - Getting Help: In this section, I talk about how we are held back by mental health stigmas. I explain how the lack of information and understanding is having very powerful and negative consequences for the children, teenagers, and communities of today.

Section Four - Our Contradictory Attitude Towards Sex: Then, I talk about how we collectively fail to address anything intimate in a meaningful way, while accepting endless amounts of sexualization and pornography. I go into detail about how this attitude is creating many problems for today's confused teenagers.

<u>Section Five - Empowerment:</u> This is the shortest section, and I basically talk about what YOU can do to speak up and make a difference, as well as the power of social media.

In 1963, women were being limited by the limiting agreement that women were to exist as housewives only. Betty Friedan wrote, "If women do not put forth, finally, that effort to become all that they have it in them to become, they will forfeit their own humanity. A woman today who has no goal, no purpose, no ambition patterning her days into the future, making her stretch and grow beyond that small score of years". **Today, all individuals are being limited by unhealthy gendered expectations, by mental health stigmas, and by a contradictory attitude to sex.**

****

Why These Issues Matter

At this point, you might be wondering 'But so what? Who cares about a low self-esteem crisis?'
   We should care about the problems teenagers are facing, like low self-esteem, because if more of us reached our full potentials, larger and more pressing problems would be solved - like world hunger.
   A famous psychologist named Abraham Maslow believed that humans were motivated to seek fulfillment. Maslow created something called the 'Hierarchy of Needs'.
   In the 'Hierarchy of Needs', the ideal and most fulfilled state that a person can be in is called 'self-actualization'. Essentially, self-actualization is what happens when a person reaches their full potential. In other words, **self-actualized people are those who are the best versions of themselves possible**, and are working on fulfilling themselves even more!
   The results of actualization are different for each person, as each person reaches their fullest potential in different ways. For some, self-actualization for some could mean creating a play, while for others self-actualization could mean reforming the education system!
   Self-actualization is awesome because self-actualized people are typically ethical, creative, and problem-centered.

Do you know someone that is self-actualized? What are they like?

_____

_____

_____

What would you be like if you were more self-actualized?

_____

_____

_____

_____

What can you do to become more self-actualized?

_____

_____

_____

_____

Unfortunately, the 'Hierarchy of Needs' asserts that in order to reach self-actualization, individuals must have self-esteem. **Without self-confidence (in most cases), an individual cannot truly live up to their full potential and be the best and truest version of themselves possible.**

And <u>this</u> is why it is important we pay attention to things that destroy confidence, and consequently hold us back from reaching our full potentials. ***This* is why it is important to call out our current expectations about gender, our current mental health stigmas, and the current way we talk about sex.**

If we remove unnecessary roadblocks and things that are holding us back, <u>I believe that more individuals could reach self-actualization.</u> And then, if we had more self-actualized people, we would have more people working towards a bright future.

<u>Sadly, we cannot make positive progress in tackling the world's many problems (world hunger, poverty, etc.) if we continue to restrict SO much potential in so many people.</u>

You should care about unhealthy gendered expectations, mental health stigmas, and the foolish way we talk about sex, because changing or removing these will allow many more people to reach their full potentials, and consequently the world to become a much happier place.

Like I said, my transformation was made possible in two short years by confidence... I believe that there are a lot of kids and teenagers out there, who have hidden potential - exactly like I did. While taking into account my privileges, I believe that when the unnecessary expectations that are holding us back are either overcome or removed, anything is possible. *I know because I am testament to that fact.*

****

The Book That Needs to be Written & Other Notes

I am writing this book because there is no other book like this one out there.

At age sixteen, I started researching and reading books to understand more about self-confidence and all of the things that my friends and I were going through.

But after a lot of reading, I became frustrated. Though some books were brilliant and helpful, some were boring and outdated and really hard to get through. And all of them had one thing in common: They were written for everyone but children and teenagers! I couldn't believe it - almost no one was reaching out to the group that needed to learn and hear empowering messages the most!

I'm writing this book because it's the book that needed to be written. This is the book I wish I had when I was younger.

I wanted a book for people my own age, something that I could relate to, and something that was fun and easy to understand. I've also always wanted to write a book. So it looks like both my wishes are coming true. :)

True, I am not an adult or 'professional expert'. But, I've spent my life right here on the frontlines, contributing and being affected by many of the problems I discuss, which has given me personal insight.

In addition to my personal experience, I have spent over two years researching for this book. I have read many books, articles, and studies, and have watched countless videos, talks, documentaries, and more. I've also conducted a survey and a few interviews. During my survey, I was able to collect over a thousand responses from females on various topics and their anonymous quotes will be inserted throughout the book.

That being stated, I write this book from the life perspective of a white, blonde, female who has come from a beautiful town. I understand that not everyone shares my experiences, and in fact that most people don't, and I understand that many won't be able to relate to me. I know my limitations and I won't try to pretend to know what I haven't experienced. Because of this, I have asked my friends to contribute their own stories to fill in my gaps - however, there are still **_many_**, **_many_** gaps that are not filled. I hope that by speaking up I will inspire other individuals of **_all_** backgrounds to share their stories, **so that way there is a truly diverse group of experiences to learn from.**

   Finally, this book is imperfect, and I acknowledge this. My goal was never to write an incredibly in depth book - as I've stated before, there are already books out there like that. **My goal was to write a book on gender, mental health, and sexualization that would simply be a starting point to your education and to get a conversation going.** When I wrote this book I was in high school, and I want it to be known this was written from my _high school perspective_. As I do my final edits, this is clearer to me now more than ever, because my thoughts have changed a great deal. Since I wrote this book, I have taken different classes and I now know much more than I did when I began, and because of that I look forward to creating much more intersectional and inclusive work from my current college aged perspective. That being stated, this book contains the thoughts of a sixteen, seventeen, and eighteen year old girl who did her best and gave it absolutely everything she had. Yes, there is room for improvement and I am aware of that. However, I believe that there is something very genuine and worth sharing from my high school perspective.

****

Thank You

   And before you read any further, I would like to thank you for giving this book a chance - thank you for believing in me :) Believing in someone is very flattering and it is something I think we often underestimate the power of, so thank you very much. I sincerely appreciate it! I hope I don't disappoint you!!!

   Welcome to a life changing journey! Grab a snack, make sure you're hydrated, and have a pen ready to go (you're going to need one)!

With respect,

Ashley Olafsen

FEMINITITY

****

Opening Quote:

"To lose confidence in one's body is to lose confidence in oneself" - <u>The Second Sex</u>, Simone de Beauvoir

"51% of 9 and 10 year-old girls feel better about themselves if they are on a diet" - Journal of the American Dietetic Association

****

Opening Questions:

Has how you identify gender-wise ever held you back? How so?

_____

_____

_____

_____

Have you ever wished you were a different gender than the one you identify with? Why so?

_____

_____

_____

_____

Have you ever been told you couldn't do something because of your gender? How did you respond? How do you wish you responded?

_____

_____

_____

_____

Are gender stereotypes a bad thing?

_____

_____

_____

_____

****

PREFACE

I believe that everyone should be able to live up to their full potentials. Unfortunately, for many, gendered expectations are a barrier that hold individuals back from reaching their full potentials. As individuals across the nation struggle with low self-esteem, poor body image, the pressure to conform, and more, it is evident that expectations about gender are having real life implications on teenagers today. **What we learn about gender affects the way we think and treat ourselves, as well as others.** This section, we're going to talk about gendered expectations, and how that has affected us teenagers.

Before we go any further, I want to make three things clear.

> **1. We (largely) learn how to be boys and girls.**
> **2. We learn how to be boys and girls from our media.**
> **3. The messages we learn about gender stick with us.**

1. **We learn how to act like boys and girls.**

I should start off by letting you know that **we (for the most part) *learn* how to act like boys and girls, based on the expectations that our culture, friends, and family has for us.** Truthfully, males and females actually aren't that altogether different - in fact, we are all pretty similar regardless of gender identity. One woman analyzed 46 meta-analyses on gender, and concluded that "males and females are alike on most— but not all—psychological variables...It is time to consider the costs of overinflated claims of gender differences".

I'd also like to note that ALL individuals learn how to be boys or girls, regardless of their actual gender identity. Therefore, we have a very narrow idea of what gender is and through gender expectations we enforce the idea that there is only two acceptable ways to present oneself.

Moreover, when I say that we learn how to be boys and girls, I am NOT saying that there are no sex differences. There are. BUT, Lise Eliot, author of <u>Pink Brain, Blue Brain</u> writes, **"What I found, after an exhaustive search, was surprisingly little solid evidence of sex differences in children's brains"**. _What she found instead was the influence of culture on our behaviors._

I could go on to cite dozens of studies from her 300 page plus book, but I will instead leave you with a fact: **We, to a large extent, learn how to be boys and girls.** After all, it's not like boys come out of the womb afraid to cry - they literally come out crying. And it's not like girls are born immediately feeling self-conscious of their body - that's largely learned.

Science shows that we humans share much more in common than often like to believe.

2. **We learn how to be boys and girls from our media.**

Thanks to media, gendered expectations exist more powerfully than ever. All ideas, including ideas about gender, can be spread and be reinforced in ways that the world has never seen before. <u>Media matters, and media makes a difference.</u>

A Kaiser Family Foundation Study found that **people ages 8 to 18 spend more time on social media than any other activity - except perhaps sleeping.** Currently, _adolescents spend 7 and a half hours every day consuming media._ **Guys. That's nearly ⅓ of our day spent on media.** And, the time spent on media is quickly rising as each year passes, thanks to the increasing accessibility.

How much media do you have? Take a second to list all of the different media related things you have (instagram, a television, etc.):

_____

_____

_____

_____

Do you think media is good or bad or both? Why?

_____

_____

_____

_____

We don't just spend seven and a half hours a day consuming media though. We spend seven and a half hours a day consuming *messages.* From our media, **we learn expectations about gender.** We are learning how to act, how not to act, what's acceptable, and what isn't. One of the things we learn is that there are only two genders - boy and girl - and we learn that we must conform to a set of expectations in order to be perceived as such.

We start understanding the influence of media at a very young age. Born to Buy author Juliet Schor writes, **"Kids can recognize logos by eighteen months, and before reaching their second birthday, they're asking for products by brand name. By three or three and a half, experts say, children start to believe that brands communicate their personal qualities, for example, that they're cool, or strong, or smart". Media is an extremely pervasive influence, changing the way kids think even before they're four years old.**

With media, expectations about gender are utterly inescapable, because they are *everywhere*. Expectations are in television commercials, on highway billboards, in our apps, and in almost every song on the radio. They're popping up on the side of the website as we try and get our 5 day forecast, staring us down and begging us to click when we watch something on YouTube - EVERYWHERE!

Media is a powerful medium that reflects certain values, people, and attitudes while ignoring others...consequently creating culture. Media might not be the sole reason why girls call each other sluts, but, it certainly contributes to an atmosphere where it's okay to be mean to other girls. Media might not directly cause sexual harassment, but it absolutely 100 percent creates an atmosphere in which behaviors like disrespecting women are acceptable. The media that I have grown up with may not be the direct cause of everything that teenagers are going through. BUT, **the cultural attitudes and expectations that <u>the media is perpetuating</u> encourage so many of these problems.**

Media COULD be a place to challenge gender expectations. It could, and it sometimes is!! **But, for the most part, media serves to reinforce and exaggerate stereotypes of the groups it chooses to reflect.**

Of course, media isn't the only one perpetuating gendered expectations. Our parents, friends, and communities are just a few of the other sources that influence our ideas of gender.

3. The messages we learn about being boys and girls stick with us.

Finally, the messages we learn growing up have a long term impact on us. This is because as we age, _our brains continue to grow..._Newer research finds that key brain development continues through childhood and the teenage years, even into the mid-twenties and later, proving that w**hat we're learning as teenagers still count**.

A Newsweek article states, "An excess of gray matter (the stuff that does the processing) at the beginning of adolescence makes us particularly brilliant at learning—the reason we're so good at picking up new languages starting in early childhood—**but also particularly sensitive to the influences of our environment, both emotional and physical.**" In other words, teenagers are still very receptive to influences, especially from influences like media.

And not only are teenager's brains still growing, but what they're learning is going to influence them for the rest of their lives. As one study writes, **children and teenagers are "laying the neural foundations that will serve them for the rest of their lives".**

So if the messages that we're learning as kids and teenagers are going to set the stage for the rest of our life...what messages are we learning? And what kind of impact are these messages having on us?

This section, we're going to find out.

We're going to start out by talking about gender non conforming and trans individuals, and then we will discuss what females learn about being females.

****

Trans and Gender Nonconforming

Though we rarely talk about it, there are many individuals all over the world who don't conform to the gender assigned to them at birth. These individuals can be transgender (someone who differs from the sex they were assigned at birth) or gender nonconforming (someone who does not identify as male or female).

These communities face great violence and hostility as gender expectations hit them the hardest. Heartbreakingly, 78% of the trans and gender nonconforming community report harassment by students, teachers or staff **IN SCHOOL**...that being stated, there are regional differences and gender nonconforming students report higher rates of harassment than trans students. Sadly, 1 in 5 members of the community report experiencing homelessness at some point in their lives...as they were either harassed, turned away, or sexually assaulted by homeless shelter residents or staff members. The community experiences unemployment at twice the rate of the general population, **with rates for people of color up to four times the national unemployment rate.** Horrifyingly 90% of the community reports experiencing harassment, mistreatment or discrimination on the job.

The problems this community is facing are severe, devastating, and seriously life-threatening.

I do not have an essay written by any of my friends who are trans or gender nonconforming, and so instead I strongly suggest you do some research of your own...the internet is a vast place and there lots of fantastic resources out there to further your understanding.

****

Cross the Line

Now, we're going to talk about the expectations female identifying individuals have to face.

During my first self-confidence workshop, something happened that I won't ever forget. My best friend lead an activity called 'Cross the Line'. Basically, she read out statements, and girls would cross the line if the statement applied to them. For example, she would read, "Cross the line if you've ever worn clothing just to fit in" and all of the girls who had worn clothing just to fit in would cross the line. Then, everyone would go back to the starting point and the next question would be read. The activity is unifying, because everyone always crosses the line at some point. And it's powerful because it allows girls to be brutally honest with themselves.

During the activity, my friend read out, "Cross the line if you've ever thought you weren't pretty enough to do something".

When she read off that statement, every single girl in the room crossed the line. *Every. Single. Girl.*

Thought that she wasn't pretty enough to do something, thought that her appearance restricted her capability as a person! Real, live, actual people thought that they couldn't do something, because they weren't *pretty* enough!

I truly have never been so devastated by something. My little sister crossed that line! My best friends crossed that line! These thirty eighth grade girls crossed that line!

This experience shocked me and made me realize something important. **Girls today are held back, not always necessarily by rights, but by the cultural expectations of what it means to be female. More specifically, girls are held back by the relentless beauty standard.** We, as females, cannot live up to our full potentials, *because our energy is being wasted*. How can we possibly find a cure to cancer if we're preoccupied with the way our hair looks? How can we end world hunger, if we can't stop crying in the bathroom because we don't have a thigh gap? **Girls are held back by the expectation of what it means to be female, and it's just that simple.**

****

The Messages We Send to Females

I believe that we teach girls three main points about being female that hold them back from reaching their full potential. Here are the main three:

1. **The most important thing a female can be is beautiful** - everything else, like personality, skills, intelligence, is less important.
2. **In order to be beautiful, you have to change yourself** - you have to lose weight, wear makeup, shave, the list goes on.
3. **You must be sexy - but not sexual.** And if you are sexual, it has to be for someone else - NOT YOU.

Can you think of any other messages that we send to girls, about what it means to be female? What are some other things that girls should or shouldn't be?

_____

_____

_____

_____

Together, these messages about what it means to be a girl is destroying the potential of females across the nation.

In this section, we're going to focus on the first two messages we send to females, and I will cover the third message in the section on sexualization later in the book.

****

What Little Girls Learn About Being Little Girls

So how do children understand what their gender is supposed to be like? How do they learn what behaviors to penalize? What messages are we sending them about being a boy or girl?

Well, it's very simple - <u>One of the first major ways that kids learn what is expected of them and others is from their toys.</u> And in America, toys are typically segmented by color so it's really easy for kids to figure out what they're supposed to play with. For example:

What color are toys designed for girls usually? _____

What color are toys designed for boys usually? _____

If you grew up in America, that was probably incredibly simple for you. Pink for girls and blue for boys.

Children learn from the color coding that girls and boys play with different toys, and the result is that girls are interested in playing with toys that are labeled as pink or 'feminine' toys...regardless of the 'kind' of toy.

Believe it or not, little girls aren't born loving pink. It's not historical, or genetic; in most cases, the pink obsession is learned. In fact, before the early 20th century both boys and girls wore white 'gender neutral dresses', rather than color coded clothing. And when color coding children began for marketing purposes, pink was considered masculine, because it was a lighter form of red - the color of strength! That's why the early Princesses are actually in blue (Cinderella, Snow White, etc.), because blue was considered more feminine!

Now I want to make something clear. I love pink, and pink the color isn't the problem. **The problem is that pink is used to strictly prescribe what girls should play**

with, and the toys girls are prescribed to play with are problematic. As Orenstein says on the color pink, "though it may celebrate girlhood in one way, it also repeatedly and firmly fuses girls identity to appearance". Let me explain a little more what I mean.

Take a moment to Google 'girl toys' or 'pink toys' and go onto a toy website, and take some notes on what kinds of toys are offered to girls.

What kind of messages do they send to girls about being female?

_____

_____

_____

_____

You may notice that a majority of pink toys designed for females deal with beauty. One Professor/researcher, Judith Blakemore, examined over 100 toys, and found that **"the toys most associated with girls were related to appearance** (Barbie dolls and accessories, ballerina costumes, makeup, jewelry, etc.". Pink toys don't usually emphasize to little girls that being smart is important - in fact, the math and science toys usually end up in the boys' toy aisle. Pink toys don't usually emphasize to little girls that being strong or brave is important - the action and superheroes are usually male. Pink toys don't usually emphasize to little girls that being loud and assertive is important - girls are supposed to be sugar, spice, and everything nice....quiet and agreeable.

Instead, pink toys usually teach girls that **beauty is extremely important, and that beauty/makeup/fashion is PART of being a female.** Pink toys marketed towards females teach little girls that girls care about beauty, and girls learn that in order to fit in they must love beauty too.

Additionally, the kind of dolls we market to females are ridiculously sexualized and beauty focused. Barbie, for example, displays and normalizes such a dangerous and unhealthy ideal body shape, and has very real consequences on girls. In one study on the impact of Barbie's, **girls aged 5 to 8 showed lower levels of body esteem, coupled with a greater desire to be thin after looking at Barbie books, compared to books with dolls that were of a healthy weight or no dolls**. Furthermore, other dolls like Bratz are unnecessarily sexualized. Once again, **the dolls we market so often teach females that beauty, or being sexy, is the most important thing a girl can be.**

However, I know that some of you will bring up the 'females are innately drawn to dolls' argument. I am not against females playing with dolls and **truthfully, it doesn't matter if females are innately drawn to dolls or not - that really is NOT the problem even in the slightest, in fact, it does not matter if females doll preference is nature or nurture because DOLLS ARE NOT THE PROBLEM.**

The problem, once again, is that so many female toys (including dolls) focus on beauty, and are unnecessarily sexualized.

And because of this, **rather than learning that power is saving the world, girls learn that their power comes from the way they dress themselves.** In her book Cinderella Ate my Daughter, Orenstein notes, "**The boys seemed to be exploring the world; the girls were exploring their femininity**".

There aren't many toys for girls that deal with being 'powerful'. Let me explain what I mean: Boys get to experiment with powerful male figures, such as powerful male superheroes, rescue heroes, and more. Yet, girls don't usually have all of those options. For example, when I was younger, my siblings and I were very interested in playing with Rescue Heroes - essentially a group of action figures. However, there was a huge disproportion of male heroes to women heroes. My two sisters and I didn't have enough females for all of us to play with, so as a result, we ended up playing with Barbies and other dolls, since there was not enough female superheroes for all of us to play with. What does this disproportion teach kids? Perhaps that females cannot be the heroes, but instead merely the damsel in distress. Aside from the problematic messages these kinds of toys send, it's important to note that **girls rarely get to experience any true kind of power through their toys, and are instead left to explore their limiting femininity. As Born to Buy puts it, "Girl power turned into sex power".** We teach girls that they can only experience empowerment if they conform to feminine standards. Instead of experiencing true empowerment, we promise females that they can experience empowerment through a LIPSTICK SHADE (!!!!) or various other kinds of beauty products.

The large, overarching problem is the fact that we teach kids that in ORDER to be accepted, **they must fit into our limiting gender expectations.** Chimamanda Ngozi Adichie once said, **"The problem with gender is that it prescribes how we should be, rather than recognizing how we are". Color coded toys prescribe what little girls and boys should play with, and those toys influence ideas about gender.**

Toys are one of the first places that children learn about gender, **so why do we limit them?** Why don't we encourage girls that they can be anything in the entire world? Why don't we tell girls that they can save the world like boys, or encourage them to get their hands dirty exploring the natural Earth? **We are selling kids a limited and prepackaged idea of what it gender means! And we shouldn't limit children - we should be doing the exact opposite!!**

And seriously, at the end of the day it's just absurd that we would limit children *through toys.* Putting so much emphasis on beauty at such a young age is uncalled for, and it's completely sending the wrong ideas to females about what is important.

Kids should have a right to choose what kinds of toys they want to play with.

And if at the end of the day kids choose gender stereotypical toys, that's awesome, because they're choosing it.

And either way, if kids want to latch onto something to prove/identify with their gender, that's good too! Let's just make sure that they're latching on to positive ideals of their gender.

What toys did you play with when you were younger? What toys did you feel empowered playing with?

_____

_____

_____

_____

_____

What is the problem with gender prescribed toys? Do you agree with what I said? Disagree? Why?

_____

_____

_____

_____

_____

****

Tween as a Concept

Before we begin the next section, it's important to note that the very concept of a tween was created by advertisers and those in business, and tween is a relatively new idea. Furthermore, tween culture is only growing. Juliet Schor, author of <u>Born to Buy</u> writes, "Tween marketing has become a major focus of the industry, with its own conferences, research tools, databases, books, and specialty firms. Part of why tweening is so lucrative is that it involves bringing new, more expensive products to the younger group. It's working because tweens have growing purchasing power and influence with parents. **The more the tween consumer world comes to resemble the teen world...the more money there is to be made**".

The concept of tweens is about money. Truth be told, it's fairly foolish from a developmental standpoint. As Lamb and Brown write, "The early marketing reference to tweens identified kids between the ages of eight and fifteen, which gives us an idea of how out of touch with the development of real kids the marketers initially were...What does a third grader have in common with an eighth grader other than being a potential target for the same products? **As a psychological category tween falls shorts; as a marketing strategy it is brilliant**". **It's profitable to capitalize on the differences...it's just really, really unhealthy for humankind.** To expand on that point I'd like to quote Schor saying, "**involvement in consumer culture causes dysfunction in the forms of depression, anxiety, low self-esteem and psychosomatic complaints**". Despite the fact that consumer culture is associated with depression, anxiety, low self-esteem and more, companies are making an enormous profit off of tween insecurity.

****

What Tween Girls Learn About Being Tween Girls

As kids grow up and become tweens, they understand that there are clear differences between males and females. Sharon Lamb and Lyn Mikel Brown, authors of <u>Packaging Girlhood,</u> note that advertisers focus on gender differences saying, "The commercials between shows sell more than products; they sell kids on how to be a cool, hip, and 'normal' girl or boy...While TV for young viewers makes some attempt to represent and mingle male and female characters, commercials are almost completely gender-separate spaces. Except for a few sugary cereal and candy ads, toy <u>manufacturers have all but given up on a world in which boys and girls play together or like the same things</u>". Rather than focusing on the human similarities both boys and girls share, ***advertisers exaggerate and create differences.*** As Peggy Orenstein writes, "One of the easiest ways to segment a market is to magnify gender differences - or invent them where they did not previously exist". Once again, it's about money.

And it's not just television commercials that sell tweens ideas about what it means to be a boy or girl. **As kids grow up, the messages about being a boy or girl become more extreme and more prevalent.**

For instance, there are clear themes and things that girls are supposed to love. School folders, lunch boxes and more set expectations for what should be important to females. This list includes: Shopping, texting, boys, the latest male musician (for example, Justin Bieber or One Direction), fashion, pop stars, and sass.

Anything I forgot to add?

_____

_____

_____

The authors of Packaging Girlhood explored the theme of 'girl/preteen culture', and in their own words, they state "What's in this girl culture? A whole lot of boy worship. They have buttons, purses, pillows, and T-shirts that say 'I love [fill in latest pop star]. Eleven and twelve year olds sometimes get crushes on stars, yes, but preteens and pre preteens? **The eight to ten year olds are given an important lesson that being part of being a teen or preteen is developing a crush on one of these teen hunks and decorating yourself and your room with proclamations of love**...We wish that there were ways a girl could admire other girls through their room and clothing accessories - such as 'Venus for President' - but that's not part of girl culture to marketers." Why do we encourage ALL girls of all sexualities to spend their time focusing on boys, rather than their studies?

Even board games are incredibly gendered. The authors of <u>Packaging Girlhood</u> went through 101 board games, and found that **the majority of games for girls were stereotypical, sexist, and had to do with shopping and boys.**

Believe it or not, even clothing reflects expectations for boys and girls. Male clothing is typically looser and easier to move around in - perfectly enabling boys for action. On the other hand, female clothing is typically designed <u>for the way it looks</u>. Lots of clothing for little girls is designed to look cute, rather than to be worn in. And, this affects what little girls can or can't do. In most cases, you aren't allowed to go explore the natural world, search for small frogs or bugs, or get your feet dirty when you're wearing frilly dresses, beautiful flats, or more. Boys have less of a chance of 'ruining' their clothing.

Nearly everything we offer to female tweens is overwhelmingly stereotypical - the problem is the lack of choice. And these board games, clothing pieces, advertisements, etc. are reinforcing and entertaining false gender expectations.

****

What Girls in General Learn About Being Girls

The messages only get more severe as we get older and older.

Girls learn that having a 'hot' body is the most important thing they can provide when tee shirts from Abercrombie and Fitch are sold saying, "Who needs a brain when you have these?" right across the boobs.

I learned that having the right kind of body was the most important thing I could offer when I was in 7th grade. I had a conversation with a 6th grade boy, and he told me that in order to be liked, I needed to have bigger boobs.

Girls learn that they always have to look beautiful and sexy when Halloween costumes sold to females are extremely sexualized. Boys are sold costumes with many options, and male costumes are about who the character is and what they can do. But female costumes are unnecessarily sexualized, and leave females little choice to be anything other than a 'sexy maid' or 'sexy minion' (which, by the way, WHAT THE HELL?!), etc. Most female costumes don't DO ANYTHING OTHER THAN LOOK GOOD!! If Halloween is supposed to be about fantasy and becoming someone different for the night, why would we want to limit who or what a girl can be? Girls need more options.

Girls learn that they have nothing important to contribute other than their appearance when Packaging Girlhood researched Halloween costumes on website and checked out the promisingly neutral 'When I grow up' category and found fifty-five costumes for boys, and only twenty-two for girls...And of the twenty-two for girls, fifteen of those costumes were cheerleaders, divas, and rock stars. One was even a french maid.

Girls learn that nothing is more important than how they look, when we obsess over a female's age, rather than a female's accomplishments. Rush Limbaugh, a famous radio host, once said about Hillary Clinton, who was at the time running for President, "Will Americans want to watch a woman get older before their eyes on a daily basis?" I would just like to say: **First of all, Hillary Clinton isn't in office to be looked at - she's running for office to do a job. Second of all, we watch every man grow older in office**.

Girls learn that what a female can do is less important than what a female looks like, when we criticize females on what they look like, rather than what they can do.

Girls learn that nothing but their body matters when, on the very day that Condoleezza Rice became America's first African American female national security advisor in 2001, the front page New York Times story mentioned, in addition to her accomplishment, the fact that her dress size is 'between a 6 and an 8'....

Girls learn that their weight is important, when curvy girls can't be depicted as a normal girls with normal emotions. Think about it - Fat Amy in Pitch Perfect isn't just Amy - she's 'Fat Amy' because it is so rare that we will depict a fat person in our media, that when we do, their fatness becomes a core part of their identity. Fat or curvy people or overweight people can never be depicted as normal people - they're depicted as fat people.

Girls learn that their body is the most important thing about them when the cruelest insult someone can deliver is not that a girl is 'dumb' or 'mean' but 'fat', 'disgusting', and 'ugly'.

We learn that the most important thing a female can do is have a nice body when radio host Bill Cooksey of WKRO said this about a very important politician: "I think she's hot .... She's tiny, she's short. She's got a banging little body on her. Facial-wise, I give her about a seven. Body-wise, I give her about an eight-and-a-half. Tight, little butt. I endorse Karyn Polito". I'm sure that she's thrilled, that after YEARS of hard work in the government, she gets to have her butt commented on, instead of her accomplishments.

It's when former TV hosts say things like this about Sarah Palin, a woman who ran for Vice President: "We want to have her over for dinner. I trust her. I want her watching my kids. *I want her laying next to me in bed.* That's the way people vote". Gross!

Or when the Senate Majority Leader, one of the most powerful positions in the country, says this "Many senators are known for many things .... We in the Senate refer to Senator Gillibrand *as the hottest member*". Forget the fact that Senator Gillibrand has worked to make the world a better place - all that matters is that she's hot. And I'll keep going.

Liz Funk wrote an entire book when she was a teenager, yet still noted "I've never received such positive feedback for anything I've done as I did for being thin".

Girls learn that nothing but their appearance is important when boys in movies and television shows and music videos only fall in love with pretty girls - instead of smart, ambitious girls. I used to be so scared of being ambitious and driven and of having big dreams, because I was so scared that no guy would ever love me - a girl who wanted the whole world. In the media, it seems like boys go after the girls with the best body rather than the girl who is smart and driven.

Women are reminded again that nothing matters except their body when influential actress Scarlett Johansson worked tirelessly making independent films for fourteen years, and she got voted....best actress? Best supporting actress? Nope. Best breasts.

Girls learn that appearance is most important when parents reinforce it from a young age. Lise Eliot writes "parents of girls tended to describe them as prettier, softer, more delicate, weaker, finer-featured, and less attentive than parents of boys described their infants".

Girls learn that all that matters about a female is her body when nearly naked models make the cover of Sports Illustrated to be celebrated for their bodies, rather than female athletes being celebrated for their skills.

And when athletic women are actually shown in magazines, they're just the stereotypically sexy ones. Lamb and Brown note, "Some sports can and do look quite solid, strong, and muscular, but magazines want sexy or feminine. So it's not the Olympic softball team that makes the cover but skaters, gymnasts, and select beauties like Anna Kournikova or sensational images such as Brandy Chastain in a sports bra or seductively posing for Sports Illustrated with nothing but two soccer balls covering her breasts". Athletic women are celebrated for their looks rather than skill.

And speaking of sports, they write: "Even in 2004, the year of the summer Olympics, the most commonly represented female sport was beach volleyball. We suspect it was because of the bikinis. The lesson is clear: Girls who play sports get attention when they look hot. After all, the U.S. Olympic swim team posed provocatively for *Maxim* after the competition".

There was also this gross comment, made by Gene Lyons about the women running for office in 2008, "To the connoisseur of American political theater, the most entertaining aspect of the 2010 election season has been the rise of the right-wing cuties -- political celebrities whose main qualification is looking terrific on television. From where I sit, in a comfortable chair in front of the tube, the GOP Cupcake Factor has enlivened an otherwise dreary campaign season". **He talks about these women as though they are simply things to be looked at, rather than people with ideas who can contribute a lot of intellect!**

We're reminded again that nothing we do matters except for the way our breasts look when a young, new politician was asked by a meeting chairman after her FIRST campaign speech "Sam, I want to ask a question all the men in this room have been dying to ask you: Just what are your measurements?" - as in, yes, breast measurements. Horrifying. I can just picture her feeling so excited to get her campaign on the road, and she's been rehearsing this speech, and she has a picture in her mind of how great it's going to go, and then she gets up there and is asked how big her boobs are. It's just so discouraging! All of that hard work and the only thing someone can pay attention to is her boobs. It's completely off topic and it's very inappropriate.

One of the most bizarre comments I found was when a famous columnist says THIS about Sarah Palin, someone running for Vice President, "The high-sheen lip gloss, the 'Naughty Monkey' brand red pumps, the black leather outfits, the winking, for heaven's sake. She's the original 'Mean Girl' — the head honcho of Orwell's 'Junior Anti-Sex League' dressed to kill. You want her, but you can't have her". I literally don't even know what that statement means, let alone *WHAT* does that have to do with *ANYTHING*??!?!?! Like you would NEVER say that about a man running for Vice President!

Girls are repeatedly told time and time again that being beautiful or sexy is the most important thing they can be.

What are some other ways girls learn that being beautiful is the most important thing they can be?

_____

_____

_____

****

In Order to be Beautiful...

And more than that, girls learn that in order to be beautiful they need to change the way they are. Girls learn that their body is not good enough as is. Girls learn that there is a variety of problems with the natural female body - your natural body hair is disgusting, your stomach can be 'too big', your face can be too pale or more commonly too dark, your arms can be too flabby, your hair can be too frizzy or curly, and even your ankles can be too fat. YOUR ANKLES! *But perhaps the most important lesson that* girls learn is that the natural female body is something to be ashamed of, and something to be changed.

This is something that all girls learn in varying degrees, depending on skin color and/or ethnicity.

Susan Douglas, author of Where the Girls Are wrote, "We learned, through these fairy tales, and certainly later through advertising, that we had to scrutinize ourselves all the time, identify our many imperfections, and learn to eliminate or disguise them, otherwise no one would ever love us". Douglas had it spot on - **girls learn how to identify their 'problem areas', and then learn how to fix their problem**

areas. Girls also learn to fear what will happen to them if they don't conform to the standard of beauty. I know I personally was always so worried about my appearance because I believed that only beautiful and sexy girls were loved, and as a 13 year old girl, I felt that I was neither of those things.

Advertisements specifically teach us what problem areas are. Advertisements have a pretty simple structure to them. First, most identify some kind of normal thing that women have on their body, and cast that normal thing as a problem. This creates insecurity and pressure, which is quite common today. In fact, I found that 71% of girls surveyed felt 'a lot of pressure to fit in'. Then, the advertisement will offer a solution to the problem area and the solution is their product!

Beauty products (usually) attempt to sell self-esteem. And many of us are attempting to buy self-esteem…. In 2015 alone, the global cosmetic market was worth 60.58 billion. **Unfortunately, complete self-esteem cannot be bought or sold - it can absolutely be encouraged by a great lipstick or some terrific heels, but self-esteem is largely internal. Self-esteem is not a commodity, despite the fact that it is being treated as one.**

One example of a marketing campaign that tries to sell self-esteem would be the infamous 'don't risk dudeness' Veet campaign. In an insulting video campaign, Veet demonstrates scenarios. In the scenario, *women turn into men when they grow leg hair*. The slogan, 'womanly around the clock' appears right after Veet hair removal products is advertised, associating shaven legs as feminine and unshaven legs as disgusting and masculine...and thus selling self-esteem in the form of shaved legs. When we see the reactions, we learn people are terrified of leg hair, especially men. We see body hair shamed, and as something that needs to be taken care of immediately.

BUT LET'S BACK UP A SECOND. HUMAN BEINGS HAVE LEG HAIR. NATURALLY. WOMEN ARE SUPPOSED TO HAVE LEG HAIR. THAT'S NORMAL. IF WOMEN WEREN'T SUPPOSED TO HAVE LEG HAIR, WE WOULDN'T GROW LEG HAIR.

Yet, we have been convinced through relentless advertising that leg hair is abnormal, gross, terrifying, and will turn you into a man.

We learn that our natural body is not good enough, and that with expensive products we can be good enough.

Another example of how we buy and sell self-esteem would be the product 'neck cream'. Now, as women age, obviously their necks become less smooth and wrinkles start to appear - THAT IS NORMAL! But, we teach women to fear growth and aging. One advertisement I saw while waiting for an appointment said 'You're only as young as your neck' - hence creating an aging and neck insecurity. And right in line with the advertising format I described above, a solution was then addressed following the insecurity. The solution is the 'world's #1 neck cream'.

Anti-aging advertisements, combined with our culture that treats older women as invisible, results in a huge sales increase. And, the APA writes "This inability to meet the culturally imposed standard of beauty may lead to body shame, lowered self-esteem, and a reduced sense of well-being".

Aging shame makes sense because we live in a society where female beauty is valued above all else, and we define beauty as youth. As a result of this thinking, we shame growth. We shame stretch marks, sagging breasts, and the weight that comes after women have babies. It makes sense that we shame stretch marks, sagging breasts, and the weight that comes after women have babies simply because those are all normal things that the female body does. And, **we commonly shame the normal, natural, unchanged female body.**

During the empowerment workshops, my best friend sometimes comments on how we teach girls to disguise their imperfections with cosmetics or surgery...For example, you don't like something about your body? Cover it up with foundation. Take on an unhealthy diet so you can lose weight, all for the purpose of looking good. **We teach girls to hide what they don't like about themselves, rather than encouraging girls to love what they view as their imperfections.**

And we buy this - quite literally. In 2013 alone, 63,538 cosmetic surgical procedures were performed on people age 13-19.

Girls have learned that in order to be beautiful, they have to change themselves. We have created an ideal standard of beauty that is so outstandingly limiting that it cannot be achieved naturally.

Have you ever bought a product because you thought it would make you look more like society's idea of beautiful? Have you ever tried to buy self-esteem?

_____

_____

_____

What do you think about this quote by Lamb and Brown? "Marketers love anxiety. They fill those uneasy spaces with products that girls can use to form a statement - bracelets, skirts, hair color, T-shirts" - Is it true? Untrue? Why?

_____

_____

_____

****

We Believe We Can Change Our Bodies

And girls really unhealthily believe that we can change our bodies and appearances to look just like the standard of beauty. Jean Kilbourne states, "Even more destructively, they get the message that this is possible, that, with enough effort and self-sacrifice, they can achieve this ideal. Thus many girls spend enormous amounts of time and energy attempting to achieve something that is not only trivial, but also completely unattainable. The glossy images of flawlessly beautiful and extremely thin women that surround us would not have the impact they do if we did not live in a culture that encourages us to believe we can and should remake our bodies into perfect commodities". We really believe that it's possible to change our bodies.

Perhaps that's why the weight loss industry is nearly a $60 billion dollar a year enterprise.

In today's media, there are so many stories on how to look like celebrities. I've seen headlines like 'Get Taylor Swift's Dream Body!' or 'Fergie's Workout!' or 'Tips from Lauren Conrad's Personal Trainer!', or even makeup tutorials that will teach you how to look *just* like Kylie Jenner.

When I was younger, I ripped a magazine page out of a magazine that told me the secret to looking just like Taylor Swift! The page supposedly had HER very own workout routine, and I religiously practiced it the beginning of my sophomore year in high school. There was a picture of Taylor in her bathing suit, and I was convinced that if I just worked hard enough, I could have a waist and stomach EXACTLY like her!

In reality, there is no way that not even 5'0 me is EVER going to have a body like nearly 6'0 Taylor Swift - we have incredibly different body shapes and our 'healthy' bodies are going to look different.

But at the time, I didn't realize that and I used to be convinced that if I just worked hard enough, I could eventually have the 'perfect' body - just like Taylor Swift. And I'm not alone - I know so many girls (and boys!) who experience the same phenomenon.

Think about how often we alter our natural body. Take a second to make a list of all the things you do to alter your body, whether it's shaving or dying your hair or painting your nails:

_____

_____

_____

_____

Now here's the thing and I want to make it clear so you don't misunderstand me. **THERE IS ABSOLUTELY NOTHING WRONG WITH CHANGING YOUR BODY AND WEARING MAKEUP AND GOING TO THE GYM OR DYING YOUR HAIR OR SHAVING OR ANY OF THAT.** Personally, there are few things that excite me more than putting on sparkly eye shadow. **Changing your body because you want to is not the problem. However, there IS a problem with how we relentlessly urge individuals to change their body in order to be accepted.**

I will respect all of your choices, and if you choose to alter your appearance that is awesome because it is totally your choice. But my next question to you is: Why do you change your body? Is it to be liked? Is it because you personally like how you look?

What is your motivation for changing your body?

_____

_____

_____

_____

I want you to think about your motivation. I hope that if YOU choose to alter your body, you're doing it for yourself and no one else.

****

Racism in the Beauty Standard

One devastating component of the beauty standard is that it's very white, with little to no tolerance of other ethnicities or races.

Can you name five television shows where the protagonist is non-white? What about three movies where the Hispanic person plays the lead? Can you think of them?! I know I can't.

There are so many girls with different skin colors that we portray as invisible, and if not invisible, a stereotype. We don't show Muslim girls in kind way, we don't show Asian females in a bold and assertive way, we don't show African American females as the protagonist, we don't show the Latina Girl as the Class President and also Valedictorian in movies, and we sure as heck don't show two Indian girls - that would be muchhhh too confusing. Instead, we don't show the Muslim girl at all, we show Asian girls as the smart or cute sidekick, we show African American females as the sassy black friend, and the Latina girl is that slut who 'got herself' pregnant.

One of the many problems with portraying so many women as invisible, is that it allows the blonde, blue eyed female to become the sole standard of beauty. When we don't portray women of different colors and ethnicities, we exclude them from a cultural acceptance.

When I was going through the answers of my survey, I read this: "I also have a request: in this book you're writing, will you please talk about race? I know it's a very hot-tempered and difficult subject to talk about but it's important and very relevant to the whole conversation of body and self-image positivity. It simply cannot be denied that if you are a black/Asian/darker-than-white, people like you are shown in afterthought. People like you are rarely focused on by the media and when you are, their faces are photo shopped lighter and somehow, they barely resemble themselves. There is so much pressure on girls of color not only to be beautiful but to be beautiful according to the status quo; to look as white as possible just to fit in. If you can't include this in the book then it's alright, I'd be surprised if you did anyway".

The reality is the beauty standard is racist and exclusive...and promotes a white only kind of beauty standard.

Another wrote to me saying, "I'm a POC (person of color) so while I do feel like media targets girls in a not so great light, they target colored girls (Indian, African American, Asian, etc.) in an even worse light. You RARELY see images of people that look like you and that can definitely take a drift on your self-esteem when you don't consider yourself "beautiful" because the people that are considered beautiful on television, music, etc. aren't what you look like".

This invisibility of an appreciation of non-white races and other ethnicities has created an exceptionally white beauty standard, where only white features are appreciated. One girl wrote, "I think the media portrays beauty in the Caucasian race. Brunettes and Blondes are portrayed as beautiful, especially with their colored eyes. And I think it's hard being Asian and trying to fit in, especially when the stereotype of Asian doesn't fit well. It's hard to be yourself when you're constantly being judged for how you look". It hurts my heart to know that Asian girls (and most likely many other girls of other ethnicities) feel this way. **Invisibility in the media often times creates insecurity.**

For example, typically, when we represent women of color we make them look white by lightening the photos. I can't include examples in this book for copyright reasons, but take a moment to Google 'white washed photos of celebs' or something along those lines.

What comes up?

_____

_____

_____

_____

_____

The message that these pictures send is that you can only be beautiful if you are white. There is simply no appreciation for women who don't have stereotypical white features. For example, we rarely show girls with natural African American curly hair or dreadlocks. The one time that a woman of color wore her hair in a more natural way, like Zendaya did, Giuliana Rancic, a host of E News! and Fashion Police made an extremely racist and unnecessary comment, saying that her hair probably smelled like drugs. If she wore her hair straight - the way white people do, Giuliana would NOT have commented that her hair smelled like drugs. Moreover, if I wore my blonde hair in dreadlocks like that, NO ONE would accuse me of smelling like drugs - it would be fashionable and complimented.

And it's not just America. Here's another quote from my survey, "I have a friend whose mother is from Trinidad. My friend is first generation American and comes from a family that is obsessed with physical beauty and attractiveness. My friend's mother has told her time and time again that she should only marry a man who has blonde hair and blue eyes. Her mother has gone so far as to buy her blonde wigs and blue colored contact lenses, despite the fact that they are not well-to-do. My friend is beautiful, with dark hair, skin and eyes, but unfortunately suffers from chronic acne. Her mother repeated tells her that she doesn't look presentable because of her skin. While I know my friend has strong willpower to fight against her mother's patronizing attitude, she sometimes remarks on how I am so much more beautiful than she (myself having pale skin, blue eyes and light brown hair). Her family also remarks on how "fat" she is, despite being a size 4 and playing lacrosse every day after school. My friend is so beautiful, but she fails to see it because of the comments of her mother and other foreign family members. While negative body views can come from the media, **I am far too often reminded that sometimes these things can come from home, too**". This quote is an important reminder that we may have biases that we have been reflecting onto our siblings or family members as well.

Have you ever commented negatively on a family member's appearance?

_____

_____

_____

Another quote that broke my heart was, "I am constantly feeling like I'm not good enough since I am different ethnicity than most of my classmates". If you feel this way, I want you to know that you are good enough. **Regardless of your race or ethnicity, you matter. And you are good enough. Don't ever let the color of your skin define your self-worth.** I know that it's much easier said than done, and that I'm not really in a position to be giving this kind of advice, but I would feel wrong not saying anything because it is so incredibly important that you know you matter.

****

Survival of the Prettiest

Rosalind Wiseman writes in her book <u>Queen Bees and Wannabe's</u>, "Adolescence is a beauty pageant. Even if your daughter doesn't want to be a contestant, others will look to her as if she is". For girls today, we don't get a choice of whether or not we're entered into the beauty pageant. <u>We automatically are.</u>

This forced beauty pageant has created something I like to call *Survival of the Prettiest.*

Survival of the Prettiest is a gigantic competition where girls compete against each other to be like, or rather to look like, the ideal version of a female. Survival of the Prettiest is fueled by cultural attitudes and the ever present media, which determine what a perfect and ideal female is like. **Ultimately, Survival of the Prettiest demands that girls sacrifice everything that makes them unique in order to be beautiful above all else - or else. The competition to look and be like the most ideal version of a female out there is never ending, time consuming, and unrelenting.**

But let me tell you the dirty little secret of Survival of the Prettiest: No one wins. NO ONE can win.

If you're fat - you're gross, disgusting, shouldn't wear bikinis to the beach and are going to be body shamed. But if you're skinny - you're 'scary thin', shamed for having no boobs, and an anorexic who needs to 'put some meat on your bones'.

If you're not toned you need to go to the gym, but if you're too muscular then you're 'too manly' and 'gross'.

If you wear makeup you're 'trying too hard', 'lying', giving people 'trust issues', have 'too much on', etc. But if you don't wear makeup, you really need to put some on because your natural face is just not good enough as is.

Being female means that you're asked to walk a fine line in all that you are. You're supposed to be sexy but not sexual and also you can't be frigid or else you'll be a bitch. You are supposed to be educated but you can't be smarter than boys and God forbid you're more ambitious.

There is ALWAYS something that you're doing wrong or could be doing better. One girl wrote, "I have definitely been very self-conscious of my body hair. It is interesting because I am skinny and tall so that side of the beauty industry has not affected me, but there is always something else that isn't right and isn't sexy". *There is literally always something else that can be done in Survival of the Prettiest.* As I befriend more and more girls, I realize that everyone struggles with the beauty standard - even those that appear to fit it. Of course, some of us struggle with it more than others because of how closely or far away we are from reaching the beauty standard - but this isn't a contest of who has been affected the most (though it is important to acknowledge that we all start at different places). This is my realization that **there is LITERALLY no way to win Survival of the Prettiest - there is always something more you need or should be.**

In Survival of the Prettiest, the ones who don't live up to the standard of beauty are choked by society...they are rejected or ignored, and slowly lose their voices and believe that they are not good enough, not female enough, not **beautiful** enough.

The ones who are gorgeous appear to survive, but the 'winners' of Survival of the Prettiest have wasted countless hours, days, years on changing their appearance...not because they wanted to or because they enjoyed straightening and curling their hair every day, but because they believed they needed to change in order to be accepted. And these human turned Barbie Dolls wasted years of their lives, years that their brains could have been used to better society.

The 'winners' might seem like they've won, but I know too many girls who I thought had 'won'. And as it turns out, they haven't won - they're affected by ravaging eating disorders and insecurity just like the rest of us. It is horrifying to realize that the girls I desperately wanted to look like growing up do not even like the way they look. To add insult to injury, these girls with 'perfect' bodies to the male eye are the girls that are often times picked on and degraded the most.

And a rare few overcome Survival of the Prettiest and accept themselves for who they are, but they are regarded as 'vain' and 'conceited' by the rest of the world.

In Survival of the Prettiest, no one wins.

It's a chilling statement. It's also true. No one can win in such a mentally, physically, and emotionally draining game.

****

Everyone Loses

Did you know that 42% of 1st to 3rd grade girls want to be thinner?

It's true. **Worrying about appearance starts young.** A Common Sense Media report states, "Children are aware of body issues and methods to control body size and appearance by the time they are preschoolers, and **many young children start exhibiting <u>socially motivated</u> distortions in their body perceptions**".

This fear of weight only grows with age. 81 percent of 10-year-old girls are **afraid of being fat.** Ten year olds!!

And it only gets worse. In one study, 91 percent of women surveyed on a college campus had attempted to control their weight through dieting.

But of course, those are just numbers and facts. Here are some quotes from females, of all ages, about the way they think about their body image:

"There are times when I sit and cry because of how unhappy I am or because I hate myself."

"I am very self-conscious, and have a low self-esteem. I try to make myself look strong and appear fearless by being a bitch. So really, it's like a double negative. I'm insecure, and mean. I'm alone with no friends and I hate how I look. I want to constantly change myself."

"For a few years I've struggled with self-esteem issues... I've always felt like the girls at school are all prettier than me and I don't feel like I really fit in."

"I think when someone doesn't like me <u>it's my fault </u>and that I need to improve myself for the next time."

"It's just that I'm striving for a goal and a dream that never came true. <u>I feel trapped inside my body</u>. I wanna get out of it."

"As someone planning on going into the performance industry, I have received an enormous amount of pressure to lose weight and make myself blander, usually under the guise of becoming more of a 'blank slate' for directors to work with. *This is erasure of the representation of my body type on stage and erasure of my personality in real life. And it's awful.*"

"I feel unhappy in my own body and I feel like I need to be thin and tall and be pretty constantly or else I'm ugly."

"I really want to be happy, but I don't feel like I'm pretty enough to be happy, *like I don't deserve it.*"

"I feel like my body is not good enough."

"I feel that people don't care about your personality, and that you aren't given a chance if you aren't as pretty and perfect as the girls around you. That isn't right."

"Society's unrealistic expectations of women are ridiculous. I constantly feel pressured to have clearer skin, be fit, wear cuter clothes, be more confident, etc. I've even felt bad for things about myself that I have no control over, like my chest size and my facial structure. *I shouldn't feel bad about the way my body and face are shaped.*"

"I'm a senior at high school and my graduation is in less than 4 months. School has been really stressful and on top of this I feel pressured to lose weight in order to fit in the right clothes for that special day."

"I have been feeling the pressure to be thin since I was eight years old and it hasn't stopped yet. I hope something will change soon."

"The whole pressure thing triggered me to self-harm and then I got made fun of and I was given a lot of crap when people found out. I just can't win here."

And it's not just Americans that are dealing with a limiting standard of beauty.
"I live in Brazil. I received the link to this by a friend and I'd like everyone to realize (if they not already do) that this is a worldwide problem. I have been called names, been

mocked, been laughed at for years and I still am. I don't believe when people say I'm beautiful and I also get extremely uncomfortable. Because for my whole life I was led to believe I wasn't beautiful. <u>I have friends who are ashamed to be seen eating. We have to hide during lunch because they can't stand the thought of no one looking at them eating.</u> ***That's how far we have come.***"

How in the world did we get here? How did we teach girls to believe that their bodies are disgusting, and how did we teach girls to have low self-esteem?

_____

_____

_____

_____

_____

****

Me Too Team, Me Too

I too have struggled with self-confidence and body image. Growing up, I had a lot of self-confidence issues. I was ridiculously insecure and spent the majority of my time hating myself and wishing I could fit in. I remember crying to my Mom in 5th grade, telling her that we needed to buy a specific brand of clothing, so I could be like everyone else.

I felt so self-conscious all the time, especially in middle school. I needed my friends' approval for absolutely everything. I just remember feeling so on edge, all the time, hoping that no one would see me. I wanted to be invisible, and I didn't want to be called on or looked at for the majority of 5th grade to sophomore year.

I hated the way I looked. I hated my 'gigantic' nose. I hated my stomach, which always seemed to be too big. I ESPECIALLY hated my thighs. I thought that they were enormous, and I never worked out, so my legs were all fat. Today still, when I sit, my thighs expand on the seat because they're not toned. I used to be so ashamed of my visibly untoned legs that I would sit on the edge of my seat during school and cover my legs so no one could see. I hated my eyebrows, because they were so bushy. The only thing that I truly liked about myself was my eyes.

I had four Taylor Swift posters hanging in my room, all which were ridiculously photo shopped. And every once in a while, I would quite literally compare every single part of my face to hers. I would look at her nose, compare it to mine, and then try and figure out a way that I could get her nose. It went like that for every single body part. Unfortunately, the pictures that I was looking at were completely fake and totally photo shopped, so I wasn't even comparing myself to a real body or face.

I was always especially insecure about my height. I hated being so much shorter than everyone else. Hated is an understatement, I absolutely RESENTED being short. I thought about it constantly, in total shame and embarrassment. I really, really let myself be miserable. People commented on it endlessly and that only made me feel a million times worse.

For example, one time I was sitting in 6th grade English class, when my homeroom teacher opened up the connecting door and looked around the room. "Ashley, come stand over here!" she said. I got up, and she had me stand next to a boy who was only slightly taller than me. The class and two teachers surveyed us and came to the conclusion that I was shorter. She then took me out of English class and into the Math class she was currently teaching. She brought me up to the front of her room and I stood self-conscious, embarrassed at the fact that every student in her class was staring at me. I had no idea why I was pulled out of class, or what I was doing next to the tallest boy in my entire grade, also at the front of the class.

"Today we're going to learn about outliers" the teacher said. I had no idea what an outlier was - we hadn't made it that far in my math class yet. She drew a graph on the board and plotted points. The majority of points were in the center of the graph, but a few stray points were very high or very low on the graph. These random points, the teacher explained, were called outliers. And, the teacher explained, the very tall boy and myself were outliers. Almost all of the students were in the middle, but there were a few outliers, people whose heights were totally different that didn't fit the trend. My whole class laughed at the example and the boy took the news splendidly, while I did my best to laugh along with everyone else. But my cheeks burned red and I started taking a few deep breaths when I realized what an outlier was. **It was confirmed, once again, I was an outlier and my height set me apart from everyone else again. This wasn't even in my head, my teacher knew too, and now so did everyone else. My biggest insecurity in the entire world, the thing that consumed my thoughts and worried me every night was just pointed out IN FRONT OF AN ENTIRE CLASS OF PEOPLE WHO WERE JUDGING ME!** My height was different and it wasn't normal. I was humiliated and felt shaken from this experience. While I know it sounds dramatic and silly, to 6th grade Ashley, this was the most embarrassing situation that could have possibly happened.

I hate to admit this, but even in high school, I would actually count, each week, to see how many days I could get through without someone commenting on how little I am. For YEARS, I couldn't get through a single week without at least one person reminding me how short I am. At least one person every single week, usually multiple people a day commented saying, "Wow, you're really short", "Are you done growing?", "How tall are you!!", "Whoa, I forgot you were so short!", "You go up to like here on me!" and on and on and on and on. It never ended. I didn't understand why the heck I couldn't get through a single week without someone saying something about it. Did it really matter that much to everyone else?? Why was it so important?? Why in the world did anyone even care how tall I am?? Whenever someone would comment, it would confirm what I already knew: My height was an embarrassment and something to be hated. The comments only reinforced how much I disliked myself, and as my self-confidence sunk lower and lower, I sunk shorter and shorter as I tried to disappear from everyone around me.

Unfortunately, my experience with insecurity, self-hatred, and poor body image isn't singular. In fact, we are in the middle of a huge self-esteem crisis. Almost everyone else feels or has felt the same way I did. Today, poor self-esteem and poor body image, is almost universal.

****

Self Esteem and Body Image

What do you think self-esteem is?

_____

_____

YoungWomensHealth.org defines self-esteem as "how much you like yourself, and how you recognize or appreciate your individual character, qualities, skills, and accomplishments". In other words, **self-esteem is basically what you think about yourself**. So, if you have a good self-esteem you are confident and happy with the person you are. If you don't have much self-esteem, you think poorly of yourself - exactly like I used to. Research shows that males' self-esteem tends to be higher than females.

What is your experience with self-confidence/esteem? Take a moment to assess yourself:

_____

_____

_____

_____

_____

_____

Interestingly, Eliot notes that 'self-esteem is more strongly predicted by the qualities associated with masculinity than those associated with femininity'. **In other words, self-confidence is typically higher when people display characteristics that are stereotypically masculine - for example, people usually have higher self-esteem when they are strong and independent, rather than submissive or passive.** Likewise, traits that are stereotypically feminine - for example, weak or expressive - are shown to predict a lower self-confidence.

Let's talk about **body image, or the way people think about their bodies**.

What do you think about your body?

_____

_____

_____

_____

_____

_____

_____

Why do you think that is?

_____

_____

_____

_____

_____

Self-esteem is extremely important. **We know from research that the way people think about themselves determines "aspirations, personal goals and interaction with others" or more importantly who they can become.** Self-esteem leads "to better health and social behavior", whereas poor self-esteem "is associated with a broad range of mental disorders and social problems".

Clearly, self-esteem matters. And so does body image. One study wrote, "As part of self-image, it's linked to key aspects of emotional and social well-being and the healthy development of adolescents. **Body dissatisfaction is tied to critical mental health problems such as eating disorders, low self-esteem, and depression**". It's time we started taking body image and self-esteem seriously.

****

Time to Change the Game

If no one can win the game, the only thing we can do is change the game.

And luckily, we have the power to change the game.

It is important to know that body image, or "one's perceptions, feelings, and behaviors toward one's body" **is almost entirely learned**. Research shows that we **learn** how to think about our bodies; we learn to love them, or we learn to hate them. **So, this means that we females have learned to dislike our bodies.**

This information is revolutionary! Women aren't born hating themselves - Survival of the Prettiest starts young and results in kids, pre-teens, teenagers, and adults who have low self-confidence and a poor body image! **This information means that we have the power to change the way females view themselves, because females (largely) learn how to view themselves! If we created this problem in the first place, we have the power to get rid of the problem!**

I believe, **I know** that attitudes can change, and I know that it is completely possible for girls to regain their self-confidence and to have positive self-esteem! I know it because I see it happening as girls leave my workshops and summer programs! I know it can happen!

With that being stated, let's do this. **It's time to change the game.**

****

Solutions

Dealing with poor body image is time consuming. It takes a huge amount of time, energy, and focus to dislike your body. Trying to fit in with the standard of beauty is hard. And everyone loses!

And, it doesn't even MAKE SENSE HISTORICALLY! Naomi Wolf writes, **"There is no legitimate historical or biological justification for the beauty myth; what it is doing to women today is a result of nothing more exalted than the need of today's power structure, economy, and culture to mount a counteroffensive against women." We're making money, but we're losing a lot of potential.**

So you know what I think?

WE NEED SOLUTIONS!!! I am proposing two basic solutions as a starting point, and then it's up to you to think of more solutions. You all have a responsibility to help this cause.

****

Solutions pt. 2

The first solution is to change our media. I would like to talk to you for a moment about the importance of media representation.

Growing up as a female, I can honestly say that I have learned that is that it is more important to be beautiful and hot, than it is to be smart, funny, brave, kind, open minded, hardworking, or pretty much any other adjective you can think of.

I think because many girls have internalized this belief, often times, girls will abandon characteristics that make them unique and true, for fear that they will be judged...If you are anything other than beautiful and quiet, you're setting yourself up for potential rejection and *certainly* judgment. You'll 'come off too strong' or be 'too much to handle' or be 'weirdly obsessed' or a variety of other seemingly negative things. **It takes a lot of courage to be yourself in your fullest form, and it's easier to remain quiet and strive to be 'beautiful'.**

So for a long time, I tried to make myself less, and I was quiet and shy in class and I failed to live up to the person I knew I could be. I didn't allow myself to be big.

I was so scared of being everything I knew I could be. I was scared that if I was more ambitious than the boys I would scare them all off and they wouldn't like me - and this makes sense because girls are taught that male validation and approval is fiercely, fiercely important...more important than personal self-approval.

In high school, I dated a boy, but whenever he tried to bring up the empowerment workshops I give or anything I was passionate about, I gave a vague answer because I didn't want to scare him away with the intensity of my dreams. And when he eventually broke up with me out of nowhere, I silently reprimanded myself for being too big, attributed that as the cause of the breakup, and vowed to be less than I was.

In reality, I have a lot to me. I am hugely passionate, I am unrelenting, driven, ambitious, and hungry for more. Senior year of high school, I became so committed to my cause that I finally allowed myself to fall in love with my big personality. And when I did, I became infinitely happier and was able to accomplish so much more.

One of the major reasons why I was finally able to embrace my big ambition was because of the character Leslie Knope from the television show Parks and Recreation. If you haven't seen it yet, go watch it right now. Or after you finish this chapter. SOON!! :) If you've already seen it, re watch it.

Parks and Recreation is about a small town government employee who has big dreams. The main character Leslie Knope, played by Amy Poehler, is wildly ambitious, hardworking, caring, really, really funny, and outstandingly passionate about her career, waffles, and friendship. She is one hell of a personality and protagonist. I started watching this show with my Mom when I was a freshman in high school. I was totally captivated by Leslie - there was so much to her and she was so successful. In fact, in one episode, she even admitted that she sometimes inspired herself - something a female should never admit to, or else she'll be considered vain.

Leslie Knope made me want to be more. She gave me permission to be my big, passionate self. She combatted the notion that girls should be beautiful above all else, and showed me that it is admirable to be kind, to be bold, to be smart. **She taught me that being myself is a worthy investment.**

Leslie Knope is white and blonde - just like me. The fact that I sort of look like Leslie Knope is something not to be under estimated. I was able to see myself in Leslie Knope, and I was affected by the power of visualization.

Research shows that visualization is a very powerful tool in sparking progress and growth. In The Talent Code, there is a scene in which a frustrated music student named Clarissa watches her teacher play a few bars of a very beautiful song. Clarissa was entranced, and "got an image of herself as a performer"; Clarissa visualized herself being able to perform the bars of the difficult and beautiful song. As a result of powerful self-visualization, she was able to "accomplish a month's worth of practice in six minutes", and her practice time was more effective than many of her counterparts. **The reason why she was able to make so much progress was because she was able to self-visualize, and she was able to identify that she wanted to be like her teacher.**

Let's break it down in super simple terms: **When there is a role model who shows you that you can do something, you're usually able to do it.** Clarissa's role model showed her that she could play the song. Leslie Knope showed me that I could be my big self.

Role models make you aspire to do more, and to be more. With a positive role model, you're more likely to reach your full potential.

This is why true, diverse female representation is so crucially important. The impact that Leslie Knope had on me is enormous, and it's partially because I look like her. *But what about the Latina girls, who don't have a 'Leslie Knope' that looks like them? Where is the African American Leslie Knope? The lesbian Leslie Knope? The Indian Leslie Knope? The curvy Leslie Knope? The disabled Leslie Knope? The trans Leslie Knope? Where is she??*

Though I was afraid to be big, and that is a personal thing, **I was largely afraid to be myself because I was scared that who I am as a person wouldn't be likable - and that is a very common thing. Girls so often are afraid to be themselves because they are afraid that they won't be liked.** After all, we rarely show girls who have any kind of personality being liked...

In place of role models, there are female bodies that conform to the standard of beauty. I will talk about this in great detail in the sexualization section, but for now I will briefly make it clear that females are barely represented - unless they take their shirt off.

The Geena Davis Institute tracked over five thousand speaking roles in popular movies and found that females only received 29% of the speaking roles, proving that females are usually responsible for shutting up and looking pretty...

However, at least females sometimes get to talk. **If you're not white, you're probably not even going to make it on screen.** The Geena Davis Institute found that a full 85.5% of the characters in G-rated films are white, 4.8% are black, and 9.7% are from "other" ethnicities.

Additionally, when females are represented, they are sexualized. Females are over five times more likely than males to be wearing sexually revealing clothing. Girls are portrayed as the sexual sidekick, rather than the leader of their own adventure.

Furthermore, right now, females are far more likely than males to have a thin body, and to be referenced by another character as physically attractive or desirous. I'd also like to note that when I say females have a thin body, I mean THIN. In fact, a study of 134 episodes of popular Nickelodeon shows found that **87% of female characters aged 10 to 17 were underweight**. With such a devastating reality, it should be no surprise that 44% of girls believe they are overweight, and that 60% are actively trying to lose weight. Our media represents such a limiting standard of beauty; **In fact, the body type portrayed in advertising as the ideal is possessed naturally by only 5% of American females.**

I was unable to find statistics on different sexual orientations or on those able bodied/minded vs. not, but I suppose the fact that I couldn't find any says more than actual statistics would.

Gail Dines, author of Pornland, explains why one body shape is such a problem, saying "They take the abnormal body and make it normal by virtue of its visibility, while making the normal bodies of real women look abnormal by virtue of their invisibility". The utter invisibility of other body shapes creates insecurity in those who don't have the single body shape portrayed.

We know that exposure to this kind of limiting media takes a toll on girls' body image, and has very real consequences. In fact, there's really no question about the fact that media plays a huge role in shaping body image. Common Sense Media reports, "There is an abundance of research (experimental and correlational studies) on the role that media play in girls' and women's body concerns. **Studies have found evidence to support both direct and indirect relationships between girls' and women's consumption of mainstream media and their idealization of certain body types and appearance-oriented behaviors**".

And, the invisibility of non-white races and ethnicities creates a white ideal, and sadly, exposure to a white ideal "in the media may be damaging to women of color who cannot match that ideal". Research shows that there is a negative relationship between music video exposure and self-esteem in African American adolescents. One girl from my survey wrote, "I hate that African Americans aren't accepted as beautiful in this society. Please make voices heard for all girls!" **If you are somehow involved in film, and you are reading this, please hear these girls. Please represent them. Their stories are just as important, and please show them as being both beautiful and capable. Please hear them, and please make their voices heard.**

We need to see gender diversity. We need to see body diversity. We need to see racial and ethnic diversity. We need to see sexual orientation diversity. We need diversity - period.

We need girls to believe that they can do anything. We need girls who want to be the heroine, and who believe that they really can be. And we can achieve this by having an excess of role models, rather than an excess of sexualized sidekicks. Everyone needs a Leslie Knope character that will inspire them to be more. If there were more Hermione's, and Leslie Knope's, and more positive strong female characters, I really believe that many more girls would be able to live up to their full potentials. **We need to change our media so that way girls are able to reach their full potentials.**

So how do we change the media? I have two ideas.
 1. **Get more women in the media.**
 2. **Use your voice to make a difference!**

1. Get More Women in the Media

Currently, men hold 97% of clout, or key, mainstream media positions...this does not leave much room for females to have control over how they are represented. **Females need better representation, and we need more women telling their own stories. We need more women writing and directing and producing.** Caroline Heldman, a Professor and media critic writes, "Media are highly influential in creating and communicating societal norms about proper roles and behaviors for men and women. If more women were involved in the production of entertainment and news media, we would see more women on screen and better roles portraying women as powerful subjects instead of passive sexual objects. **More images and more diverse**

images of women in media would lead to a revolution of identify and leadership if millions of little girls grew up thinking of themselves as fully capable, ambitious human beings instead of bodies to be worked on in order to get validation through male attention". Hearing women's voices and allowing women to tell their stories is a simple solution.

2. Use Your Voice to Make a Difference!

This is the more realistic of the two solutions, the easier solution, and truthfully it's probably more effective. You have got to speak up and make a difference, because there are so many ways that you can use your voice to make a difference. I challenge you to take two of my ideas and act on them. Here are a few of my ideas below:

- Call out a magazine in a tweet for skinny or fat shaming
- Write a letter to a television station and ask them to create more positive media
- Send in a customer complaint to makeup companies who advertise negatively
- Go to the movies to support awesome, strong female led films
- Create your own movie or video that's positive
- Write your own story that stars two best friends who are both unique and smart
- Sign my diverse media petition at change.org/p/diversemedia
- Write a slam poem calling out the media industry for it's unrealistic expectations
- Host your own fashion show
- Tell your story on Facebook or in a video
- Write an email to someone involved in the film industry asking for better media
- Tweet your criticism of that sexist movie you saw

What other ideas do you have?

_____

_____

_____

_____

****

We Need to Become Self Confident and Body Positive

The third solution is to become self-confident and body positive ourselves. Change begins with us.

I want to start off this section by making it clear that self-confidence and body positivity is a choice. It's not an easy choice, but it IS a choice. **YOU are the one who gets to determine what you think of yourself.**

Something that I've always said at workshops is that you get to define beauty for yourself, and that the media/boys/anyone else can NOT define beauty for you. But this time I want to strengthen my point and really focus on it more. A few months ago, a friend of mine essentially said that he wasn't attracted to me because of my height. The reason why I'm bringing this up is because if a boy had told 16 year old Ashley she wasn't hot because of her height, I would have believed it. I would have thought, 'A boy doesn't think I'm hot because I'm short, so he's right, I'm NOT hot'. And I would have cried a lot. After all, a boy not liking me because of my height was one of my biggest fears.

But when my friend told 18 year old Ashley I'm not hot because of my height, it literally didn't even phase me. Instead, I thanked him for being honest and I meant it...after all, I have no control over his personal preferences. The reason why I barely cared that he didn't find me hot, was because I knew he was wrong!!!!!

Kidding - sort of. For real, I knew that it didn't matter what he thought of me, hot or not, because HE does not get to determine if I'm beautiful or not. I do. I am the only person that can. And I choose to view myself as beautiful. Despite the fact that lots of boys aren't into me for what I look like, I still choose to view myself as hot. And despite the fact that I'm under five feet and models are a foot taller than me, I still choose to view myself as attractive because I am the ONLY one who gets to determine my beauty. **Just because someone says something about you does not mean that it's true.** At the end of the day, you are the only one whose opinion matter on your appearance, and you are the only one that gets to decide if you're beautiful or not.

So in that case, let's question how we view beauty, and then redefine it! Why should only white, blonde, toned, big breasted females get to be beautiful? Why can't women with black skin and curly hair get to be beautiful too? Who said Indian women can't be beautiful as they are? Why the heck does our standard of beauty have to be so limiting and unattainable? And, why can't personality and ambition and intelligence be beautiful??

I call bullshit on this whole unattainable and limiting beauty standard thing. Sorry media, but **I'm just not buying it anymore.** Beauty isn't measured by waist or breast size, by skin color, or by the space between a female's thighs - to heck with that.

I believe that beauty is up to the individual. **I believe that beauty is inclusive, not exclusive**. I believe that differences are beautiful. I believe that people who are undeniably true to themselves are beautiful. I believe that compassion and thoughtfulness and big, curly hair is beautiful - equally as beautiful as straight hair. I don't care if a person is heavy, in the middle, skinny, tall, short, blonde, a brunette, white, black, or any other skin tone - I believe that anyone whose cheeks are flushed with passion and excitement is beautiful.

So, how will you define beauty? After all, media doesn't get to determine what beautiful is. Nor do boys. Or girls. Or literally anyone. So, how are you going to define beauty? We all have personal preferences and the capacity to appreciate differences - acknowledge what you really think, not what the media wants you to think!

What is beautiful to you?

_____
_____
_____
_____

I am proud to announce that I think I am beautiful. :) I am so proud, because I have learned to love the parts of my body I once hated!

And obviously I have moments where I'm filled with insecurity, and I'm not perfect with body image and self-esteem, but that's okay because **self-love is forgiving.**

So, how did I get to a point where I'm giving workshops talking about positive body image? And what can YOU do to become body positive and self-confident? Well, you're about to find out.

****

Accept Your Body

First, accept your body. You don't have to love it yet - just accept it. Let me tell you something right now: Your body is going to change as you get older and grow up. Your body might get bigger, it might get smaller, it might get taller, and someday maybe even shorter. The reality is that as we age and grow up, our bodies are GOING to change. And right now, a lot of you guys are going through puberty and the reality is that your bodies are going to change now more than ever.

We can try and fight our bodies from changing. We can try and fight the eventual wrinkles with wrinkle cream, we can try and lose the weight we gain after and if we someday give birth, and we can fight the college freshman 15, or the weight people usually put on their freshman year of college by dieting and being the only one of our friends not enjoying the pizza delivery at 2 am. That's no fun though.

We can try and fight our bodies from changing, but wouldn't it be so much better just to accept them? What would happen if you accepted your body...if you stopped fighting it and just accepted it and met your body where it was? What if you stopped judging and constantly evaluating your body? What if, instead of striving towards that one seemingly perfect body type that is white, skinny yet curvy, blonde, tall, and nearly hairless, we accepted that our bodies are going to change and grow?? What if, instead of wanting that one body "perfect" body shape, what if we loved our bodies FOR that change, not despite it??

What if, just maybe...what if you viewed your body as a work in progress?

I did an online survey in high school and I collected over one thousand quotes and opinions on body image and self-confidence. One girl wrote, "Beauty is presented like a narrow box in the media and I fail to see the merit of appreciating and striving towards something that is physically impossible and potentially life threatening to try and attain...we are all works in progress, and I think that is beautiful". And I LOVE that attitude - **I am a work in progress and THAT is beautiful!!**

This year, freshman year of college, was not my best for body image. I put on several pounds, and it was a small shock. It used to take me months and months to put on a pound, and because I'm so short every pound feels like it counts a lot. Anyway, I felt very worried when I started splitting my leggings, outgrowing my pants, and worst

56

of all the black and white skirt I spent so much of my own money on at H and M. First semester, I felt really self-conscious of my body and I tried to lose weight by working out and dieting, which to be honest I'm kind of ashamed to admit because I'm the one that's supposed to be above it all and it's not like I'm new to giving workshops.

I wish that I had remembered that my body is a work in progress, and should be appreciated as such. We are ALL works in progress, and THAT my friends is what beautiful is. Second semester I started to feel much more comfortable in my slightly bigger body, and I really know for sure now that I am a work in progress and that is what is so beautiful.

****

Stop Blaming Your Appearance

Then, stop blaming everything on your appearance. I used to blame everything and anything that went wrong on the way I looked, more specifically on my height. I actually thought that the reason why guys didn't like me, was because of my height. I actually thought that no one could possibly like someone who was so embarrassing to be seen with. That was my legitimate mindset. I knew that if I could just be a little bit taller, everything in my life would be great - Boys would like me, I would be popular, everything would work out! Every night, before I went to bed, I prayed to God that I could be just a little taller.

I am not the only girl that has blamed her body for things that are not our bodies fault….so many of my friends have blamed their problems on their insecurities.

However, **our bodies don't deserve to be blamed** - they literally are not at fault whatsoever, and it's devastating that we have learned to blame our bodies. You're the same exact person thin as you are fat. You're the same exact person tall as you are short.

We need to change our mindsets, not our bodies. If we want to achieve a healthy body image, we have got to stop assigning unfair blame to our bodies.

Have you ever blamed your body or appearance for something?

_____

_____

_____

****

Don't Put Yourself Down - Talk Yourself Up

Another thing we need to do is stop putting ourselves down, and start talking ourselves up. Very often, we are our own worst enemies. One girl from my survey said, "I never criticize other people, only myself. For example, I've said in this survey that physical looks are extremely important but that only applies to me. I rarely ever judge someone on their looks or say that a girl is too fat or too ugly. I'm only hard on myself".

I used to constantly comment on how fat and untoned my legs were, and I have recently started to notice how 'gross' I perceive my arms to be. **Sadly, research shows that 93% of young women engage in "fat talk", or talking poorly about their bodies, in everyday life offline.**

Have you ever talked poorly about your body, or commented to yourself negatively on how you look?

_____
_____
_____

We have got to start talking ourselves up. If we look at ourselves in the mirror, and say 'wow, I really like my eyebrows', **we are eventually going to like our eyebrows.** That's what I did - I love my eyebrows because **I chose to and because I told myself I loved them repeatedly.**

You can do this too. Start looking in the mirror, and instead of yelling at yourself about your flaws, notice things you like. **Start by making a list of things you really, genuinely like about your body.** You might not be able to come up with them right away and that's okay. That's okay :) Don't stress yourself out. You can always come back to it.

Things we love about our bodies:

Me (Ashley)	You
My eyebrows, because they are prominent and strong.	

My dimples, because they're super cute and make me look happy.	
My shoulders, because someone once complimented me on them, and ever since I've appreciated them.	
My waist, hips, and legs. I actually really like the way that they curve.	
My smile, because smiling is awesome.	

Once you stop putting yourself down, you'll be able to start talking yourself up. It sounds really silly, but before I take a shower or whenever I undress, I'll take a moment to look at myself and to appreciate my body. I'll say things to myself like 'Ashley, I really like the fact that you have curves and you know what? You're not super tiny waist is okay, and it's worth loving'. It's silly but it helps.

What are some positive things you can say to yourself about your body?

_____

_____

_____

****

Wear Clothing You Feel Awesome In

Something that I wish I knew earlier is that wearing clothing and makeup you feel comfortable in is SOOO important to self-esteem.

Growing up, I would always try to wear tight cami tank tops. However, the camis are designed for girls with 100 percent flat stomachs, which is not the case for my belly. My stomach would always stick out and then I would feel disgusting and self-conscious. You never, ever should have to feel that way towards your body. Wearing clothing that empowers you, rather than clothing you feel self-conscious in, is going to make a difference, and this is a lesson that I very recently learned...

First semester, I would go to parties as a college student does, and I would look around and compare myself to all of the other girls and feel so out of place and so completely awful about my body and face in comparison to them. Halfway through first semester, one of my friends came to visit me and gave me a shirt that I felt really, really good in. I felt genuinely good in it and when I went out that night, I didn't feel self-conscious - I felt amazing. I then realized what a difference clothing and makeup can make to your self-esteem.

So take a minute now and think about what empowers you? Does makeup empower you? Or your natural face? What kind of clothing empowers you? For some girls modesty is empowering and for others skin is empowering...what empowers you?

_____

_____

_____

****

Pictures Are a Must

In my best friend Maddie's #PartyLikeBodyPosi video, a few girls mentioned how they feel body positive when they take and share pictures of themselves. I am a HUGE fan of photo shoots, and the reason why is because having pictures of yourself that you feel good about is AMAZING for your self-esteem.

Something that I recommend is that you try having a photo shoot with a friend...step out of your comfort zone. And if not a photo shoot, dedicate some time to take some selfies. Take all kinds of pictures, too. Take pictures of yourself without makeup and learn to find the beauty in that, and take pictures where you're not smiling either. It's empowering to have pictures you like.

****

Stand Up For Yourself

And then once you're able to talk yourself up, you **need to stand up to the people who put you down.**

I'm going to tell you a story that I cringe thinking about.

When I was a sophomore, one of my best friends was a senior guy. At the end of the day, I was standing by my locker, collecting my things, when he walked by. I joined him and then a very tall friend of his started to walk by us. My friend introduced the two of us, saying "Ashley, this is X and X, this is Ashley". X looked at me and asked, smirking, "Are you a dwarf?"

My heart stopped. All of my insecurities started flooding back. I couldn't believe that the first thing someone would comment on when they looked at me was my small stature. I started to laugh, and say no, and he immediately asked me how tall I was. When I politely refused to give him an answer, he continued. He then pretended to look at our mutual friend in amazement, and pointed at me like I was some kind of animal. Cheeks flaming, I walked straight ahead. I was so embarrassed of the whole situation that I cried myself to sleep that night.

I was also disappointed in myself for laughing and going along with him. I wanted to let him know it wasn't okay to comment on my height and I wasn't someone to mess around with. So the next time I saw him, I was standing outside of History class, before the bell. His eyes lit up when he recognized me, but before he could make fun of me again, I started speaking. I'm pretty sure I opened up with a curse and said two or three sentences that were crude, loud, and to the point. I was so exhilarated by the prospect of standing up for myself, but looking back I regret the immature way I handled it.

The next time I saw him was after school, and auditions or callbacks had just finished. A few of my theater friends and I were waiting to be picked up, when he came out of nowhere. He joined the friend group I was standing with, and I didn't want to deal with him, so I walked to another group of friends. I could still hear him though, and he actually started talking about me. He was saying things like 'How tall do you have to be to be a legal midget? Does anyone know?' and 'How common are legal midgets?' Since I had tried playing it cool one time, and screaming another, I decided to try ignoring him. When I didn't give him a reaction, he just got louder. At this point, I tried to pull out my IPod, but I couldn't get the music to play. He literally started pointing at me, and I don't remember what exactly he said, but he involved the group of my theater friends. When he started talking directly about me, and I could clearly hear, I started to tear up. You have to understand, he was talking to a group of people who I looked up to and admired, and wanted to be like. So when he started talking to them, he really hit a nerve. I grabbed my stuff, and sat outside in the freezing cold, crying.

It sounds lame that I was so hurt by his comments, but I was and I am not ashamed to admit it. I know that many other girls and boys are affected by rude or unnecessary comments as well.

I decided that this whole exchange needed to end, and I needed to end it once and for all. So the next time I saw him was in the library after school. I was with two of my friends, and I called his name very politely, and asked if I could talk to him. He looked at me, smirked, and said no, because he had a band lesson to go to. I responded, 'I'll be quick'. I then delivered a 30 second rehearsed speech. He laughed at me the entire time and mocked me, but he stayed for the full time and didn't leave. I said something about how first, I wanted to apologize for swearing at him because that was the wrong way to do things. I explained to him that I was actually insecure about my height, and that I didn't appreciate him picking on me or commenting on it. I then told him if it continued I would go down to guidance.

After I stood up for myself, he stopped talking to me about my height. The fourth thing that we need to do is to **stand up to the people who make you feel self-conscious about our bodies.** I want you to know, that **if someone is commenting on your body and you don't like it, you need to tell them to stop.** It is wholly unacceptable, and you need to stick up for yourself and tell them to stop. In some cases, they might not even know what they're doing. In other cases, they sure as heck know what they're doing. Either way though, you need to inform them that what they're doing is wrong. You can politely ask them to stop, or explain to them that it actually hurts and it isn't okay for them to comment on your body. <u>If they refuse to stop, go tell a teacher or guidance counselor or someone you can trust.</u> I know that you might be worried about being a 'snitch', but at the end of the day, we really can't keep tolerating this behavior.

This is an anonymous paper one of my best friends wrote for me, and I hope you will all take the time to read it:

"I don't know many things, but I do know that junior year is a rough one. There's a lot of pressure coming from all different areas in your life, and it often made me feel like I was trapped in a box.

My problem with junior year really started about three weeks into school. I went through something traumatic, and it immediately changed my perspective. I saw the world as a bigger, scarier place.

I was vulnerable, confused, upset, and looking for an outlet. I tried boys, alcohol, self-harm... Nothing seemed to work. So naturally, the self-harm grew worse and the other outlets started to create other problems that just transformed me into a bigger mess.

Just as I thought I had things under control, it started. I had two boys in one of my class that would relentlessly tease me. Tell me things like "You wish you were as pretty as your friends, don't you?" or "Oh my God, who would ever want to touch your ass… You really shouldn't be wearing those pants".

It ruined me.

I cried and cried, and my mental health only worsened. It became an everyday thing, I grew scared of the class. It was hard work to go through the entire thing pretending to be invisible and keeping my composure. And then one day, after I attended one of Ashley's first seminars, I realized that it had to stop.

I told one of the boys that it had to stop, that it hurt, that it was affecting me so much more than he knew. That he didn't know what my life was like, that I didn't need his opinion, that it's MY BODY and I can do what I want with it.

It felt good. The world got brighter. I was honest with my real friends, I let them lift me up and pull me out of the hole I had buried myself in. I picked myself up and I moved on, because that's what you have to do.

I'm writing this for Ashley because I know I'm not the only one who experienced something like this. These boys were my friends. They were people I trusted, people who knew me. It's shocking how far some people will go to put you down just because they're insecure about themselves. But they won't stop on their own- You HAVE to tell them.

It's not about feeling one hundred percent confident in yourself in this case. **It's about knowing that you are so much better than what anyone else has to say, and that they don't have the right to say it. I cannot express enough how important it is to speak your mind and to let yourself be heard. Honesty is the most powerful tool I've ever used in my life, and I know it sounds corny, but it's true. I am a better person today because I told people whose opinion was ruining me that THEY were wrong and I was right because it was MY BODY. It's completely one hundred percent yours and you shouldn't ever let anyone else say anything that makes you upset about it.** You shouldn't turn and try other outlets or never wear shorts or hide under your Mother's baggy t-shirts.

You need to join the MOVEment. You need to speak up for yourself. **It doesn't matter if it's a joke to them. As long as it's not to you, something has to be said. It's your body, it'll always be with you.**

Join the MOVEment and show it some love".

You have GOT to stand up for yourself.

Have you ever stood up for yourself? Have you ever had an experience where you wish you stood up for yourself?

_____

_____

_____

_____

_____

****

Stop Putting Down Others

And then, once you stop putting yourself down, and you ask other people to stop putting you down, **you need to learn to stop putting others down for their bodies.** We're all on the same team. We are all, as females, going through the same exact things, and are quite literally (please notice the high school musical allusion) all in this together. When we rudely comment on other women's bodies, we're hurting women a whole. **We shouldn't be fighting against each other - we should be working together.**

One girl from my survey wrote, "I see so much hate between women. It can be a girl calling another girl ugly because she keeps her hair in a ponytail and dresses in t-shirts and baggy jeans, or a girl calling another girl a slut because she can looks really cute in her outfit". I know I personally have put down girls for their clothing choices, just because they were different from mine. Even the other day a friend of mine was commenting on how she dislikes Kylie Jenner's makeup because she thinks it's just too much - but who cares! It's not hurting anyone and it's Kylie's right to embrace her individuality and to explore with makeup! Have you ever contributed to that kind of thing?

How so?

_____

_____

_____

Unfortunately, we're not doing any good by being rude about other women. Courtney E. Martin writes, "The more critically and less compassionately you view other women's bodies, the less you will have the capacity to accept yourself". In other words, **if you view other women's bodies with jealousy, hatred, and judgment, you're going to have a more difficult time accepting your own. Likewise, the more compassionately you view other women's bodies, the more you will have the capacity to love your own body.** We need to end body shaming - both fat and skinny shaming. **It is never okay to shame any kind of body.**

It is truly so important that we learn to stop putting down other people's bodies. I'm not sure we realize what a powerful ally we can be in everyone else's quest for self-confidence and positive body image. In my own personal journey for a positive body image, I received a lot of support from my friends. My theater friends especially were so accepting and encouraging. They would always compliment me, on not just my body, but my acting skills too. It is so important to have a group of people who are accepting. **The same way a group of critical people can bring down your confidence, a group of encouraging people can boost it.** I don't think I could made it through middle school without them.

I want you all to know that YOU can boost people up, and you can have a serious impact on self-confidence.

Have you ever made a difference in the way a person views their body image?

_____

_____

_____

****

No More Apologizing

Sometimes, when I don't wear makeup, I APOLOGIZE for looking the way I do, and I will put myself down and say things like 'No, I look gross, I don't want to take a picture' or 'Ew, I'm so sorry, I didn't have time to put on makeup'. To be honest, I've even stayed home before because I felt so insecure about my appearance and I didn't want anyone to look at me.

Have you ever apologized for the way you look? Why?

_____

_____

We shouldn't have to apologize for the way we look, but to me it's become second nature. This is a consequence of the fact that girls are taught that their body and appearance is inherently gross, and that it needs to be changed. Well, guess what!

From here on out I refuse to apologize for my appearance. Why in the world should I be sorry for being my radiant, sometimes very sleepy self?? **I want to love my body in all forms**, and I want to love the way I look without makeup, at 6 am, and no more a apologizing is a way to get there. I urge you to join with me, and to **stop apologizing for the way you look. You have nothing to be ashamed of,** even if you've been convinced that you do.

****

You Are Not Your Body

Additionally, it is important to realize that we are not our bodies. I want to recount a part from <u>Perfect Girls, Starving Daughters</u> that really resonated with me:

"My friends' therapists recently asked her, 'So how are you?' She answered, 'Oh, I'm okay, feeling kind of fat this week'

'No, but how are you', he questioned again.

'What do you mean?' she questioned. 'I just answered that'.

'No, how are *you*?' he asked for the third time.

'I'm okay, I told you', she spat back, frustrated with what appeared to be a weird psychological game.

'You realize that you are not your body?' he finally explained. **'You realize that your body is only one aspect of who you are?'**

....Almost every girl I know lives as if how she feels about her body is representative of how she feels about everything else. It doesn't matter how successful or in love or at what place she is in the rest of her life, is she feels unhappy about her body, she is unhappy in general.

Martin continues to then say, "**We are not our bodies. Our souls are not our stomachs. Our brains are not our butts.** A lot of women have lost track of the truth that how we feel about our bodies does not have to be indicative of how we feel about ourselves."

You are not your body. *You are not your body..* Our bodies, are different than our minds. Our bodies, are separate from who we are as people. There is a separation between our bodies and who we actually are! We grew up believing that we had to measure ourselves in terms of our bodies, but that isn't true. In fact, our bodies and who we are as people have nothing to do with each other. Our bodies have literally NOTHING to do with who we are! Nothing at all!!!!

I used to think badly about myself a person, because I disliked the way I looked. **I did not realize that who I am as a person is different and separate from what I look like. Recognize that you are more than a body, and you're one step closer to positive body image and a healthy self-esteem.**

****

Become a Person You Really, Really Like

Sophomore year of high school, I started to think about who I wanted to become. **I wanted to be ambitious, driven, educated, creative, bubbly, a good person.** After I thought about who I wanted to become, I worked so that way I could become her. Today, I am proud to say that I am the person I wanted to be.

Now it's important to like yourself as a person, because when you like yourself as a person, your thighs and height and body starts to matter less. **Literally who cares what my stomach looks like - it's what my personality is like that matters!** When I started to like myself as a person, I kind of stopped thinking about my body because it's just unimportant. My brain and who I am is what matters.

You all should really take time to think about what kind of person you want to be, and what characteristics you want to have. If you're not sure who you want to be, or where to start, start by thinking about characteristics you admire in other people. For example, I really admired my older friends who were intelligent and educated, so I wanted to be that too.

So in that case, who do you want to be? What qualities do you hope to have and what kind of person do you want to be?

_____
_____
_____
_____
_____
_____
_____
_____
_____
_____
_____

I think it's also important to think about the qualities we like about ourselves. This also might take time, and that's okay. Take your time, and if you don't know, come back and fill it in later - what do you like about yourself?

Me (Ashley!!)	You (!!)
I like the fact that I'm open minded. I wasn't always so open minded, and I love that I appreciate everyone and have an open mind to different perspectives.	
I like that I value friendship.	
I love that I am so ambitious and creative. I love that I am always hungry to do more, and that I have the capability to create whatever I want to.	
I love that I get excited really easily. It's a fun trait to have.	
I like and am glad that I work hard and have a strong work ethic. I'm really grateful for	

that trait.	
I like that I recognize there's always room for improvement. There is always is something that I can do better, or some way that I could be better, and I'm glad that I don't settle.	
Speaking of settling, I'm glad that I don't settle anymore. I'm glad that I know my worth.	
I like that I am a good public speaker and a good writer. I'm really proud of those two things. I might not be great, but I work really hard at writing, and I rehearse a lot of public speaking, and I'm proud of myself for how much time and effort I put in.	
I like that I have started to make decisions that are right for me. It's a pretty huge step, and I'm proud of what I do.	

Begin to identify the things that make you you. And then start to appreciate them. **When you start to appreciate who you are as a person, your body will become less important and a lot easier to love**.

****

Surround Yourself with Role Models

Another easy way to become confident and body positive is to surround yourself with role models and people who have made an impact on the world with their mind. When you are surrounded by people you admire for more than their bodies, you start to want to become more than a body.

96% of females who answered my survey asserted that they feel that the models used in beauty advertising are not a realistic representation of women today. So when beauty advertising fails, sometimes it's up to you to surround yourself with powerful role models.

In the television show Parks and Recreation, the main character's entire office is covered in pictures of powerful women who she admires. I replicated what she did, and I have a section in my bedroom designed to empower and inspire myself.

On my wall, I have pictures of Emma Watson, Leslie Knope/Amy Poehler, Jennifer Siebel Newsom, myself, Leymah Gbowee, Lupita Nyong'o, Lorde, Malala, and more. These are all women who have either inspired me or who have excelled at what I hope to. There are role models out there for whatever you are interested in, who can inspire you to be bigger and better!

What do you care about? What do you find interesting or are you passionate about?

_____
_____
_____
_____

Now, Google role models and pioneers in that field! For example, if you're interested in medicine or being a doctor, the first female doctor would be a terrific role model. Who did you find?

_____
_____
_____

There are always people out there. **It's so important to surround yourself with who you want to become, because you really can't be what you can't see.** Creating a space in your bedroom or a space on the cover of your notebook to fill with inspiring people is a great starting point.

****

Get Angry

I have three more tips for you. The first tip is to allow yourself to get angry. It is a lot easier to have a good body image, when you realize how annoying and harmful it is when you had a bad one in the first place.

Once I got really angry that such awesome people were facing self-confidence issues, I started realizing that all of the time and energy we spend on reaching obnoxiously ridiculous standards **holds us back.** And then I was pissed - Women are being cheated, and women cannot fight for equality, because we don't have the energy to do it. We are bogged down by beauty standards and foolish expectations that take up our time mentally and force us to constantly focus on something that we can truly only semi-change.

I am not playing Survival of the Prettiest anymore. When I started getting really angry, I started committing myself to getting a better body image. I was so bothered by this terrible phenomenon that I wanted to seriously change it. **And I knew that if I wanted to change an entire culture, I would first need to change myself.** And so I did and here I am, and here we are today.

I'm going to beat the game, and I have stopped worrying about society's expectations of me. **And instead, I am reaching my full potential. I am devoting my time and energy not to diets, but to making the world a better place.** I hope that you will be able to get angry and start to devote your energy to things that are more worth your time. As Courtney E. Martin says, "You don't need a diagnosable eating disorder to be powerfully affected by these issues. If you spend precious time and energy worrying about your weight, instead of your soul, you have been cheated. If you waste your sharp intellect on comparing and contrasting diet fads instead of the state of the world, we are all cheated". **It is far time we stopped being cheated, and instead, we started cheating and changing the game.**

****

Educate Yourself

My second to last tip for you is to educate yourself. It is so freeing to be able to look at advertisements and say 'Hold up, MY body type isn't the problem - **this advertisement and its portrayal of women IS the problem!**' I seriously encourage all of you to learn more about the messages of the media and more about the beauty standard, because that is when you start to gain control and power. If you're not sure where to start sign up for my weekly newsletter at ashleyolafsen.com

****

Use Your Voice and Potential

Finally, use your voice and potential to stand up for positive body image. When you speak up, you WIN! And THAT'S how you rise above the beauty standard. Use your voice to start clubs, to start a petition, to write to beauty magazines and television shows. Use your voice to tweet, to create an app, to instagram a body positive picture.

How else can you use your voice?

_____

_____

_____

_____

****

Forgive Yourself

Having self-confidence and a positive body image isn't easy. It's hard. Be forgiving of yourself. Self-confidence isn't something that happens overnight - you have to really work for it and put time and effort into loving yourself.

****

Choose Confidence

As I conclude, I want to repeat myself: **Self-confidence is ours to decide.** It's up to you. Not the media. Not your parents. Not your friends. Not your teachers. **Self-confidence is up to you. So what are you going to decide?**

****

Discussion Questions

Was there anything that really stood out to you in this section? Why?

_____

_____

_____

What did you relate to?

_____

_____

_____

Did any of you learn anything about yourself?

_____

_____

_____

Why is it so difficult for females to have a good body image?

_____

_____

_____

Do you think that we as girls contribute to this body shaming of each other? How so?

_____

_____

_____

Have you surrounded yourself with people who bring you up or people who bring you down?

_____

_____

_____

Have any of you overcome any insecurities? How did it make you feel?

_____
_____
_____

How have your insecurities affected you?

_____
_____
_____

Who would you be if you didn't have those insecurities?

_____
_____
_____

Why is it so important that we address issues like body image, media, and self-esteem?

_____
_____
_____

Why is it important to show different races and ethnicities? Why is it important to show different body shapes in the media, too? Why is it important to have a diverse media?

_____
_____
_____

What action will you take to change the way we treat the female body today?

_____
_____
_____
_____
_____
_____

COMPETITION

Opening Quotes:

"I think there is too much pressure these days to looks and act a certain way, which makes us girls insecure." - Anonymous survey taker

"Coming from an all-girls private school, I see it all first-handedly. There is so much pressure and competition to do well, academically, as well as the need to look a certain way. I myself am stressed out constantly cause I feel that I have to do good and get into a good university later on..." - Anonymous survey taker

"The constant competition and impossible standards of beauty we're held to has caused a lot of self-doubt in my life. I wish things were different." - Anonymous survey taker

****

Opening Questions:

How do you treat females? Not just your friends?

_____

_____

_____

Do you compete with others? How so?

_____

_____

_____

Do you find yourself getting jealous when other girls succeed? Do you feel threatened?

_____

_____

_____

Do you or have you ever excluded anyone?

_____

_____

_____

Have you ever been excluded?

_____

_____

_____

Have you not talked to a person because of what you've heard about them?

_____

_____

_____

Have you ever cyber bullied anyone?

_____

_____

_____

Have you ever been cyber bullied? What was the experience like?

_____

_____

_____

****

We Can't Make Progress Divided

One of the major issues females are dealing with right now is competition among women. Let me be clear from the beginning - competition itself isn't inherently bad. But, competition among women is not as positive.

While I was researching, I came across something that really changed the way I view the world and I'd like to share it with you all. Naomi Wolf wrote, "In the 1980s, it was evident that as women became more important, beauty too became more important. **The closer women came to power, the more physical self-consciousness and sacrifice are asked of them. 'Beauty' becomes the condition for a woman to take the next step**". In the margin, with red pen I scrawled, "*This* is a way to keep women competing!" **What I meant is that beauty ideals are a way to keep women divided. When we compete, we drag other females down rather than helping one another rise up.**

When we compete, we are divided, and when people are divided nothing gets accomplished but hatred towards one another.

And when we are divided, it is impossible to unite for a common cause. In other words, we can't move forward and make the issues I've talked about better for females, until we are able to stand together instead of working against each other. **We simply cannot join together if we are too busy competing to be be the most beautiful.**

We are only powerful when we stand as one. I sincerely believe that widespread female friendship and support is ***critically imperative*** to any kind of advance we hope to have. In order to change the way women are treated, we need to start by example. This means we need to treat each other with kindness and respect. We need to support each other, instead of dragging each other down. And most importantly, we need to learn about other perspectives so that way we can do our best to support ALL women - not just richer, white women.

When we drag each other down, it makes it okay for everyone else around us - not just guys, but the media, our larger society, everyone - to drag us down.

****

How We Teach Girls to Compete

In this section, we're going to talk about competition and ways that females are taught to buy into the idea that we should be competing. This competition obsession seems to start out innocently with the 'fairest of them all', and then gradually manifests into 'Who wore it better?' columns, until it results in insecure women who gossip about each other because they feel threatened.

When girls are little, they learn that only **one** person gets to have the happily ever after. In most princess movies, there is usually only one princess who gets to be valued as the best, or the 'fairest of them all'. In fact, other females aren't even shown usually, unless they're the villain. The princesses don't usually have any genuine female friendships and are lucky if they get to be friends with an animal, teaching girls that they need to be the very best in order to fulfill their fairytale dreams.

As we get a little older, girls are constantly being pitted against each other. This happens in the books we read, the movies we see, and the media we are constantly being exposed to. **There can never just be two individuals who are both equally awesome in their own ways, instead, there's always competition between girls to fight for the top status. Girls are constantly competing for the 'best' hair, makeup, body, for boys, status, etc.** Think about it.

In magazines, we get to be part of the female competition and choose what star wore the outfit better. Frequently, there will be sections devoted to girl vs. girl created drama, failing to recognize that both girls are able to wear the same thing in their own unique, spectacular way. **Furthermore, beauty magazines encourage competition over hair, makeup, nails, bodies, and essentially anything else you can think of beauty related.** One word used frequently in these magazines is 'best'. **Women are constantly being asked to be the very best, and best is singular. There cannot be two who are the best. There is one, specific type that is the best, and if you buy the right products then maybe you can be the best...and it's important to note that the specific type you should be is white and straight.**

And we understand that if you don't follow the trends, or you don't compete, you're a social reject. One girl from my survey expressed, "As a girl in middle school there is a lot of pressure to be 'perfect'. You need to have perfect hair, style, grades, etc. There are people who only care about who you are friends with or if you own a Michael Kors bag. It's so hard to feel like I am good enough when I look at myself compared to others. My thighs are bigger, my hair is frizzier, my boobs are smaller, my stomach isn't flat, I don't have a thigh gap... the list could go on for days. Nobody would pick the girl with the nicer personality over the girl with the nicer looks...". This girl is in middle school, and she's worrying about designer handbags instead of her childhood. That's awful.

It's even part of board games! Games like Pretty Pretty Princess have girls competing with other girls to be the 'prettiest' - I mean that's quite literally Survival of the Prettiest right at work, for goodness sake!

And once again - I'm not anti-competition. I love competitive games (especially those done in French class with my best friends). **Competition is not the problem - it's what we encourage females to compete over.**

****

We're All Feeling the Pressure

With competition fueled by the relentless media, girls are feeling the pressure to compete. In fact, my survey found that 70% of girls feel pressure to compete, and girls constantly wrote about competing with each other in the comments section. One girl wrote, "My school is one where most of the competition between students is about grades", whereas another wrote, "I am a 12 year old in 7th and I feel as if sometimes there is a ton of competition between girls...what you wear and who you like and your personality and looks...The girls in my huge group of friends compete, but not visibly. Instagram likes and photos, the cute boys that want to hang out with you, the clothes that you just bought at the mall...We all love each other, but there is an unspoken competition between us all. I realized this a while back and have always been wayyyy better friends with the guys". It's overwhelming how many things we compete over. In other words, as one survey taker put it "Girls are all in completion to be 'that girl'. The girl everyone wants". There's a lot of competition and we're aware of it.

A lot of times, we buy into the notion that females shouldn't get along. I remember saying in middle school how much I 'hate girls because they cause so much drama, I like boys soooooo much better'. I had literally learned to hate other girls, despite the fact that I AM A GIRL!

I remember feeling like I had to compete with everyone, and I remember always feeling like I was miserably losing the competition. I felt like I didn't have the best anything - not the best clothing, not the best hair, certainly not the best relations with boys, not the best friend group, nothing. For a majority of my middle school years, I treated other girls like they were to compete with, instead of to befriend. A girl wrote to me, "I think girls like you and me treat each other like it's a race. They want to be at the top of this list of popularity". Just like her, I did treat other girls like it was a race to grow up. I would judge, evaluate, gossip, and compete with other girls. Girls who had it together threatened me and I would hate them instead of acknowledging how terrific they were.

****

Time to Take Responsibility

This chapter, I hope to examine ways we hurt each other. <u>I'm not saying that females should take all the blame.</u> That would be foolish - quite frankly, the media, society, and other influences are to blame in some ways. I'm saying that we need to add ourselves into the equation, and look at way we are participating.

One girl from my survey recognized this and wrote, "I think a lot of the problems women face in the world today are self-inflicted. Women gossip about each other, pressure each other, and tear each other down too much for anyone to cultivate any sense of self-esteem". We may have been led by the media, however, we are somewhat responsible. Another smart girl agreed, saying "I think that other girls sabotage other girls' confidence in the teen years. There's a bunch of jealousy and that affects confidence. If you're pretty, other girls are jealous and try to bully you or tear you down so that can ruin self-confidence". **Competition hurts everyone.**

So I ask you, right now, to examine the way you treat other girls. **Once we acknowledge that we are hurting, instead of helping, the situation we are in, we can take responsibility. And once we take responsibility, we can work to change our behavior.**

****

Comparing Yourself

Do you compare yourself to other girls? How so?

_____

_____

One way that we drag females down is by comparing ourselves. **When we constantly evaluate, rank, and compare females against each other, we refuse to acknowledge the beauty of differences.** When I do workshops, almost all girls admit to comparing themselves to other girls in their school. One girl wrote, "All my friends are tiny and skinny so I always compare myself to them, which does not help my self-esteem much". I know I used to do this. Looking around, I would notice all of the things that other girls had, that I lacked. And it made me feel real crappy.

One girl wrote, "There is just a lot of pressure in our society to compare ourselves to the "ideals" that the media portrays, and often this pressure take advantage of girls when it shouldn't. Sometimes it can be difficult to be happy with who you are or how you look when you are constantly being compared to others and sometimes criticized for either how you look or how you act". While it is sad to compare yourself to realistic people, it's even more upsetting that so many girls compare themselves to celebs or models - being that what they're comparing themselves to is *very* fake. Cindy Crawford, a famous model, once said "Even I don't wake up looking like Cindy Crawford" - because she didn't even look like herself in her photos!

We shouldn't be comparing ourselves pictures of women who aren't our age, who have been through plastic surgery, who are photo shopped, and have used other extreme measure to alter their body.

When we compare ourselves to other girls, we fail to appreciate how everyone (including ourselves) is beautiful in their own way. Taylor Swift smartly said, "Other women who are killing it should motivate you, thrill you, challenge you and inspire you rather than threaten you and make you feel like you're immediately being compared to them. The only thing I compare myself to is me, two years ago, or me one year ago". I absolutely love her outlook, and I'm really taking it to heart. **From here on out, the only person I will compare myself to is me, and the way I've acted in the past.** I'm going to continue what I do now, and reflect constantly on my behavior and what I've learned to try and be the best I can be. It sounds cliché and kind of lame, but it's a hell lot better than judging our self-worth against other girls' appearances. We need to view other girls supportively, instead of viewing them with hatred and jealousy. I encourage you to appreciate others and yourself, instead of evaluating and comparing.

What will you do moving forward about comparing yourself?

_____

_____

_____

****

Popularity

Do you worry about popularity?

_____

Do you treat people a certain way based on their popularity or yours?

_____

_____

Another way we keep girls competing is through the power system of popularity. Popularity is a problem because it divides people and makes one person more worthy than another. However, <u>**perhaps the largest problem with popularity is how we choose to define it.**</u> Currently, the media defines popular girls as people who are white, skinny, straight, stereotypically beautiful, slightly to outright catty, self-centered, judgmental, and fairly stupid. Many of these popular girls are cheerleaders or pop stars, though there are exceptions. **Popularity is extremely exclusive and very limiting.** After all, have you ever seen an Indian female depicted as popular? Probably not.

There's really no wonder why kids want to be popular - popularity appears to get them everything! Juliet Schor of <u>Born to Buy</u> writes, "marketers have defined cool as the key to social success, as what matter for determining who belongs, who's popular, and who gets accepted by peers". **Of course, this is a brilliant marketing strategy because kids will spend money in order to be considered cool.**

So, popularity is partially determined by how much money each individual has….which means that **the poorer kids lose.** In this way, popularity is racist. Schor writes, "When cool is marketed as expensive, lower income and minorities cannot afford" to be cool. By all accounts, popular is unfair.

Here's the thing about popularity: When we value popularity, we value those who can conform and change themselves to fit our expectations. Now, it goes without saying that kids are impressionable. Kids want to fit in, and want to be loved - which is all well and good. So, the problem is that at a time when children are learning how to be accepted, <u>we teach them that in order to fit in, they should acquire the traits of someone popular.</u> And as stated before, the traits associated with someone popular aren't exactly positive. **Right now, we're teaching girls that popularity means giving up who you are and putting on a catty face.**

In addition to learning who is popular, we learn how to identify those who are unpopular.

When I say unpopular, what comes to mind?

_____

_____

Unpopular people are usually depicted as smart, but they're portrayed as weird, and antisocial and they dress unconventionally. More often than not, they're non-white or disabled.

When media has the kids who do drama or the kids who are overweight with glasses as the 'unpopular' ones, *that's a huge signal to all the kids watching the movie what an unpopular kid looks like. More than that, it's a huge signal to children that they shouldn't display the characteristics that makes a person unpopular.* So, this brings us to our next problem with popularity:

Popularity stifles individual differences. In order to be popular, you have to conform to the expectations of what a popular person is like. Popularity rewards the people who those who are willing to commit. So kids learn that if they really love science, if they use a wheelchair, or if they like to ride horses in their spare time, that they shouldn't be those things, because that might make them unpopular. And, they may reject those parts of themselves, and give up who they are, or what they love in order to be popular. This is a true shame, because it is the individual differences that make us so utterly wonderful.

If a person refuses to conform to society's standards, they must face the consequences of unpopularity. One girl wrote, "As an athlete in a small school, I get looked down at a lot. I don't wear makeup. Sweats and track pants and hoodies are common for me. I don't try to get all the guys. The girls half the time look at me like I'm dumb or something for actually enjoying gym and making soccer my life...But being unlike them is fine for me. I don't want to change who I am to become like one of them". Though I do not encourage or like the negative way she spoke about other females, I chose this example because it shows that she is rejected for refusing to conform. All of this further separates and divides females.

Have you ever given a part of yourself up, in order to be liked?

_____

_____

_____

_____

_____

_____

It seems as though many teenagers and children have. One girl wrote, "The people around me have pressured me into doing a lot of things; wearing makeup, dressing nice, even self-harming. For a while I was bullied for being different". There's nothing wrong with wanting to be accepted - However, we teach girls that in order to be accepted, they must give up who they are as people and look and act a certain way.

Furthermore, children are learning that unpopular people should be treated poorly. Kids understand not only how to identify someone as unpopular, but they understand that they should treat the people are unpopular in a not super nice way. When I was concerned about popularity, I stopped talking to people who I considered to be 'below me', and I was embarrassed to be seen with them.

Perhaps these power relations are reinforced by the media. 'Popular' or 'cool' characters generally don't talk to nerdy or uncool characters. In fact, the popular characters are usually 'out of whoever's league' and it's a comedic joke whenever an unpopular character attempts to talk to someone that isn't of the same social status.

Have you ever talked or not talked to someone just because of their status?

_____

_____

The pressure to be popular, exaggerated by our media is working. One girl wrote, "I'm fourteen, pretty young actually. I'm a freshmen in high school and I feel a constant pressure to fit in. While other girls in my grade are out hooking up with guys and getting drunk, I'm on tumblr or on Netflix. I wish I could say that this doesn't bother me but it does. Sometimes, I wish that I could be invited to those parties or that

I could be getting with those guys. When I was little, I was the nicest little girl ever and so confident in myself. However, ever since middle school people in my grade have been constantly beating me down with insult after insult so much that I am no longer myself. I just want to be one of those popular girls everyone loves". It is so sad to me how many girls give up on the confident person they once were.

We must reject popularity and learn to appreciate the differences in people. Individuality is SUCH a beautiful thing. There is something so captivating about people who do their thing, and have their own passions.

I constantly hear people crapping on others for their hair choices, what they're wearing, their decisions, their hobbies, their passions and on and on and on.

Have you ever done this? I know that I have…

_____

_____

Who cares? Who cares if you don't like their pants?? Who cares??I Stop putting other people down just because they're different than you. Realize that they're on their own path, and their path doesn't hurt or affect you! Treat other people like works in progress; I cannot emphasize enough how important it is to respect others! Once you start accepting everyone and appreciating the differences and understanding that different things work for different people, you'll stop gossiping because you'll be able to *tolerate the differences*! So that's a huge positive to appreciating other people!

Thoughts?

_____

_____

_____

_____

I want to conclude by making a few final points about popularity:
The concept of popular vs. unpopular is created by us every day. *If we can create it, we can end it.* Everyone is insecure, everyone is unhappy, and it's keeping us females separated. End popularity by refusing to let it separate you. Talk to everyone. Judge no one. Also:

- Never, ever, ever judge someone by their popularity or what you've heard about their reputation. You don't know them. Believe me, you have no idea what they're really like. Take the time to get to know a person before you pass any judgment on them. Don't miss out on great people like I did.
- Popularity isn't the real world. If you're having a tough time with it, just keep in mind that it isn't going to last forever, and people will eventually grow up.
- Don't ever measure your self-worth by popularity. Ever. You are so much more than your social status. Never allow popularity the power to restrict, limit, or define your self-worth.
- People are people. You can talk to anyone you want, popularity isn't holding you back. You're holding yourself back. *No one* is 'out of your league' or is someone you can't talk to.

What are you going to do regarding popularity? Do you need to change your actions in any way?

_____

_____

_____

_____

How are you going to respect both people who fit in and those who stand out?

_____

_____

_____

_____

****

Exclusion/Gossiping

Do you gossip?

_____

Have you been gossiped about?

_____

I was gossiped About in 6th grade. There was a girl who pretended to be my best friend. While I was believing her act, she came in and told all of my other friends lies about me. In the end, all of my previous best friends turned against me because they believed the lies. I remember sitting in the lunchroom, time after time again, by myself or with a few girls, and she would come over and apologize to me, saying 'I'm sorry I can't sit with you, it's just that you're not really cool and none of the others girls like you'. She was so sugar sweet nice to me and then she'd go behind my back and write me mean letters and notes. In fact, she wouldn't even write them herself because she didn't want them to be traced back to her. She would dictate letters and have my previous friends write them out and deliver them. For months, I received hurtful letters saying that no one wanted to be my friend and that no one liked me. The worst part was, after they were delivered to me she would come over and pretend to be concerned, as if she hadn't totally hadn't been involved. And she grabbed them out of my hands and threw them out, so that way I would have absolutely no proof.

Even if I did have a letter for proof, I don't think I would have gone for help. Looking back now, I'm not sure why I didn't tell anyone. I could have told my parents, it wasn't like I didn't have anyone to tell. I think I didn't speak up because I felt so helpless. I just remember feeling so defeated, and I was so quiet and little that I probably thought it was best to keep it all to myself. I slipped up once, after I had eaten lunch by myself again. I was coming down the stairs and I saw my ex best friend and started crying. I remember saying, 'Please make her stop, I didn't do anything - please make her stop'. My ex best friend pulled me into the bathroom. She told me that none of them liked the girl that was being so mean to me.

But that didn't change anything either. Despite that one bathroom interaction, my ex best friends still stayed the heck away from me. Sixth grade was hard. I had girls in my classes who were friendly to me, but we were never close enough to hang out - they were just temporary school friends. As a result, I ended up befriending a couple of guys.

Except that didn't work out either. She accused me of flirting with all of the boys and made fun of me for 'thinking that all the boys had crushes on me'. I knew they didn't, and I knew that we were just friends, but that didn't stop her.

In sum, 6th grade sucked. She bullied me, she excluded me, and she gossiped about me. She took away all my friends and broke my sad little eleven year old heart.

She did this, as I later found out, because she was jealous of the people I was friends with. Instead of competing with me and hurting me, she could have quite literally just joined our group of friends.

This is my worst experience with gossiping. Though instances this extreme don't happen to everyone, they do happen. I'm not the only one who has a negative experience with gossiping. During Cross the Line, we have two statements we always read. The first is "Cross the line if you've ever gossiped'. The second is "Cross the line if you've ever been gossiped about". And almost everyone will cross the line together. Almost all of us have contributed and been affected. by gossip, including myself. Including myself, as much as I hate to admit. In fact, I found that 87% of girls from my survey were aware of a time they had been gossiped about. **Gossiping and being surrounded by gossip is almost unavoidable.**

Here's the thing about gossip: Gossiping or bullying someone hurts EVERYONE involved - NO ONE is a winner. Gossiping hurts three main kinds of people: 1.) The ones involved in the gossip or bullying 2.) The one being gossiped about and 3.) The bystander.

Let's break it down:

1.) The ones involved in the gossip or bullying: The person who is gossiping or bullying is hurting themselves because they are filling their hearts with hate instead of love. They are denying positive, healthy friendships, and they're going to be labeled as a bully or problem. *And once they have a bad reputation, they're going to have a hard time breaking it.*

Solutions:
First, understand that there is a difference between gossiping and venting. Gossiping is when a person spreads negative information about another person. On the other hand, venting is expressing your feelings, with the intent of getting it all off your chest so you can find a solution.

There's nothing wrong with venting, if it leads to a solution. However, gossiping and judging are completely unnecessary and disrespectful, and will only cycle hate. If you have a problem and need to get it off your chest, go talk to a guidance counselor about it, and come to a real solution. This way you can avoid gossiping.

Additionally, take some time to think about what kind of impact you want to make on other people. Our habits and what we do *are* going to affect other people. And it's up to us to choose if we want to hurt or help other people.

What are you going to do regarding gossip in the future? Why?

_____

_____

_____

What are other things you can do if you are the one gossiping?

_____

_____

_____

2. The one being gossiped about: Here's the problem with gossiping in black and white: Gossip creates reputations. Except, gossip is usually false. So, untrue gossip creates untrue reputations. As a result, girls will be unfairly judged and will be treated poorly by others.

And here's the problem with untrue reputations: People act on your reputation and call you names and judge you based on it, and never get to know the real you. In most cases, gossip isn't even true and we end up judging people for things that are entirely false and wrong.

Any idea what your reputation is?

_____

_____

How accurate is your reputation?

_____

_____

Reputations are kind of like stereotypes, in that **both reputations and stereotypes are beliefs that we hold about people.**

The harm with stereotypes, or reputations, is a little thing called stereotype threat.

Ever heard of it? Can you guess what it means?

_____

Stereotype threat is a well-known phenomenon that, *"refers to being at risk of confirming, as self-characteristic, a negative stereotype about one's group"*. It's basically the idea that **people will perform according to the stereotype given to them**. The stereotype 'threat' is that people with negative stereotypes may (and usually will) live up to their negative stereotype - even if it isn't actually truthful. **In other words, stereotype threat is the scientifically accepted belief that people will fulfill beliefs about them.**

Several studies have been done on stereotype threat, and science shows that people perform according to their stereotypes. So let's apply stereotype threat to a larger level.

How do you think stereotypes or reputations affect the world and people around you, like people of color or women or other groups?

_____
_____
_____
_____

How do you think the reputations of people you go to school with affects them and the way they behave?

_____
_____
_____
_____

How does your stereotype or your reputation affect you?

_____
_____
_____
_____
_____

Here is the problem: When we create negative reputations for people, we run the risk of having people adapt to them, because they believe it to be true. When we create negative reputations about people, we restrict human potential and ability, something that no one deserves.

The reason why gossiping is so dangerous is because it creates reputations, and there's a good chance that girls will believe these poor reputations because of stereotype threat. And when girls are dealing with stereotype threat, they learn to limit themselves because of ridiculous notions...The harm of reputations, created by gossip, is that sometimes reputations holds individuals back from being the best and most authentic person they possibly can be. Here's the bottom line: stereotypes and negative reputations are limiting.

Have you ever had an experience where you acted according to a stereotype that wasn't true to you?

_____

_____

What stereotypes have held you back? For example, I held myself back using the 'girls aren't good at math' excuse.

_____

_____

_____

Clarification: Nothing wrong with fitting into a stereotype - if you are a girl who happens to love baking, props to you my friend; I'm right there with you :)

Solutions:

Keep going. If you're brave enough, you can deal with not having a great reputation. And all of you are brave and capable. **Just because a person says something about you doesn't make it true. You determine who you are, and you define yourself.**

3. The bystander: The people overhearing gossip, without saying anything lose as well. Here's why: **Reputations hold us back from getting to know the very amazing person behind the bad reputation.** Chimamanda Ngozi Adichie put it best when she said **"The problem with stereotypes is not that they are untrue, but that they are incomplete. They make one story become the only story."** Perhaps part of the reputation we are hearing about is correct, but regardless of whether or not it's true, it is INCOMPLETE. Yes, that girl you heard gossip about may drink on the weekend - but there is so much more to her! And by believing the limited gossip you hear about a person, we <u>hurt ourselves, because we believe that our limited knowledge is the whole picture.</u> **We believe that their reputation is the whole truth, and as a result, we don't ever get to know them past the reputation.**

For example, when I was in high school, there was a guy who I thought was very attractive. I was interested in his vibe and how effortlessly cool he seemed. However, he had an AWFUL reputation and I so did not approve of the things he was associated with. I knew his reputation, and I refused to look past it.

And then, a little later on, I actually took the time to get to know him. I had an open mind, allowed him to be whoever he wanted to be, and ignored what I had heard about him. I judged him based on how he presented himself to me, not on his previous actions. And guess what happened? We ended up being together for six months. As it turns out, he was so much more and so much greater than his reputation.

I bought into his reputation when I was younger, and as a result, we didn't speak once. If I bought into his reputation all throughout high school, I never would have gotten to experience any of that. Never! I chose to have an open mind towards people, regardless of stereotype or reputation. And I was greatly surprised. **Take the time to make your own judgment.**

Have you ever had an experience where you looked past someone's reputation?

_____

_____

_____

_____

Senior year has been a really eye opening, because I've learned to extend this open mindedness to 'popular girls' in my grade.

For the past maybe eight years, I've heard gossip about things going on in the 'popular' friend group. My friends and I would comment on their 'trashy' clothing, their partying ways, and their willingness to be with boys. Granted, I didn't know them that well, but I mean I knew them because we were in school together - and besides, haven't you seen their latest insta??? I mean the beer bottle is right in the picture, talk about stupid!! I talked badly about so many girls to others, based off of what I had heard or seen online.

Then, I got to actually know them. Or rather - they got to know me. One by one, they started to reach out to me for advice. Me! Out of literally nowhere, they trusted me enough to ask for advice. Or they came to an empowerment workshop. And was I in for a surprise. Turns out, I have never been more wrong about a group of girls in my life.

These girls that I had been mean to, turned out to be incredible people. They are smarter than I ever thought, they put effort into everything, and they are funny and good friends. They surprised me more than anyone else ever has.

I knew their reputations. I didn't know them. And it absolutely kills me, because I spent so many years gossiping about these girls for their habits and what I believed them to be. Instead of being their best friends!

That's the thing about reputations - they hold you back from making amazing best friends! I can't believe that I bought their stupid reputations for so long - I cheated myself of amazing friendships for years!

Too often in my life, I have judged girls on what they wore to a school dance or what they did on the weekend - rather than judging them on the content of their character and their REASONs for doing what they did. Too often, I have judged girls on a part of who they are, rather than on who they *actually* are.

Reputations and stereotypes, even when they have some truth, are still **incomplete.** In reality, we have no idea what another person is going through. No idea. We have absolutely no right to judge someone off of their reputations. Ever.

Have you ever judged someone without getting to know them?

_____

_____

_____

_____

_____

How are you going to treat people moving forward?

_____

_____

_____

_____

_____

_____

Solutions:

The best thing you can do when you overhear gossip is to speak up and against the gossip. The next best thing you can do is work to understand the people being gossiped about.

I am Catholic and I have a strong faith in God. I am currently reading The New Testament in the Bible, and one of the things that is really having an impact on me is the way God and Jesus feel about compassion and understanding. One of the things that God tells us is to love our enemies as though they were our neighbors. It's a radical idea. And it's an awesome idea because it is so compassionate and full of love, rather than hate. Of course, today we probably don't have many 'enemies', but if you take it a little less literally I bet you can apply it to your life. For example, there are a few people I dislike because they are very rude to me, or just disrespectful to females in general. Now, it would be incredibly easy for me to hate them, being that they don't particularly like me or my values. But, what does hate accomplish?

Instead, I am working to like or to understand them. I am nowhere close to the point of loving my 'enemies' or the people I dislike, and I have a ways to go. But, I am doing my best to feel compassion and understanding towards others. At the very least, I have stopped feeling hate towards the people that I previously disliked.

I am ashamed of my younger lack of compassion, and I am disappointed by my previous lack of understanding. **I hope that from here on out, you will look to understand people, instead of judging them.**

We especially can't judge people based off of the way they've acted to us in the distant past. I'm not talking about two weeks ago, I'm talking about two years ago. The person that they were they were to you when they were in 7th grade won't be the same person when they are when they're a freshman. You've grown and changed, and they should be allowed to as well. **Keep an open mind to change.**

Finally, stereotyping and reputation is something that divides and affects all of us, not just females. Are we going to let that happen? Or are we going to use our voices and join together, regardless of reputation?

****

Name-calling

Have you ever called another girl a slut, a whore, bitch, etc.?

_____

_____

_____

Have you ever been called any of those names? How did it feel?

_____

_____

_____

_____

Two months or so ago, a girl completely opened up to me and spilled her entire dilemma. She told me that over someone she trusted had taken a picture of her while changing, and she thought he had deleted it...yet last night, she found out that someone had put the picture in a group message, and an entire group of boys had seen her butt without her consent. She was scared that everyone would lose respect for her, she was upset because she never consented to any of this, and she was worried that the story would be twisted. She wanted all of the pictures completely gone. I felt horrible watching her speak - she was so distressed and kept repeating how violated she felt. I had NO IDEA what to do, other than assure her that it was going to be okay and that we were going to get this figured out, so I offered to take her and our mutual friend to go talk to my guidance counselor.

Here's the part that I want you to know: At one point, we started talking about how frequently boys and girls will call her names like slut and whore. She said something that has stuck with me, and I don't think I'll ever forget it. She looked down and softly commented, 'You know, when people call you a slut and whore so often, you really start to believe them'. She had started to believe that she was in fact not worthy of respect, that she was someone who deserved being called such a negative seeming term.

When we use words like sluts and whores, we teach girls that they are not worthy of respect. After being called names so many times, girls start to believe that they should be called names and that are in fact sluts and whores. Because slut is an insult, naturally, these girls' self-esteem go downs. And research by Professor Carol Dweck backs this up, AND relates this kind of bullying to a larger level. She writes, "Victims say that when they're taunted and demeaned and no one comes to their defense, they start to believe they deserve it. They start to judge themselves and to think that they *are* inferior".

The problem with calling girls names, especially sexually shaming names, teaches girls that they're not worthy of respect. And we teach women they are not worthy of respect, they're going to have lower self-confidence, they'll tolerate unhealthy and potentially abusive relationships, they will quiet their voices, the list goes on and on and on.

Name calling is just a part of going to school and being a teenager. Hell, it's just part of life. The names may change depending on your age, but they're always there. Being 17, I hear words like slut, whore, bitch, skank, ho and so on every single day. It's easy to get drawn into. And if we're being honest, I'm ashamed to admit that I have called girls names like sluts and whores. I've judged girls on what they're wearing and have called them slutty. I have called girls who I don't even KNOW these words, and I have called them names literally based on what I've heard about them. I regret my actions, and I don't do it anymore, but I want to be honest with you all.

From a high school perspective, I think that the most name calling comes at high school dances. I HATE high school dances. I HATE everything about them, because there is NO way to win. **Dances are a catch 22 - you're damned if you do and you're damned if you don't.** If you do grind, you're suddenly a slut. Everyone thinks you're easy and loses a lot of respect for you. Even the teachers make fun of you - I'm not kidding, one of my teachers revealed to me that the teachers refer to grinding as 'nut to butt' dancing. But if you don't grind, you're prude, lame, no fun, and a whole range of other names. One of my friends actually got called a 'bitch' the other day for refusing to grind at a college party. And you feel super out of place. You can't win. You're going to be called names by both kids and adults no matter what.

We're all at different stages and comfort levels regarding everything sex related. I talked about just grinding, but this goes for kissing, sex, and everything in between. We all mature differently. People do different things and we should never, ever shame someone because we ourselves are at a different place. **Everyone is a work in progress, and everyone is learning. It is unfair and cruel to judge a product that is not finished. I cannot emphasize enough how cruel it is to judge a person who is learning.** Growing up is hard enough as it is. Let's not make it harder for anyone else and shame their sexuality - everyone should be free to learn and figure it out.

I don't refer to girls as sluts or whores anymore. And it feels awesome. I respect that people make sexual choices that I wouldn't, but they're in control of their own sexuality and I have no right to judge them and tear them down.

At this point, I would like to introduce a concept to you called slut shaming. **Slut shaming is when you make a person (usually female) feel guilty for having sexual desires.** Too often, we call women who are confident and open about their sexuality sluts. And even more often, we call hesitant girls who are learning sluts. And even more often than that, we will call girls who 'LOOK promiscuous' sluts. One major problem of slut shaming is that women of course do have sexual desires, because of the fact that they are human and humans have sexual desires. **Another major problem with slut shaming is that there's a double standard - men and boys are actually encouraged and praised to have sex, whereas women are shamed for even dressing in a sexual manner.** Girls and boys have extremely different sexual standards and sexual codes. So when we slut shame, we give females a hard time for something that we ignore when men do. Some examples of slut shaming would include:

- calling a middle school girl who is wearing a short skirt a slut
- saying that a girl who kisses a boy that she isn't dating is 'slutty'
- saying that a woman who has sex is a whore

Wiseman discusses the fear of being called a slut in <u>Queen Bees and Wannabes</u> saying, "Girls often feel like they have to choose between being themselves and displaying a sexy costume, which is a huge conflict. If a girl opts for the costume and acts the part, she'll get the boy's attention, but she'll also risk the girls' resentment - and the spiteful talking behind her back. <u>So she'll try to achieve the impossible by pleasing groups with two competing agendas.</u> She might also feel that once she interacts with boys in a sexual way, she won't be able to hang out with them without her sexuality being the only thing they value about her. <u>These conflicting emotions and</u>

confusion increase when girls accuse each other of acting like sluts. For younger girls, the threat of being called a slut defines the limits of acceptable behavior and dress". **Girls are expected to be sexy and we're told from media and advertising that it is our duty to be sexy, but as soon as we wear a skirt short enough to be sexy, we're a slut and shamed.**

Recently, there was a huge debate about school dances because my principal just cancelled all high school dances with the exception of Junior Prom and the Senior Boat Cruise due to the increasingly sexual nature of the dancing. My town has a private Facebook group that many of the mothers have joined. The Facebook group is a mystery to us kids, and we're always curious about what exactly happens in this group. Apparently the mothers had a debate and so one of my friends hacked the system and created an account for her mother. She joined the group and told us about her findings during class.

My heart is so angry and sad right now. So many of these moms criticized girls for their short dresses. SO many mothers made horribly rude comments about what other parents were letting girls wear, and seriously shamed girls for wearing short dresses. **While I understand how they might find short dresses inappropriate, it breaks my heart because they don't understand that we are in this constant dilemma of trying to please, and we can't ever win. Instead of being upset at a fifteen year old girl for absorbing the media's messages, maybe adults could channel their fury and use it to change culture.** By blaming girls instead of the culture, they are contributing to this huge problem of slut shaming. If adults truly have a problem with short black dresses, they could be part of the solution, and take steps to speak up and change the culture that's lying to girls and telling them that their worth lies in their sex appeal, and that sex appeal is short black dresses. **Additionally, adults are teaching their children that it's okay to criticize what someone else wears, and it's okay to determine what another person wears.**

Wiseman adds, "When it comes to the slut reputation, girls accuse each other of two things: acting like a slut, and being a slut. The fear of being accused of acting like a slut controls girl's actions in a particular situation. For example, when your daughter chooses what to wear to a party, she's trying to balance looking sexy while not coming off as slutty (i.e. being attractive to boys yet not incurring the wrath of other girls)". **It is a constant balancing act, but with slut shaming, there is no way to win. You're supposed to look and act sexy, but as soon as you actually do, you're a slut.** You're shamed. The author of The Lolita Effect writes, regarding girls trying to deal with sexuality alone, "**Societies judge them, but extend no helping hands: they must struggle with these situations on their own**". I saw this tonight, when so many adults said the rudest things about girls in short dresses, and I am so saddened because (though they may be well intentioned and I respect that) they are hurting more than they are helping.

Have you contributed to slut shaming? Have you contributed to name calling?

_____

_____

If you answered yes, we all make mistakes. And I'm proud of you for admitting it! Having evaluated your role in slut shaming, what are you going to do about it? After I evaluated my role, I stopped calling girls names. I don't call girls sluts and whores and bitches and other names anymore. I refuse to contribute to a system that brings down and divides and shames human beings. I absolutely will not hurt another person and divide females even further with a few words. What will you do or not do here on out? Make it realistic, and something you can follow through. If you'd like to even make a plan of words to cut out one at a time, and need more space, flip to the back.

So what will you do or not do?

_____

_____

_____

_____

_____

_____

I talked a lot about slut shaming and words that shame sexuality, but there are so many other words that are used to name call. In high school, names often have to do with sexuality (slut, whore, etc.) but there are plenty of alternatives. Words like bitchy, mean, rude, weird, gay, try hard, etc. are all examples.

What are common words you use to describe people you don't like?

_____

_____

_____

The obvious news about being name-calling is that it sucks. One girl wrote, "I was bullied almost all my life because I have ABS (Amniotic Band Syndrome) on my hands and feet. Often, I would be called names. As I get older, it bothers me more and more and high school has been hard. I've always wanted to just fit in and be popular". It's such simple logic to state out loud, but being called names hurts. It straight up sucks.

How have words been used against you?

_____

_____

_____

_____

_____

_____

The good news about name-calling is that it's fairly easy to stop. We are completely in control of it. We choose how we are going to use words. So, I would now like to ask you: **How are you going to use your words?**

_____

_____

_____

If you fail and don't use your words for good, try again. Don't give up. This is all going to take some time. **You are a work in progress, just keep going :) You got this!**
      I hope you will choose to end this ridiculous separation, keep an open mind to people, and stop *all* name-calling.

****

Being Assertive

At this point, I want to talk about how to stand up to bullies, how to confront your friends/partners when things aren't going so great, and how to talk through difficult conversations. **Learning how to effectively communicate is unbelievably important, and it needs to be talked about.**

I am not always a great communicator. But, I have had successful difficult conversations, and I'm proud of the way I've handled them in a mature way. I don't have all the answers, but perhaps I can offer some insight on how to communicate.

Communication Tip 1: Always have difficult conversations in person

Always. There is absolutely no exception. Do not initiate a difficult conversation over text, Facebook message, email, anything. If someone tries to initiate one with you over text/etc. simply tell them you would love to talk about it, but you would like to talk in person. Then find a time that works for both of you. If you're having a problem with a friend or loved one, **you owe it to them to talk in person.** And if you don't get along with the person, it's important for them to see and hear how serious you are about the conversation. The only time you should have a difficult conversation over the phone (talking, not texting) is when you are either a.) In danger or b.) When it is geographically impossible to.

Communication Tip 2: Talk directly to the person you need to

Always talk directly to the person you need to - don't talk to friends of friends to get information. If you talk to their friends or someone else, you'll end up getting false information and then you'll be all upset over something that isn't true. If you don't directly address the person you need to talk to, miscommunications could and will occur. Don't play games and talk to others, get the story from the person him or herself. It is incredibly important you hear their own thoughts, directly from them.

Communication Tip 3: Don't bring extra people

There's nothing more ineffective than a conversation that's supposed to be happening between two people that ends up happening with six people. I remember when I was younger, friends would always say 'I'll come with you, I'll help you talk to her' and there would end up with too many people and no real solution. It's nice to have supportive friends that want to help out, but conversations (usually) work best when only the people directly involved are there. The other thing is that if you bring extra people, the person you're talking to is probably going to feel ganged up on, and like they need to

101

defend themselves. If you want to have an open, honest, genuine conversation, the person you're speaking with needs to feel free to speak without limiting their words, in order to keep their reputation up in front of other people. Having a conversation between you and the other person is best (assuming it's safe to do so), and I would recommend limiting it to just those involved, unless the extra person is a guidance counselor.

Communication Tip 4: Never post online about the person indirectly
Posting indirect slights about whoever it is you're having trouble is going to hurt more than it helps. It's going to create tension and the person will be upset with you from the very start. Believe me, difficult conversations are hard enough as it is. You don't need to fuel the fire and add another thing to be worked up about.

Communication Tip 5: If it helps to write out what you want to say, that might be a good idea
If writing out how you feel will make the conversation easier for you, go for it. I know it's helpful to me personally. Just make sure that a conversation follows.

Now that you have a few basic communication tips, here are comments about two potential conversations you might have. The first conversation is about one you initiate, whereas the second one is focused on what to do if a friend comes to you for any kind of help. These are just guidelines, and I am giving you all an extremely basic structure, so feel free to add or take away parts of the conversation to fit what you need it for.

If you need to have a difficult conversation, here are a few points to keep in mind...

Point: You can do this
Difficult conversations can be scary, and in the past year alone, I've cried over at least two of them. Don't let the fear hold you back though. I believe in you and *difficult conversations are necessary and important to have.* I cannot emphasize that enough. And you never know, they might surprise you. One of the conversations I cried over upon realizing I needed to have it, completely surprised me. Our friendship got so much better, and I walked away with a completely clear chest. It's okay to say "This is hard conversation to have, but I think we need to talk about it". It's okay to admit that

you're a little unsure and to acknowledge that it is awkward. I've done that plenty of times. Just know that you are more capable than you think, and whatever the outcome is it's much better to have an outcome than to keep going in circles.

Point: Make the person you're confronting feel valued

Doesn't matter if they're your friend, or the person that's been bullying you. If you need to have a difficult conversation with your friend, tell them how much you care about them and continually remind them throughout the entire conversation their strengths. When my best friend talked to me about how distant I was being, she made it extremely clear that she was being so honest because she cared about me and she missed me and wanted her best friend back. It is so critical that you remind people of their self-worth, and the things they add during difficult conversations.

Point: Take some time to understand why you feel the way you do

What has lead you to having your opinion? Why do you feel so upset? Figure out the root of the problem, because it's going to be helpful to understand the depth of your emotions. Then, you can even share why you feel that way. For example, the reason why I was so upset by a boy calling me a 'midget' as a Sophomore was for the surface level reasons (I felt humiliated, I'm not a midget and I don't like being incorrectly identified). But, the deeper reason as to why I felt so upset was because I was deeply insecure about my height, and had been for years. The reason why I was so upset at being referred to as short was because I was embarrassed that he picked on my biggest insecurity. I was especially ashamed that he picked on something I hated in the presence of front of my older friend, a person I really looked up to! Understand the underlying problem. Once you understand it, you can voice it and add explanation to the conversation.

Point: Always explain how you feel

Honestly, there's probably a good chance that the person you're confronting doesn't know that they're hurting you. For example, last year a few guys were making comments about my friends weight and appearance - really cruel comments that had her afraid to go to class every day. She finally confronted them and told them that their comments really hurt her. As it turns out, the guys had no idea whatsoever and to them it was all just jokes and they didn't mean to hurt her. I don't understand how they didn't realize it was horrible, but this kind of misunderstanding seems to happen time and time again. Another person I know had her friends always making fun of her poetry and her emotions. Finally, she had enough and outright told them how rude it was and how much it hurt her. Once again, they had no idea that it was so hurtful to her. I think in a lot of cases, people truly don't realize that they're being mean. That's why it is so important you explain how you feel. And even if they know that they're doing something wrong, you should still tell them how you feel. In every single difficult conversation, it is critical to talk about how you feel and why you feel that way. Open up. Be vulnerable. Be brave. I know you can be. If you're not sure how to start, you can begin with 'I don't know if you know this or not, but I feel...when you....'

Point: Take responsibility
It's helpful to talk about the role you played and own up to the things you did that weren't so great. I'm not telling you to put the blame on yourself - I'm just telling you to recognize that you (in most cases) played a role. This is completely possible to do while you still address the things that the person is doing.

Point: Listen
After you've said your part, take some time to listen! And I don't mean passively listen, I mean actively listen to what they are saying and take some time to understand their side of the story. I would strongly recommend looking at the tips below for advice on what to do if someone else is talking to you. The authors of Difficult Conversations state, "You can't move the conversation in a more positive direction until the other person feels heard and understood". Everyone wants to feel understood, and it is important you take the time to seriously consider their points.

Point: State directly what you want
If someone is bullying you or hurting you in some emotional or physical way, make it entirely clear what you want the outcome to be. Do not hedge your statements. For example, say 'I want you to take down all of those pictures' or 'I want you to stop calling me names' or 'I want you to stop texting me' or even 'I'd like to be friends with you, but after the way you treated me, I'm going to need some space. Friends don't treat each other like that and if you want to be my friend, you're going to need to prove it', Give direct statements that completely get the point across. Do not say what you'd maybe like, or it'd be nice if; be 100% clear about what you'd like the outcome to be. Being straightforward is absolutely critical to hard conversations. Additionally, I

104

would also suggest following up with what you will do if what you'd like to happen doesn't. For example, 'I've given you a warning, but if you continue to call me names I will go to guidance'. Or 'If you don't delete that picture, I will go to the school resource officer because that is unacceptable'.

Point: Get Help Always

I would also like to make two other points here: 1.) Never, ever be ashamed to take your problem to administration or guidance. Or to your parents, or to the police, or to anyone you can trust. Your problems deserve to be addressed and they deserve to be taken care of. 2.) It's okay to go straight to the solution, if the solution means taking action. If you think it's a better idea to go straight to the police or straight to guidance, or straight to a trusted adult, that's okay. You be the judge - some situations are dealt with better and more correctly when they are immediately brought to guidance/etc. Guidance is also just a great place to go to talk about what you can do. If you're unsure of the step you'd like to take, go to guidance. Most counselors are extremely helpful.

What to do if someone comes to you for help:

- **Thank them for trusting you.** Opening up is scary, so make sure they feel like it was the right decision to trust you. You could say 'I am so proud of you for telling me, thank you for trusting me'.
- **Give them sympathy and a confidence boost.** Everyone loves sympathy and feeling good, so tell them how awful it is whatever they're going through, and remind them how great they are. For example, 'I can't believe something that terrible would happen to someone as terrific as you. I'm really sad about this, you don't deserve this at all'. However, this will only work if you're genuine and you actually mean it. Don't flatter or be fake - mean what you say.
- **LISTEN.** That's all. Listen. Don't cut them off. Just let them get it all out, and really, really listen to what they're saying and why they're saying it.
- **Acknowledge their feelings.** Acknowledge how they're feeling. You could say, 'I understand that you're really devastated right now, I would be too' or 'that sounds really tough'.
- **Understand what the problem is specifically.** Ask questions to understand what or exactly why the person is feeling this way. State to them what your understanding of the problem is, and make sure it matches theirs. Do some digging to get to the why they feel the way they do.

- **Ask them what they want to happen.** Have them figure out what exactly they want the end result to be.
- **Then put together a solution or plan.** Now that you know what you want to happen, you can begin to put together a solution. You could even make a list of possible ways to reach your solution.
- **Remind them how much you care about them.** Very important.
- **If you need to, go talk to a trusted adult.** Talking to an adult brings a lot of clarity and can really help. And if the first adult doesn't work out, try again. You can't give up so easily, keep trying.

How can you use what you just learned?

_____
_____
_____
_____
_____
_____

Other thoughts/notes:

_____
_____
_____
_____
_____
_____
_____
_____

****

Friendship

In the media, we don't really have many good examples of female friendship. Furthermore, when we do see female friendship, it's typically based off of shallow things, like mutual admiration for a girl's hairstyle. The authors of <u>Packaging Girlhood</u> analyzed messages girls receive from books, television, and other media forms and stated, "One very sad thing about almost all of these movies is how female friendship is not treated as an important part of a girl's life - this is at an age when girlfriends can be everything to girls. It takes a backseat to the romantic interest. Best girlfriends are introduced as an accessory to the lead girl, but they rarely developed as characters and rarely go on adventures. They never rescue friends and very seldom become part of the plot". Female friendship is devalued time and time again, with competition prevailing.

****

Conclusion

Naomi Wolf, author of The Beauty Myth really had it right when she wrote, "The terrible truth is that though the marketplace promotes the myth, it would be powerless if women didn't enforce it against one another. For any one woman to outgrow the myth, she needs the support of many women. The toughest but most necessary change will come not from men or from the media, but from women, in the way we see and behave toward other women, in the way we see an behave toward other women". She wrote this in the 90s. And here we are, twenty years later, still dealing with the same exact problem.

We can blame the media and other people for only so many years. **While they may contribute to all of the problems listed above, we need to take a look at ourselves and see if and how we have contributed.** And we need to take responsibility for our actions.

If we fail to treat other women kindly, things are not going to get better.

Imagine what would happen if instead of feeling threatened by each other, we worked together?! Imagine if we had mutual admiration, rather than fear that we won't be the best??

I have accomplished some of my best work alongside my best friends, and I know that I would not be capable of creating such powerful workshops if it was just me alone. **We need each other.**

Now I'd like to share a secret with you:

In this societal desire to keep us insecure, hating ourselves, and competing, a huge mistake has been made. A mistake so big, it threatens to ruin everything if exposed. We females are supposed to not get along, we are supposed to be jealous of other girls, we are supposed to look better than everyone else, we are supposed to fight over boys.

We are supposed to share nothing in common, and be constantly displeased and disassociated from other girl's drama.

However, we all share something in common. We have all been affected by the beauty standard. And if not the beauty standard, we have each been touched by the media's negative influences one way or another, or at least the expectations of our gender. Though we certainly have varying experiences and levels of experience with the beauty standard, we still share that experience. We are literally ***all in this together - cue the <u>High School Musical</u> music.*** We have something common to bond over. We have something that can bring all females together, regardless of age, status, anything! This is a huge, life changing concept! We don't have to compete anymore - we can bond over something that we all share, that something being self-confidence and the media!!

We have the power to change this female hierarchy, one that no one is winning. We just need to support each other and work to educate ourselves so that way we can truly support everyone. One of my favorite things about self-confidence workshops, is that all of us girls are together as one energy. Self-confidence workshops are so powerful, because there are so many of us in the same room and we are all crying at the same things, and making the same connections. **It makes you really feel like you're part of something bigger, and it makes you feel like there's something really powerful that girls can come together over.**

We can use self-esteem as a way to bond, and today, we can realize that other girls aren't enemies to be competed with or gossiped about - but that they're actually our own personal strongest allies in defeating the ridiculously unfair beauty standard. We can challenge what we've been taught to believe. And once we stop competing, we will be free to embrace girls as friends. I don't compete with girls anymore. **I recognize that every girl is different than me, and spectacular in her own individual way. I recognize that some girls make lots of choices that I wouldn't personally make, but it's okay because I don't know them or their story of why they're making that choice!**

All of this begins with acceptance of others. Live with a 'That isn't right for me, but that's great for you' attitude. Yeah, maybe that girl has a million tattoos and a ton of piercings, and I personally would never get a whole sleeve of tattoos - but she isn't hurting me, I have no reason in the entire world to dislike her or be mean to her, and it's her choice! Yeah, maybe that girl posts a picture of her boyfriend every single 'man crush Monday' and maybe I'm super annoyed - but why should I be annoyed? She's happy with her boyfriend, she's making her own choices, and I have no reasons to judge or be mean to her for a legit social media post. Yeah, maybe that girl's wearing preppy clothing and I only wear grunge - but WHO CARES SHE CAN ROCK WHATEVER SHE WANTS EVEN IF IT'S DIFFERENT THAN ME! It's all about tolerance. Start thinking about what you're thinking towards other people, and begin to correct and respect others.

It is at this point that I would like to invite you to join me in celebrating Galantine's Day. This is a day that Leslie Knope celebrates each year, on February 13th and I think it should be a national holiday. Galantine's Day is a day to celebrate female friendship with your female friends while eating waffles. I honestly can't think of a better way to spend a February 13th and I hope you will join me in celebrating female friendship :)

I want to end this section with a few reflection questions about friendship, because change starts with you. I cannot emphasize how important it is we support each other. We have been divided for far too long.

****

Reflection Questions

So I ask you, what are you going to do to end this division?

_____

_____

_____

_____

_____

_____

_____

_____

What are some characteristics of a good friend?

_____

_____

_____

Tell me a little bit about a great friend, and what makes them a great friend:

_____
_____
_____
_____

What kind of friend are you?

_____
_____
_____
_____

What kind of characteristics would you like to have as a friend?

_____
_____
_____
_____

Would you want to be friends with yourself?

_____
_____
_____
_____

Don't forget everyone, you've gotta be your own best friend, so make sure that you're someone you want to be bffs with.

If you're not sure how to be a good friend/make a new friend or how to support other girls, here's a few ways to get you started:

-Literally just smile or say hi
-Or message them saying "I think you're cool and we should be friends because you seem awesome!!!" (That's what I do tbh)
-Compliment people on things you really admire / be sincere and genuine
-Compliment people on things that they have the potential to be good at

-Send good luck texts or cards or give a hug before important (or regular) events

-Give a card or send a text after the event congratulating them or asking how it went

-Ask people questions about themselves

What are a few other things you can do to be a good friend?

_____
_____
_____
_____

How are you going to use the messages in this book? What's your plan of action?

_____
_____
_____
_____
_____
_____
_____

Other thoughts from this chapter:

_____
_____
_____
_____
_____
_____
_____
_____

MASCULINITY

****
Opening Quotes:

"The Act Like a Man box controls boy's behavior in countless destructive ways. For example, boys want to have strong friendships, but many boys don't feel they can talk to even their closest friends when they're upset because they'll be teased. Asking for help is often the same as admitting you're weak and sensitive. And I'm not just talking about social problems boys' experience. When boys have learning disorders, they don't ask for help because it seems weak and shameful. But overall, one of the most profound things the box teaches is that the easiest way to prove you're 'in the boxness' is to demean and dismiss girls and out-of-the-box boys." - Rosalind Wiseman, Queen Bees and Wannabes

****
Opening Questions:

What pressures do boys face that girls and gender nonconforming individuals don't?

_____
_____
_____

What kind of pressures do boys and all other individuals share?

_____
_____
_____
_____

What are the pros of being a boy? What are the cons?

_____
_____
_____

****

Introduction

Originally, when I decided I was going to write this book, I planned on writing it just for girls. I didn't want to try and tackle anything that guys have to deal with, because I have no experience as a male.

With the help of some friends though, here we are. It's a start – not the end of the conversation.

****

Why This Chapter Was Written & More

This chapter was written to expose problems boys are currently facing. This chapter was also written to discuss potential solutions to the toxic standard of masculinity we have created and expect boys to live up to.

Sadly, there is not very much information out there about the state of boys emotionally. The books I could read for research were limited, and there isn't an excess of studies. I have asked some of my male friends to write about their experiences to better understand what it's like (and to have boys represent boys), and I have otherwise relied on what I've observed, a few books, TED talks, videos, and a studies. It is also important to immediately acknowledge that males experience masculinity differently based on expectations for their race. That being stated, this chapter is a very basic introduction to masculinity.

I hope that by speaking up, I will inspire boys to share their stories to give you a more complete and educated version of what it is like to be a male in today's society - I know they will do a terrific job filling in my many gaps.

****

The Standard of Masculinity

Today, many boys are held back from reaching their full potentials due to a limiting standard of masculinity.

So, what is the standard of masculinity? After talking to boys and doing research, here is a list of things that boys must do or be like in order to live up to the standard of masculinity.

In order to fit the standard of masculinity, boys should:

- be good at sports (extra points for football)
- be tall, muscular, and good looking - boys feel pressure 'to be big'
- be well liked and to have a friend group
- to be in the popular group
- put 'bros before hoes'
- 'get' lots of girls, especially the 'good' ones; 'it's like a contest to see how many girls you can hook up with'
- have an 'impressive' penis
- have a 'big', muscular body
- watch porn
- judge girls on their bodies/talk about girls bodies
- drink the right sports drink
- look nice or to 'wear expensive clothing from the most hip stores'
- have nice shoes
- be 'the first one to get it done' - upon further questioning, this applies to both blow jobs and sex
- disrespect girls
- listen to the 'right' music
- be in girls instagrams/on their social media; 'if you get in a really good girls instagram, then you've scored'
- compete against other boys
- not show emotion/vulnerability or any kind of weakness
- be funny and 'in charge'
- be self-sufficient/financially stable (later on)

What else would you add to the list?

_____

_____

_____

Clearly, we have many expectations for how a boy should and should not act. Unfortunately, this has consequences.

****

The Problem with Masculinity

Like females, males are also failing to live up to their full potentials because they are consumed with gendered expectations. Our standard of masculinity is outstandingly cruel because we expect boys to act in one strict, confining way - with no appreciation for differences. In other words, the standard of masculinity urges that boys strip the parts of them that make them authentic and individual - forcing boys to become someone that they aren't.

Most boys are really struggling to fit in with these insane standards. One of my friends really struggled with the standard of masculinity.

He noted, "I remember going through middle school and being a pretty bitter individual. I wasn't athletic or "cool" or confident or someone who talked to many girls (the real pinnacle of coolness for guys). And the guys who were all of those things frustrated me for a few reasons. They weren't the most mature, they acted out a lot, they were very loud, etc. However, they always seemed to be having the most fun out of anyone. And especially as an adolescent, it's easy to merge the ideas that not only are they the 'manly men', but that that's how you talk to girls and both of those things make you 'popular'.

Since I didn't embody any of those things, I assumed there was something wrong with me and that I should just accept my role as being a 'loser'. But just because I accepted that didn't mean I never made friends; I made many friends as I went throughout middle school, yet my self-image was always warped until the end of middle school. I felt discouraged from talking to people and trying to make new friends, I felt I had to remain quiet and try and blend into the background, and I felt that there was no hope for becoming anything more than some geeky kid who did well in school. It made me feel small and insignificant, like I was just floating beneath the surface and view of others.

However, this isn't who I am, and these were not traits I felt were me. When we behave not authentic ways, we get nauseous, and that was the sickly feeling I remember. I like to consider myself much more authentic now in my life, and who I am embodies the opposite of how I felt in middle school; I love talking and interacting with people, I am much more dramatic with my presence and often ignore the worry of standing out, and I have full confidence I can change and be who I want. This confidence is the most important thing to provide hope in an adolescent; some amount of control over one's own fate and being is often enough to give kids security in their choices.

It took me until high school to start to realize that the problem wasn't that there was anything wrong with me, but that it was the way we viewed masculinity and what a man 'should' be."

As my friend explained, the expectations we have for boys are truly impacting the way boys view themselves and the world...**What we teach boys about being 'boys' is having real life implications. Boys are holding themselves back from being their authentic selves, due to an intolerant standard of masculinity.**

We have created such a ridiculous amount of pressure to 'be a man' that in my high school, at lunch time, boys won't buy a salad unless they're in a group. I kid you not.

I REPEAT. OUR STANDARD OF MASCULINITY IS LITERALLY SO RIDICULOUS THAT SOME BOYS IN MY HIGH SCHOOL WON'T BUY A SALAD ON THEIR OWN, BECAUSE THEY'RE WORRIED THAT THEY WILL LOOK (AND I QUOTE) 'UNMANLY'.

****

Masculinity is Learned / Masculinity is Fragile

The way we socialize boys plays a HUGE role in the development of males and turns small differences into enormous gaps. In reality, *boys learn how to be boys through learning what is expected of them.* Boys learn about what a 'boy' should be like through their parents, their friends, their teachers, their siblings, the media, their culture - the list goes on.

A great example of how we teach boys to be boys is noted by a researcher called Judy Chu. She spent a year studying a group of preschool age boys, to better understand masculinity and how boys form perceptions of themselves. Contrary to stereotypes that depict boys as clueless, emotionally impaired human beings who don't need close relationships, Chu found that "the boys in my study **demonstrated a remarkable ability to be astute observers of their own and other people's emotions, sensitive to the dynamics and innuendos within their relationships, and keenly attuned to norms and patterns within their social interactions and cultural contexts** (e.g., being introverted or extroverted, reserved or outgoing), **all of these boys sought to establish and sustain meaningful connections with others**".

She described the young boys as:

"1. attentive, in the sense that they could listen carefully and respond thoughtfully as they engaged in their interactions with others:

2. articulate, in the sense that they could describe their perceptions and experiences in a clear and coherent manner;
3. authentic, in the sense that they could conduct themselves in ways that reflected their thoughts, feelings, and desires at a given moment; and
4. direct, in the sense that they could be forthright and straightforward in expressing their meanings and intentions."

However, halfway through their pre-k year, Chu noted that the boys started to change - in order to fit in with the expectations of their gender. In fact, they began to show signs of becoming:

1. "inattentive, as they learned to focus more on impressing people than on engaging people (e.g., in their efforts to connect with others)
2. inarticulate, as they learned to withhold their personal insights and opinions (e.g., for the sake of preserving their group affiliation and peer relationships);
3. inauthentic, as they learned to display attitudes and behaviors that did not necessarily reflect their own interests, preferences, and beliefs (e.g., in order to accommodate to other people's expectations);
4. indirect, as they learned to obfuscate their meanings and intentions (e.g., in their attempts to avoid causing or getting into trouble)."

The boys in her study started out their year of pre-k very genuine with their behaviors, yet by the end of the year they started to become inauthentic **as they learned to fit into expectations of them. She wrote, "The boys' adaptation to masculine norms were largely motivated by their desire to identify with and relate to the other boys. Regardless of their actual interests and personal preferences, boys who wished to fit in (e.g., be one of the boys) and to be accepted (e.g., be with the boys) learned to conform to, or at least not deviate too much from, culturally prescribed and socially imposed standards for acceptable and desirable behavior for boys"**.

This is incredibly important because it raises a very big point: Many boys take on characteristics that we expect of boys **because they want to fit in**...And acting in an emotionless/ 'it's whatever', sometimes angry, kind of way is considered an acceptable male behavior. **Acting in an expressive, emotional way could get a young boy labeled as 'flamboyant' or 'gay' or 'sensitive' -as though gay men are somehow less man than straight men.** Chu witnessed the young boys take on personas they had seen, by stating "Most commonly, the boys' posturing involved mimicking things they had heard or seen, usually in the media". **I argue that many boys try to live up to the on the hyper masculine standard not because it's who they are, but because it is what is expected of them.**

And it's no wonder why - we have created a standard of masculinity that can never be satisfied. Michael Kimmel once said, "We've constructed an idea of masculinity in the US that doesn't give young boys a way to feel secure in their masculinity, so we make them go prove it all the time". This elusive, barely reachable form of masculinity is terrific for companies, because they can use their advertising campaigns and products to offer comforting reassurance and masculinity to insecure men! I had to take out pictures of advertisements for copyright reasons, but notice that many advertisements for men acknowledge that the product is for men, and call the product 'manly'...in an attempt to reassure men that they're buying something that can reaffirm their masculinity.

I'm telling you, we have really created something real incredible here. We have created a world where we convince literal male human beings that they're not male enough, and that in order to be a 'man', they need to buy products and act a certain way.

****

We Teach Boys 3 Lessons

We teach boys many messages about being male. But they boil down to three main messages:
1. Boys are anti-female; boys must reject any part of their personality that could be considered feminine.
2. Boys are important and more important than girls - boys are encouraged to take up space, to make noise, and to claim the world that is theirs.

3. Boys are always straight and always sexual - boys must be sexually aggressive, and with many females. Furthermore, boys are not responsible for their sexual urges or how they respond to them.

In this section, I am going to discuss the first two messages we teach about masculinity, as well as the consequences boys are facing because of these expectations. I'll discuss the third expectation later in my book. So let's begin!

****

Boys Are Anti-Female

One of the first messages we teach about masculinity is that boys should be the opposite of the stereotypical female. Truthfully, our entire standard of masculinity revolves around being 'anti-female', and it can be summed up as a disassociation of anything feminine.

For example, we quite literally use the phrase 'like a girl' as an insult. We discourage boys from running like a girl, from crying like a girl, from hitting like a girl, from doing anything LIKE A GIRL. It's literally so ingrained in our culture that it's part of our vocabulary.

In today's society, being compared to a female is a severe threat to one's masculinity (which says a lot about the way we think of females). And because of this, boys will do everything they can to distance themselves from being perceived as feminine, or consequently weak.

****

Boys Are Big

Here's an example of how masculinity is anti-female: We consistently encourage females to be as small as possible. Girls are urged to diet, to have flat stomachs, to lose weight. Girls are lead to believe that the worst thing they could possibly is large, chubby, overweight, or God forbid - fat.

And because being small and skinny (except for the boobs and butt) is what is expected and valued from females, **the standard of masculinity asserts that boys must be as big as possible.** If girls are small, than boys should be big - otherwise, they risk losing their man card and are considered weak, scrawny, small, etc. If girls are supposed to lose weight, than boys are supposed to gain muscle - otherwise, they'll be ridiculed.

Our media and culture constantly reinforces the idea that boys should be big or rather 'masculine'....and it starts young. Action figures like 'The Hulk' that little boys play with are just as disproportionate as Barbies are for girls. All you have to do is search 'toys for boys' to see how early on, little boys are learning that men are physically large.

And as boys age, the extremely muscular action hero toys are replaced by video games and movies. Sadly, there isn't much research on the way men look in the media - but it really isn't that hard to see. Take a look at any popular video game for boys or any popular TV show or movie and the hero or male protagonist is frequently going to be ripped and huge - The Hulk, Thor, Wolverine, The Rock, etc.

Many boys are struggling with body image, presumably as a result of the idealized big, muscular body shape. In fact, nearly 18 percent of boys are *highly concerned* about their weight and physique. As the study puts it, "High concerns with muscularity are relatively common among adolescent boys and young men". Sadly, boys are engaging in unhealthy and potentially dangerous behaviors to look a certain way.

Media plays a role in idealizing a certain body shape. Two meta-analyses found **a significant relationship between exposure to muscular media images and men's negative self-images** (body dissatisfaction, low body esteem, and low self-esteem). And, we know from Schor that "heavy television watchers have their views of the real world shaped by what they see on the screen".

In addition to feeling a lot of pressure to look a certain way, there are other problems associated with our hyper masculine body image standard. For example, "Boys in the study who were extremely concerned about weight were more likely to be depressed, and more likely to engage in high-risk behaviors such as binge drinking and drug use". **Once again, the consequences of gendered expectations ARE HAVING SERIOUS IMPLICATIONS ON TEENAGERS TODAY!!!!**

As one of my friends says, "Accepting my body was a battle in and of itself. In addition to my lack of muscle and awkward build I have quite a few motor tics throughout my body causing me the need to twitch in my eye, my arms, my ankles, my toes, my hands, and my shoulders in varied patterns throughout the day. I still am not sure how many people acknowledge these tics in me, but since I feel every single one it contributes to a very self-conscious way of thinking. As a result, I started thinking more

120

about other parts of myself and how they were viewed by people. Whether it was the standard teenage acne that many people go through in varying degrees, or simply whether or not I was considered attractive.

Petty physical threats and muscle flexing are tools used by some stronger individuals to get their way and their point across. I struggle often with not being taken seriously because of my much more scrawny build and lack of muscle mass, and I can get very insecure and self-conscious about it. I mean, looking in the mirror my immediate reaction to the skeletal, geeky teenager in bright colored fashion is not 'wow, what a man!'

The magazines and ads I see of the attractive men surrounded by women are of only barely a variety of body types, typically being muscular, calm, cool, handsome, and confident. These are not things I really see in myself. But then I had a realization, I wasn't unhappy with my body until I thought other people weren't happy with my body and wouldn't accept me".

The reality is that lots of boys are spending time worrying about their bodies. We have created so much pressure for boys to look a certain unrealistic way, and that is seriously taking a toll on boy's body image.

We need body diversity in the media for male characters because middle and high school boys shouldn't have to spend their time consumed with worry over their biceps.

Side Note: There's **<u>nothing</u>** wrong with working out or becoming muscular or the 'ideal' male body shape - the problem lies in all of the pressure to conform to one desirable body type.

****

Boys Are Emotionless...Except For Anger

Another message we teach boys about masculinity, that is anti-female, has to do with expressing emotion. We have feminized emotion, and consequently we've discouraged boys from showing emotion like hurt, sadness, or pain. We teach boys that crying is a sign of weakness...crying is 'for wimps' and no self-respecting male should be seen crying. We urge boys to 'man up' and to not cry.

Boys also learn the lesson that only men who 'man up' get laid - something that boys feel a lot of pressure to do. Gail Dines writes that in pornography, men are shown as 'soulless' and 'unfeeling', with 'zero empathy, respect, or love for the women that they have sex with, no matter how uncomfortable or in pain these women look'. **Boys learn that men who are awful and don't care are exactly the kinds of men that women want to be with - which is ridiculous.**

This whole no emotion thing is a huge, enormous problem because, contrary to popular belief, boys have emotion. **Research shows that boys feel all of the same emotions as girls, and that they just learn not to show it.** In fact, research shows that men might even feel emotion even more strongly than females. In some studies, "men respond even *more* intensely to strong emotional stimuli such as a violent movie or an impending electrical shock". However, boys learn to disguise emotion and to hide it as a young child.

When we view emotion as weak, and urge boys to be strong, the result is that thousands of males are forced to deal with their pent up frustration, hurt, and anguish all on their own. We don't allow boys to express their emotions in a healthy way, and instead encourage them to keep it to themselves. And that's so devastating and quite frankly unfair and dangerous. Because when we teach boys that admitting to one's emotion is a weakness, **boys don't get the help they need. And this silence surrounding emotion is an especially ridiculous standard to have considering that males commit suicide more frequently than females - in 2014 alone, white males accounted for 7 of every 10 suicides.** Furthermore, boys "are at greater risk than girls for most of the major learning and developmental disorders - as much as four times more likely to suffer from autism, attention deficit disorder, and dyslexia". **If we discourage boys from getting help, they're not going to reach their full potentials.** Rather than telling boys to just 'take it', we have to encourage boys to speak up and to talk to guidance counselors and parents when they're feeling low. Boys shouldn't have to feel the heavy burden of dealing with their hurt on their own - that's lonely and sad and has negative consequences. **Emotion isn't a weakness and it's important to show feeling -** *it's what makes us all human.*

Furthermore, the whole not showing emotion thing becomes even more dangerous when you incorporate the 'violent' part of masculinity.

****

Boys Are Violent

Girls are stereotypically supposed to be submissive, passive, and are encouraged to 'play nice'. And in a society that treats masculinity as the opposite of femininity, boys are stereotypically supposed to be dominant, powerful, and 'in charge'. What's interesting about this dynamic is that we view power in a very ironic way, and we teach boys that to be powerful is to be violent. And the combination of manhood as not showing emotion, yet showing anger and violence is unhealthy, to say the least.

I believe that if we encouraged boys to speak up and get help, we would see a lot less violence. After all, the way boys learn to act on violent behaviors is to an extent learned. Eliot notes that the level of aggression and violence varies by culture, and the "enormous range of aggressiveness in different cultures shows that this behavior is not hard-wired but highly modifiable by environmental and social teaching". Eliot continues writing, **"Boys are not destined to be violent but learn whether and when such behavior is acceptable and even heralded, depending on social circumstances". Boys have the capability to be incredibly compassionate. Yet, we are forcing them into a toxic form of masculinity where compassion is not valued.**

Messages about violence and masculinity start young. One way boys learn about masculinity is through their toys. Psychology Professor Judith Blakemore identified over 100 toys and classified them by gender. She found that most boy toys have to do with violence, stating **"the toys most associated with boys were related to fighting or aggression (wrestlers, soldiers, guns, etc.)". Therefore - we teach young boys to associate masculinity with aggression.**

Of course, there are many toys for boys that promote saving others or saving the world - but they're still learning **to associate masculinity with power (rather than compassion!), and they understand that power is associated with violence.**

Some people make the argument that boys are naturally drawn to boy toys. However, most studies are done when children are old enough to understand expectations about their gender...so perhaps the studies show more about gender expectations than they do true science. One study contradicts past findings, and found that boys and girls, up until one year old, are about 'equally attracted to dolls'. This challenges the notion that toy preferences are innate, and suggests **"that sex-related preferences result from maturational and social development that continues into**

adulthood". In other words, as children learn to understand social cues, they learn to conform to gender norms and rules.

One article reiterates, saying "Moreover, developmental psychologists have found that children are very aware of the importance placed on the social category of gender and highly motivated to discover what is 'for boys' and what is 'for girls'. **Socialization isn't just imposed by others; a child actively self-socializes.** Once a child realizes (at about 2 to 3 years of age) on which side of the great gender divide he or she belongs, the well-known dynamics of norms, in-group preference, and out-group prejudice kick-in". In other words, once children realize how they're supposed to respond as a member of their gender, they will prefer their own toys and be opposed to the other genders toys. **In that case, toys serve as a way for children to affirm their gender and social standing.**

Furthermore, boys learn that they will be rejected if they play with 'girl toys'. This insecurity and rejection is fostered by advertising, as it works in advertisements favor. Schor got a President of an advertising agency to open up and say, "Advertising at its best is making people feel that without their product, you're a loser. Kids are very sensitive to that. If you tell them to buy something, they are resistant. But if you tell them that they'll be a dork if they don't, you've got their attention. You open up emotional vulnerabilities and it's very easy to do with kids because they're the most emotionally vulnerable". Boys who play with female toys won't just be a dork - they'll be 'like a girl', the worst thing they can possibly be.

Boys may also be rejected by their parents. Eliot wrote, "In dozens of studies, parents have been found to respond more positively when their young child picks up a sex-appropriate plaything, such as when a boy uses a hammer or a girl pushes a toy shopping cart'. Consequently, parents usually respond more negatively when kids play with a toy that the other gender is 'supposed to play with".

And back to power. Having control over other people and exerting force through violence *is* powerful. But is that really the kind of power we want boys to be desiring? Truly, power should be about standing up for what's right, or making decisions that are beneficial but tough. It's interesting, because we teach boys such a fake kind of power. As Wiseman puts it, "The irony of this cultural definition of masculinity is that it represses courage - not the kind where a boy will fight someone if challenged, but the moral courage to raise his voice and stand up for what's right".

Think about it - if a boy stands up for another person, or for social justice, there's a good chance he would be called a 'fag'. We seriously need to redefine what it means to be courageous.

And more than that, we're already enabling one sex to feel powerful, and not the other.

Aggression continues to be a critical part of masculinity, as violent toys turn into violent video games. The problem with violent video games isn't that they 'cause' violence, but rather as Wiseman puts it, they "normalize violence, humiliation, and degradation, especially of out-of-the-box men and women. They also normalize all of these dynamics as entertainment." **When aggression is normalized, boys learn that violence is an expected way of handling problems. And, when behaviors are normalized, people are more likely to replicate those behaviors.**

Furthermore, Schor notes that research shows that there is a link between violent media and aggression. In July of 2000, major medical associations and the United States Congress "issued a joint statement confirming a causal connection between the viewing of media violence and violent behaviors".

Black and Latino males are especially portrayed as violent in nature. Media rarely shows men of color, unless they are acting like 'thugs' who have just gotten into trouble. In this way, men of color face a different set of challenges with masculinity - men of color are constantly perceived as violent and something that needs to be controlled and disciplined.

The point that I want to make in this section is that when we tell boys that they can't feel hurt, pain, or sadness, boys have no place to show it and it becomes pent up energy. So, boys show their emotion in other ways - specifically violent ways, being that anger is an acceptable emotion for boys to feel. When we teach boys that they are powerful and always urge boys to prove their masculinity, they're going to.

****

Boys Are Not Compassionate

Additionally, we have feminized compassion, love, and friendship and consequently discourage guys from showing displays of affection. If a boy does show affection, he'll be considered gay or unmanly or feminine. It's gotten to a point where guy on guy affection is so threatening to masculinity, that boys have to say 'no homo' before hugging or after saying something nice, just so that way they won't lose their man card. Furthermore, a guy who shows affection to his girlfriend - rather than being completely in charge at all times - is declared to be 'whipped' (a word that interestingly enough references violence and abuse). There's just one, small problem to this entire no affection/compassion standard.

Well, boys are...I hate to break it to you but....boys are human. And humans **need** love and affection in order to thrive. We know from overwhelming amounts of research that friendship and love is not only important, but necessary to happiness! In fact, we know from Chu that **"the single best protector against both psychological and social risk is having access to at least one close, confiding relationships in which one feels truly known, accepted, and valued".** When people have a strong support system, they are able to better cope with stress and whatever life throws at them. **It is absurd and dangerous that we would discourage boys from being authentic and open with people, if the power of friendship is the thing that protects them most from psychological and social risk!** I can't even imagine what it must be like having to keep everything hidden, especially from my friends...true, healthy friendship is built on openness, honesty, and comfort. Life without being able to confide in friends and family must be very lonely.

I believe ALL boys are born capable of being loving, compassionate, kind, and open. I believe it because I've seen it! But - how can we expect to boys to be compassionate and expressive if there are few male role models of compassion that are idealized and glorified? They can't become emotional, compassionate, and brave men with the current role models they're expected to look up to. Popular music artists like Eminem and Chris Brown sure as hell aren't promoting empathy or communication skills. Rather their music emphasizes how great it is to degrade women and use them as sexual objects. These are the first two male artists I thought of, but they are both part of an entire music industry that has a lot of artists who all have a lot to be ashamed about. Our boys deserve better role models. And so I would like to offer you a kind hearted role model to help you out...one of my friends wrote:

"Be compassionate and loving to those around you. I can't tell you how many people value when you comment positively on how someone looks or acts. It makes the person's day to say such words. It makes you feel good about yourself as well.

I didn't compliment people in middle school, let alone talk to a lot of people. I was so scared to show others how I felt. I tried to give off a 'cool' presence wherever I went, have the desired masculine exterior. I now realize today that I just gave off the impression of a geeky shy kid for most of middle school. I realized, at the beginning of high school, nobody talked to me because they didn't know me. I decided to change that halfway through my freshman year. I wanted my voice to be heard. I had good ideas and positive notions. I told others how I felt about tests, I showed how I truly felt in social gatherings, I commented on my feelings. I joked about awkward situations and laughed at personal shortcomings.

I showed that I was a person, and people responded to that. They themselves recognized that all the crap they were dealing with wasn't unusual. It was just life. I recall my parents telling me similar statements. I would break down crying, back in middle school, because everyone expressed such ease. I externally did the same, but internally was an emotional wreck.

Once I had people respond to my thoughts and emotions, I formed some of the best relationships I ever had. I could talk with these individuals for hours, be myself, and earn confidence that I needed to get through the day. I showed that I cared for others; I showed that I would do embarrassing things to brighten the mood. I broke out of my cold, exterior shell, and have never looked back. My life has become much more exciting and pleasing. Being emotionless, simply put, is boring. Live a little guys!"

Furthermore, this whole strong, emotionless thing takes a serious toll on our view of Fatherhood. Currently, fatherhood is deeply devalued and we place much more importance on mothers than fathers - which is quite frankly unfair for men. Men aren't usually offered paternity leave, and men who take time off to spend with their kids are ridiculed. Professional baseball player Daniel Murphy took off a mere three days from his career in baseball, to spend time with his newborn. He missed the first two games of the season, but, he was there for the first few days of his son's life!! Sadly, he was ridiculed by radio hosts. One radio host, Mike Francesca, who has called paternity leave a 'scam' and a 'gimmick' said "Go see the baby be born and come back. You're a Major League Baseball player. You can hire a nurse to take care of the baby if your wife needs help". And he wasn't the only one. A radio host by the name of Esiason said that he would have made sure his wife had an (medically unnecessary) C-section before the season began, so he would be able to attend opening day. In addition to being criticized for taking three days to spend with family, **men are more likely to lose single parent custody in divorce courts...About 1 out of every 6 custodial parents are fathers.**

Unfortunately, this devaluing of Fatherhood starts young. Most toys neglect anything that has to do with Fatherhood, and we don't exactly encourage little boys to play with dolls or to care for another any kind of animal or doll. Furthermore, few domestic toys are marketed towards boys and so boys learn that a male's place is outside the home.

So, the first lesson that boys learn about masculinity is that they must reject any part of them that could be considered feminine.

****

Boys Are Important

The second overarching message we teach about masculinity is that **boys are important, and more important than girls**. Continuing on the theme of masculinity being the opposite of femininity, this makes sense. If girls are stereotypically passive, subordinate, and quiet, than it would make sense that we would encourage boys to be aggressive, dominant, and very present.

****

Examples of Male Importance Through Representation

One of the ways that we teach male importance is through representation. I don't say this to blame ANYONE or to make anyone defensive- I say this because it's the sucky reality and I want to call attention to it. **Straight white cis males are constantly OVERrepresented, in contrast to pretty much everyone else, and this reinforces the idea that specific males are more worthy of being seen and heard.**

For example, take something like reading. When we are first learning to read, we are learning initial stereotypes, beliefs, and expectations about people; we are learning about our expected gender roles, and what our place should acceptably be in the grand scheme of things. As one study said, "Children's books provide messages about right and wrong, the beautiful and the hideous, what is attainable and what is out of bounds - in sum, a society's ideals, and directions. Simply put, children's books are a celebration, reaffirmation, and dominant blueprint of shared cultural values, meanings, and expectations". Historically, this statement rings true through the ages; **books are and have been constantly put out to reflect the ideals of the society**, in order to educate the younger generation...and because we are growing and learning, the messages we learn in books are important and are going to stick with us.

One absolutely enormous study researched gender in 20th century children's books. They analyzed the representation of males and females in over five thousand books. The books that they looked at span a shocking 101 years. They concluded that, **"Gender representations reproduce and legitimate gender systems'**. Here are some of the interesting things they found:

1. Males are represented nearly twice as much as females in titles
2. Males are represented 1.6 times as often compared to females as central characters
3. Book patterns of representation are tied to feminist activism and backlash

So first, males are represented almost two times as much as females in titles. Right away, all children begin to understand that male narratives are more worthwhile reading. As the study puts it, **"Not showing a particular group or showing them less frequently than their proportion in the population conveys that they group is not socially valued"**. When we show women less frequently than males, we teach children from a very young age that women and girls are not as important as boys and men. In fact, "As a whole, existing research on children's books largely aligns with concerns about symbolic annihilation by suggesting that the underlying message conveyed to children **is that women and girls occupy a less central role in society than do men or boys"**. When we have less women in titles, we reinforce the idea that women's stories are not as important, and not worth reading. All children learn this message, which is so detrimental because ***everyone*** is learning to see females as less important.

Second, females are less frequently central characters or rather protagonists in children's books. This huge difference has "implications for the unequal ways gender is constructed. The disproportionate numbers of males in central roles may encourage children to accept the invisibility of women and girls, and to believe they are less important than men and boys, thereby reinforcing the gender system". Hold up: ***The disproportion may encourage children to accept the invisibility of women and girls, and to believe they are less important than men and boys.*** These may be just children's books, but books are a "key source and in reproducing and legitimating gender systems and inequality. The messages conveyed through representation of males and females in books contribute to children's ideas of what it means to be a boy, girls, man, or woman". They may be just books, but the books teach children the importance and what it means to be a man or women. Currently, we are teaching children that men are more important than women, whether we intend to or not. And here's the thing - the problem isn't that males are in central roles in stories - that's totally, 100% cool. The problem is that a very large **majority** of books have males in central roles, while females are close to non-existent. **The problem is that this gender disproportion is so common and so present.**

And the lack of female representation only increases as we age. For example, let's take a look at a study that researched video games and gender. The study suggested that, "videogames, similar to other media forms, are sources of information that children and young adults may use to determine what behaviors and attitudes are considered appropriately masculine and feminine. **This analysis revealed a significant sex bias in the number of male versus female characters found in the games and among the way in which the male and female characters were dressed. Of the 597 characters coded, only 82 (13.74%) were women. The Nintendo 64 games had the fewest number of female characters, and the majority of the female characters wore clothing that exposed more skin than the male character**s". In video games, once again, men usually play a more central role whereas women play secondary characters who are greatly sexualized. **Furthermore, race comes into play too.** Research shows that there is a significant underrepresentation of not only females, but of non-Caucasian races and ethnicities. **So, while the white man is overrepresented, everyone else is underrepresented.**

This underrepresentation holds true in movies and popular culture as well. Despite the fact that females are just over half of the population, males outnumber females 3 to 1 in family films. Even more staggering is the fact that this ratio, as seen in family films, is the same as it was in 1946.

Females are consistently underrepresented across nearly all areas...literally, it's so extreme and prevalent in our culture that a gender disproportion is even present while looking at board games. One study from <u>Packaging Girlhood</u> found that out of 101 board games, men are almost always central characters. They found that males almost always outnumber females in board games, and are more often authority characters. Think about it for a second...Mr. Monopoly, the body in Operation...the list goes on. Even Guess Who had 18 males to 5 females. And, while they found males on the game boxes that were builders, firemen, cowboys, world leaders, doctors, millionaires, and astronauts, they found that females were depicted as nurses and shoppers. So gender stereotypes are quite literally being reflected on game boxes, in the form of career choices.

The study on board games also found **that twice as many boys were shown in action and, _only_ male characters were ever shown winning the game. On the other hand, girls were depicted as "watching, waiting, reacting, catching, or poised to act". Gender differences are so subtle sometimes, but once you start to recognize them, you won't be able to stop.**

We are constantly being exposed to male importance - it's even part of our education systems. Take a moment to think:

Who wrote the books you read in English?

_____

Whose accomplishments did you learn about in science?

_____

Now try listing all of the famous men you know from history class, versus the famous women you learned from history class.

_____

_____

_____

_____

_____

Now try listing famous non-white individuals you learned about in history class.

_____

_____

_____

_____

What do you notice?

_____

_____

_____

****

Why Representation Is Important

As a female, it is very discouraging not to see yourself reflected...it is especially frustrating to almost never learn about female contributions in class. Especially in science class - when you don't see yourself included in science classes, it just reinforces the idea that STEM, or Science Technology Engineering and Mathematics, is white male dominated and women, especially not women of color, aren't part of it.

In March of my senior year of high school, I gave a speech in Atlanta on how to get more women involved in STEM and IT careers. I explained that women need to see role models and stressed that female representation is so important. I talked about how in AP US History Junior year, I learned about Jane Addams, an unbelievable woman who is famous for her social work and activism. It sounds kind of foolish, but before learning about Jane, I didn't realize that pursuing social justice could be a career...I always saw volunteering as kind of a side gig, but after learning about her, I started to think about the fact that I really could make a difference, and for a career! If Jane Addams was able to make a difference big enough for her to be written about in history books, I suppose so could I! I could be just like Jane! I started to envision myself as a kind of modern Jane Addams, and she sparked my imagination with what I could be. Prior to learning about her, I didn't really consider that women could make a very big impact on history - I had only really learned about women collectively as kind of a side note in history class. I really believe that learning about her is one of the reasons why I want to devote my life to a cause. No one else that I've ever learned about has ever had this kind of impact on me, and it's largely because we really don't learn about notable females!

If we want girls to dream big, we need to show them people they can relate to. And this applies to all social identities of a person. If we can't see ourselves, we will lose interest. And science proves this.

One study gave Yale freshmen an article to read about a student named Nathan Jackson. In the story, a boy named Nathan came to campus not sure what he wanted to pursue, developed a liking for math, and ended up having a happy career in a university math department. Additionally, the article included brief facts about Nathan, like his hometown and birthday. For half of the students who read the article, Nathan Jackson's birthday was altered to match the student's birthday. It was such a small detail change, yet, when the students were tested on a math problem, the students who believed they had the same birthday as Nathan had significantly more positive attitudes about math, and they persisted a whopping 65% longer on the math problem.

Can you believe that? If there's that much of a difference with one birthday, can you imagine how powerful examples like that with gender would be?

Having a role model really makes a huge difference. I send out an online email newsletter every week, and a few months ago I included some of my writing. The piece I shared was about how important it is that we have female STEM exposure in the media and in the classroom. I quickly got this message from a girl I go to school with, "In seventh grade, we were supposed to pick a scientist from a list to research, and I ended up picking Dorothy Hodgkin. I found out that she had done amazing work with investigating the structure of biomolecules and she was the third woman to win a Nobel Prize in chemistry. Learning about her is THE reason why I am interested in molecular biology and want to study it in college!". This girl had ONE exposure to a female scientist she admired (and now she's going to study molecular biology). She learned about males as well, but they didn't inspire her the same way Dorothy did.

We have got to start showing females in equal representation to males. Though boys are important (and deserve to feel important), females of all colors, ethnicities, and sexualities are too. It is difficult for girls to be what they can't see. Everyone deserves to have their stories told. Everyone deserves to feel like they are important...regardless of gender, race, skin color, ethnicity, orientation, body type, and other identities. We need to foster female growth and show ALL girls role models, because as one of my friends put it, '**What we teach to girls today determines how far they go tomorrow**'.

I always wonder who we girls would be, if we were shown role models the same way boys would be...who would we be, if we learned about over 50 Presidents that were female? Or even women in political positions that hold power? What would we accomplish, if we grew up being exposed to amazing women throughout history who shaped the world for the better? **What would happen if women were unrestricted, encouraged, and given the opportunity to dream big and know that anything was possible?**

I don't know. I want to find out though.

The overrepresentation of males, specifically white males, is a significant issue as it excludes many. This is the second large message we teach about masculinity.

****

Boys Should be Sexually Aggressive

The third message we teach about masculinity is that boys should be straight and aggressively sexual - with the exception of Asian men, who are rarely portrayed as sexually active. This expected aggression makes no sense. This concept has HUGE consequences on teenagers today, and has certainly affected many people I know. However, I'm going to cover this in the next section of my book.

****

Our Masculinity Standard Affects Boys

The standards we have for boys is truly affecting the way boys view themselves, others, and how they handle situations. We are encouraging boys to live in a way that isn't always authentic, and they are the ones facing the consequences for the expectations WE have created for them.

My best friend has a very telling story about how we teach boys masculinity. This is his college essay:

"We do not see the world as it is, we see the world through the eyes of which we see ourselves. For the first sixteen years of my life, my view of the world was grey-scale and appalling, my words were meaningless, and my actions motivated only by fear. I have been many things in my life, I've been a victim, I've been a thief, I've been a bully, I have been lost and I have been hurt. But above all, I have been changed, I am no longer a lost boy. I am a warrior, a lover, a poet, and I am wholesome. I am who I am. I am who I am and this is my story.

As a child I was warm, petite, and shy. I had a strong sense of empathy and compassion and even recall one scenario of crying in 1st grade when my friend squished an ant. I was filled with hope, optimism, and dreams. I entered sixth grade shorter than five feet and weighing a little less than 100 pounds. Being small, shy, and insecure, I was an easy target for bullying. I didn't understand why people refused to leave me alone, be it for the clothes and big glasses I wore, the way I spoke, my size, or even the way I learned. The bullying was the start of a series of events that I allowed to lead me astray.

Both my parents are recovering drug addicts and alcoholics. My mother began struggling with mental illness and relapsed by abusing pills while I was in sixth grade. In seventh grade, I broke my arm skiing one night and was taken to UMASS Memorial hospital by ambulance. By chance, this was the same night my Mom tried to take her life by overdosing on Valium. We ended up in the same hospital that night, except on different floors, but hers was locked. When I was released, I spent the better part of two days searching the house for an apparent suicide note she left behind for me, just so I could try to make sense of everything. She began the process of her two year recovery, including a immediate weeklong inpatient program in the psych ward, followed by a long outpatient program. The ordeal hurt me deeply, but I **refused to validate my emotions, I repressed them in hopes that they'd just 'go away'.** I figured at thirteen years old, it was time for me to grow up, and become the warped image of a man my childish mind had conceived.

Instead of manifesting itself on the surface, repressing that experience affected my identity in powerful ways that I failed to notice. **I became afraid to feel, and was deluded into believing that to be kind and to be open was to be weak.** I created a false image for myself of who I wanted to be. Unbeknownst to me at the time, I became what I hated, I became a bully. I was filled with so much pain and resentment towards the world and my situation that I would take it out on others. **I perpetuated the cycle.** I fantasized about the image of dabbling with drugs, and while I had no experience at the time, this is what I pretended and in turn it is how my classmates perceived me. Between seventh and ninth grade, despite all my moral deviancy, I still had the audacity to look in the mirror and tell myself I was good person. It was somewhere during this time that I lost myself, I could no longer see the way nor the light of the world, all I could see was the six inches in front of my face.

In ninth grade my mom was starting to get a hang on her mental illness, while that eliminated a source of pain, I was left with all of the damage I had done to myself internally. Ninth grade was the same time I began experimenting and abusing drugs. They were my vice that I thought allowed me to escape reality, and they contributed to my crippling insecurity and lack of identity. My drug abuse led to the overdose of my friend. While we both took the same dosage of a dangerous research chemical, he began to displays symptoms of a seizure and I knew I had to get help. We were both admitted to the ER that night. I have never prayed so hard in my life for someone, and if given the chance, I wish I could have traded places with him. Thankfully, we both escaped with our lives and our minds. This was a tipping point and forced me to re-evaluate my life.

During this time, I was blessed to have three male role models in my life, which never gave up on me, even in my darkest times. My Father, who taught me not only how to love, but how to laugh in even the toughest of times. My coach, a retired Marine Sergeant, who taught me how to stop running and fight, be it in the ring or my personal vices. And my counselor at the YMCA, who taught me how to lead and the importance of perspective. They taught me how to be a man, and they taught me how to live righteously.

I reached a point in my life where I was done running from who I was, and felt courageous enough to begin the battle for my spirit. I knew that darkness could not survive in the presence of light, so I knew I had to shine inside myself. I began to get the best of my demons in 11th grade, and began a steady progression towards becoming the person I am today. **For so long I was afraid to look inside because I didn't know what I would find and if I'd like it, but doing so was the best decision in my life.** One night while I reflected on my moral inventory and what I've done, I took the leap to look inside, and what I found caused me to break down into tears. Buried beneath all the walls I had built up, beneath my ego, and beneath my pain, laid a soul. I realized that what I only truly had inside was love. Through this realization, I became self-actualized. **I realized that the true strength and grit that I sought after long ago is not achieved by being cold, it can only be gained through the fortitude of being vulnerable, and that our capacity for love was not. It was no epiphany, it was just coming to my senses.** I became aware of who I was.

I've become who I am, and I became a man. I've become someone who no longer speaks just to speak, I've become a powerful man of action. From the time I wake up to the time I go to sleep, I do my best to do everything with love, from how my words leave my mouth or how my feet touch the earth beneath me as I walk. I've become resilient and unbreakable, kind and compassionate. I have become myself."

My friend's story tells a lot. He starts out as a kindhearted little boy, full of love and compassion, but was soon struck down by the standard of masculinity and was bullied for not conforming to it. As he aged, he repressed his hurt and pain, rather than expressing it and getting help - typical of boys, as we encourage them to 'suck it up' in order to 'be a man'. But, as a result of repressing so much pain, he ended up taking it out on others. He was in his own words, a 'bully' and he believed the lie we tell boys - he believed that to be kind and open was a 'weakness'. He, like so many other boys, took on a persona and lived under a mask and became a person that he once would have hated. Then, he turned to drugs as a way to cope with how he was feeling....though he utilized drugs, coping methods vary and are common ways to deal with the pain and pressure of growing up. However, he is an incredible person who was blessed to have good role models. With mentors to guide him, and through true strength and perseverance, he overcame the standard of masculinity. And finally, he became the man he is today - compassionate, full of love, and undeniably himself. He is an exceptional friend and I feel so blessed to have him and his unconditional love and friendship in my life. My friend is a success story, as he conquered the standard of masculinity and was able to become the most genuine version himself...I hope that he will inspire other boys to consider the person they are, and I hope he will encourage boys (and truly all of us) to live in an authentic and genuine way.

His story shows that boys are truly affected by the standard of masculinity, and that it holds them back from reaching their full potentials.

A better ideal of masculinity would be beneficial. So in the meantime, let's talk about what boys themselves can do to become authentic.

****

How to Overcome the Standard of Masculinity

I have a few tips from my male friends on overcoming the masculinity standard.

But first disclaimer from one of them: **"There is nothing wrong with being stereotypically masculine in any sense - if that works for you.** There is definitely nothing wrong with being physically strong and tough. **The reason that the masculinity standard is not healthy is not because the traits involved are horrible things to be, but that it is often the singular ideal of what "real men" have to be.** That being said, it is very difficult (especially in middle and high school) to overcome it".

In order to become authentic, a great deal of self-reflection is necessary. As one of my friends says, "Being a runner, I have a lot of time to reside in my own head and reflect on the day. In this day and age, whenever there is a lull in the day where nothing is going on, it has never been easier to hop on a phone or computer and distract oneself. But what this causes is a strained relationship with the self. **A strong**

intrapersonal relationship is necessary in forming a stronger self-identity and confidence. Without self-reflection, I would not have been able to see the error of my ways and finally take a stand against that horrible game of 'the draft'. As the lovely Ashley Olafsen puts it, 'Taking time to reflect on who you are and who you want to be is an important step to becoming who you truly are or who you truly want to be'".

Now time for some personal reflection!

When is the last time that you behaved or said something in a way that is not true to what you believe?

_____
_____
_____
_____
_____

Are you comfortable being yourself even if you lack support?

_____
_____
_____
_____

What can you change that you are not happy with?

_____
_____
_____
_____
_____

List some things that you are happy with about yourself.

_____
_____
_____

Are you prepared to disagree with a whole group of people if it's necessary?

_____

_____

_____

_____

Are you going to live tomorrow the same as today? Or are you going to change something?

_____

_____

_____

_____

Furthermore, realize that if you're a guy, you're a man. That's it. You don't need to prove anything in order to be a real man - you're a real man SIMPLY BECAUSE YOU IDENTIFY AS ONE. As one of my friends says,

"Over the years I've come to realize some simple solutions to this dilemma and I am able to say proudly that I am who I am...I'm more traditionally feminine than some of my female friends (from overall expressive speech and body language to bright colors and interest in different kinds of fashion), I could barely scratch someone in a fight, I could hardly give someone a serious threat if I wanted to, and I'm one of the most emotional people that I know. However, I am a man, a "real" man. And no matter what anyone says, I am correct in saying that.   I was happy before appearances and status and muscle really became hot topics of conversation, but I still had a body I was once happy with. And, I am happy with it. If there were something I could change and wanted to change, I'd do it. But if that happens, I'll have decided on my own."

Another one of my friends also has a really good tip. He says:

"Enjoy things that make you unique. **Express those things**. When you express these unique qualities or talents, you find life to not be so overwhelming. You gain the confidence you need to take on the world.

I was a science nerd for most of my high school career. I loved going to chemistry and biology classes. One of my teachers suggested I do Science Fair, and I got hooked. I worked both my sophomore and junior years in the Science Fair. I put in all my effort into my junior year project. I spent the previous summer combing through cancer research papers. Unrelenting curiosity and self-taught determination pushed me to keep reading through each paper to find a topic that I could latch onto. Finally, I narrowed down the search to two specific cell lines to research. I decided on GSI compound E's effect on the Notch Signaling pathway in breast adenocarcinomas.

With my research topic locked down, I presented the proposal to my Science Fair coordinators. Although concerned with the level of commitment required for this project, they nonetheless approved, commenting on my passion to pursue it. Without any connections to the medical field, I sent out proposals to doctors in the cancer research field. After two months of writing and submitting numerous proposals, I came in contact with a doctor at UMass Medical School. During the interview, I conveyed my passion to pursue my research on the Notch Signaling Pathway. The doctor explained that she usually had only accepted graduate students to work in her lab. Praising how well I presented the material while illustrating my understanding of complex medical terms, she recognized my desire to pursue this experiment and offered me lab space. I worked under the hood after school for six months, three days week. I managed every aspect of my day so I could balance this time consuming project, while maintaining my grades within a rigorous course load. I learned lab protocol, attended lectures, and nurtured the cell lines. **I am currently working on getting my research paper published.**

I loved that year in Science Fair. I did what I enjoyed. Not many teenagers can say they would love to sit down and read research articles that are meant for biochemistry academics, let alone learning how to do lab protocol. I went against the 'norm' and was proud of it. **I didn't earn my popularity for what I did, but knowing I could work with cancer gave me an incredible amount of confidence. I can say now that I stand tall today. I know I can accomplish great things, and I am truly the only one who can stop myself from achieving that greatness."**

My friend figured out his passion and explored it - despite the fact that it wasn't cool. And from that, he gained a true kind of confidence. He had bigger and better things to care about than high school. My story is very similar to his. Giving self-confidence workshops isn't a very traditional route that most high schoolers take, but I was doing what was right for me. I was engaging in material that I really cared about, and I was learning and my mind was growing. And from that, I gained a true kind of confidence. This is because fitting in becomes less important when you have an exciting passion to care about. Find your passion and go crazy with it. Your confidence will rise to a ridiculous extent.

Here are some other tips on confidence, right from another amazing friend:

"It's fairly universal that as we go through life, one of our root goals is to feel good about ourselves. This is a want that underlies pretty much everything that we do, from choosing our friends to watching TV to how we act in school and at home. We choose the friends that we do because they make us happy; we watch the TV shows we do because they make us laugh or excite us; we act the way we do because it feels right and matches up with who we are, and that makes us feel good.

So, we all want to like ourselves. But there's a common misconception that I wish I knew during my days in the adolescent landmine zone known as eighth grade. I used to think that in order for me to achieve this feeling of self-appreciation, I first needed others to appreciate me. My goal upon entering high school was to be THE single coolest human being that's ever stepped foot in those halls. I figured that if I could be a leader and have all my friends and peers look up to me, THEN I could feel good about myself.

From my experiences of being male, there has always been an unspoken competition of who is the dominant one, or the alpha. Being young and naive, I equated being a leader with being the alpha. When I thought of being a leader, I thought of being better than everybody else. I thought of being smarter than everybody else, better looking than everybody else, funnier than everybody else. My definition of being a leader and a role model meant being perfect in every way possible. I wanted to be that person who could walk into rooms and have everyone be like "Yes! Thank God he's here to grace us with his brawn beauty and slick wit! I am forever grateful!"

Ew, right? You can see what a terrible, egotistical mindset that was. Since I was so focused on trying to outshine others, my focus was on their thoughts and opinions of me. After every joke I made in class, I would quickly glance around and make sure at least one person laughed--and if nobody did, my day was RUINED. "*WAY TO GO, YOU BLEW IT!*" If I got below a certain letter grade on any assignment, I literally feared for my future altogether. And don't even get me started on social media. If I got less likes than I had hoped for it was borderline apocalyptic. I was so hard on myself! Perfectionism cannot coexist with confidence because it teaches you to get down on yourself for your flaws. It can't exist in confident females and it can't exist in confident males.

Confident people know when to care.

I wish I had been told earlier that the little things that we often times get hung up on are so insignificant to everyone else. For example, awkward hall encounters were an issue for me for a long time. I always do this thing where I think I see someone that I know in the hall and say hi to them really enthusiastically. At the time, I thought I might as well have gotten down on one knee and asked them to marry me in the middle of the hallway. Now, when I do that stuff, I don't think twice about it. I think, "Hey, I probably just brightened the heck out of that person's day!" and move along. But back then, making mistakes or not meeting my goals was unacceptable and called for a self-pity party.

This perfectionist mindset was so unhealthy that I eventually developed Obsessive Compulsive Disorder. In short, OCD is when you have an obsession (mine was proving myself to my peers) and when that obsession comes into your mind, you have these compulsive behaviors to temporarily make that obsession subside. My compulsive behavior was trying with everything in my power to be perfect, and also, avoiding situations that I appear weak in--which were a lot. I very rarely talked in class because I was afraid of sounding stupid. I never posted on social media because I was afraid of being mocked or not getting any likes. I didn't make any effort to talk to new people because I was afraid they wouldn't like me. And the worst thing that could happen was somebody not liking me, because, as a guy, I HAD to be well liked.

This made me a very paranoid, stressed, and insecure person, because, as we all know, mistakes and imperfections are a part of who we are and happen every single day. What's worse is that being paranoid and insecure is considered unmanly, causing me to further spiral. This is one example of MILLIONS that demonstrate the devastating effects that gender expectations have on the male psyche. It is not uncommon to see depression, anxiety, and other mental illnesses result from boys trying to out-do each other to be the 'perfect' well-rounded guy with brawn, brains, and a penis the size of South America.

What I wish someone had told me is that the order doesn't go "respect from others" → "respect for yourself." It's the opposite. You MUST without exception have respect for yourself in order for others to have respect for you. Allow me to repeat that.

You must first have respect for yourself in order for others to have respect for you.

This is a solid base-line for feeling genuinely good about yourself, but I thought that this was the ultimate key. I thought I had discovered the meaning of life when I realized this. *DUH! Just be really into yourself and act like you're better than everyone else. Once people know you love yourself, they'll love you too. Yes, perfect.* WRONG AGAIN, PRE-PUBESCENT SELF. I was still in that mindset of comparing myself to others. And although I appeared to be more comfortable with who I am, I was not fully there yet. I had learned to develop what is called outer confidence. I learned to disguise my lack of inner confidence and true self-respect by putting on this fake persona.

Now, with outer confidence, it would be harder to tell that in fact I still didn't like me for me. I liked me for being better than others, specifically guys. But, there are several problems with this mindset. **When your self-worth is measured in terms of how others are doing compared to you, you aren't in control of it because you can't control other people**. You just can't do it. So, how I felt each day was dependent on the feedback and actions of other people. I had no control over my happiness or confidence.

So, to compensate, I did a few things that nearly all people with only outer confidence do. These descriptions will probably sound familiar to you.

When put in a situation where I felt inferior or uncomfortable, I used to put on the "too cool to care" persona. You see this person in class slumped over, not paying attention, glaring, sometimes even scoffing at either the teacher or someone who is excited about the lesson. But, in reality, the "too cool to care" people are merely trying to bring down the enthusiastic people to their level because they feel intimidated by them excelling in school. This happens not just in academia but in sports, extracurriculars, and nearly every other place where some people excel more than others. **People with inner confidence are genuinely happy for other people's successes even if they themselves have not yet succeeded.**
Confidence has nothing to do with being better than others. It has everything to do with being better than the person you were yesterday.

I kept this in mind when I didn't make the Varsity soccer team junior year, and a bunch of my best friends did. Instead of becoming jealous of them and feeling inferior, I congratulated them and was genuinely excited for them. They had earned it and I respected that. I also didn't feel bad for myself either, and walked away that day eager and optimistic about the other opportunities I had for fall activities. I joined the cross-country team, got in better shape, and made new friends who I still hang out with today. And because I reacted so well to my soccer friends making the team, I maintained the same healthy relationship with them that I had before--no conflict necessary.

An issue that a lot of outer confidence people encounter is that they get into conflicts easily and often. The other outer confidence persona is the "I'm better than you" persona. This is the persona that comes out when the outer confidence person feels superior. These people get into arguments and social conflicts left and right. They seize opportunities to put others down either to their face or behind their back, but freak out when someone questions their superiority. They react negatively to criticisms because they are afraid of being exposed as weak. Thus, instead of people respecting them like they want, people are either afraid of them or just put-off by them. The important distinction between inner confidence and outer confidence is that people with inner confidence are happy with who they are when no one else is around. **People with inner confidence are happy with who they are when no one else is around.**

The beautiful thing about inner confidence is that when you have it you don't need to rely on complements, Instagram likes, your grades, your weight, your muscle mass, or your reputation to feel good about yourself. You rely solely on the fact that you are content with who you are, what you've done, and what you are capable of doing. Whether or not you think you have inner confidence, you can further develop it from doing these things:
And realize that from here on in, when I say confidence, I mean true, inner confidence.

Things Confident People Do	Things Confident People (Usually) Don't Do
Own up to their mistakes Confident people know that nobody is perfect, including themselves. I mean, you all saw how destructive perfectionism was when I was younger. Making mistakes is natural, and owning up to them is courageous, admirable, and relatable. You'll earn people's trust. **Accept _constructive_ criticism**	Put others down on purpose Lie - confident people accept the truth even when it is hard to Get down on themselves → you may be disappointed with yourself or something you did, but you use it as a

When other people have feedback for you suggesting how to improve, NEVER take it personally, as hard as it is sometimes. If anything, you should thank them. These people want you to do your best. You should want to do your best, too.

Give _constructive_ criticism

When you notice that you have a problem with the way things around you are working, never be afraid to speak up. Remember, you're confident, so you don't have to put people down in the process and create conflict. It's so nice. But it does take confidence to be honest.

Talk about their beliefs, passions, and desires

Confident people express these things freely because they realize that their beliefs, passions, and desires are what make them who they are. And they love who they are and want to share it.

Accept reality and the truth

Confident people are aware that there will be obstacles in their lives that they need to overcome. They accept reality because they have faith in themselves to overcome those obstacles.

Introspect

Confident people take the initiative for constructive criticism on themselves through self-reflection. If they are feeling a negative emotion, they examine themselves to figure out why. If they are disappointed about how something went, they find what went wrong and fix it for the future. Confident people do this because they're not afraid of what they might find deep in their inner thoughts.

Set their expectations high but are not afraid to fail

If you have any inkling that you are capable of doing amazing things, you really, truly are. But should you

learning experience to grow from

flaunt - they don't feel the need to

talk negatively about others in a **non-constructive** way

criticize people for being passionate

search for approval → they find it within themselves

| not meet your goal, you now have a learning opportunity that you can use to grow and keep in mind for next time. | |

Know that you have what it takes to be confident. It is completely within your control. Confidence is not a personality; it is a mindset that anyone can adopt. You can be introverted, extraverted, inverted (math jokes), or anything else in between. But realize that, like any goal, confidence takes dedication.

Confidence is a skill that you need to practice every day.

There will be days when you don't feel as good about yourself as you usually do. This is natural. But they are not bad days. They are challenging days that you can get through and come out on top, even stronger. You may finish reading this and realize that you're not as confident as you thought you were, or perhaps you may finish and realize that you're more confident than you thought you were. And both are completely ok, as long as you realize that you are capable of becoming even more confident. We all are. I am. Ashley is. All of your role models are. We all want to feel good about ourselves and boost our self-confidence more and more. When you close this book today (or exit out on your tablet), be aware that every person you interact with is currently working on his or her self-confidence too whether it appears so or not. Brace yourself because I'm going to drop a High School Musical reference right now; we're all in this together.

So give someone unsuspecting a complement the next time you see them. Praise people for chasing their passions. Lift people up. I promise they will do the same for you. Let's help and support each other–all genders aside–along the way to inner confidence. Imagine how much happier our world will be."

My friend is a beautiful example of someone who has risen above the standard of masculinity and truly become his authentic self.

****

How Do You Contribute?

Additionally, we need to re-evaluate our own biases and how we contribute to the limiting standard of masculinity.

Our own gendered expectations and bias can in fact impact the way boys act. After all, we all have expectations of how boys should act.

So, take a moment to think about how you have contributed to reinforcing the masculinity standard....

Have you ever told a person to 'man up'?

_____

_____

Have you ever used the phrase 'grow some balls' or 'take it like a man'?

_____

_____

Have you ever told a boy to stop crying, or discouraged him from showing emotion?

_____

_____

What other ways might a person contribute to enforcing the limiting standard of masculinity?

_____

_____

_____

_____

****

Changes We Need to Make

The good news about masculinity is that we have created the current standard of masculinity. **So, if we simply changed our perception of masculinity and encouraged a broader perception of it, THINGS WOULD GET BETTER BECAUSE THERE'S NOT MUCH INHERENT ABOUT MASCULINITY!**

One of my friends thought of something absolutely wonderful. We put a lot of pressure on some individuals to be a 'real man' and we similarly put a lot of pressure on some individuals to be the ideal woman. However, what if we put the emphasis on being the best version of a human we could possibly be?

"What is the difference between a real man and a real woman? Why should there be a difference? We are all humans with similar goals, emotions, and experiences, so instead of focusing on what a man should be, why not focus on what the ideal human should be? Because that is truly what we should strive for. Does the ideal person use their strength and size to feel powerful and threaten people weaker? Does the ideal person refuse to cry or express themselves emotionally? Does the ideal person treat anyone like sexual objects, pieces of meat, or points in a game, and yet shame other groups of people for being sexually liberated? I say that no, he or she does not. This person would be sympathetic and empathetic, try and help people, strive to fight for justice and the common good, and try to be someone that he or she is proud to be and would find as a role model.

Why must a real man be anything but an ideal human? It should not be different than any standard that women have. And yet it is. If you are proud of yourself and who you are, strong or skinny, sexually experienced or inexperienced, masculine or feminine, then you are the ideal individual. We humans come from a variety of different backgrounds and experiences, even among people who look very similar, their experiences could be radically different. Since we come from such a diverse species, I think it strange that we try and place so much emphasis on what traits are the ideal ones rather than encouraging self-expression of masculinity, femininity, or humanity. If there is one ideal to strive for then we end up with a large number of people who will never reach that ideal, and it is a problem to tell someone that they have not reached their full potential because they do not possess the traits of a 'real' man or woman. We allow people the chance to self-actualize if their true potential can be reached regardless of sex or gender.

We give people this opportunity by demonstrating kindness and taking the focus off of trivial things. When a young male is not putting effort into the refusal to cry he can learn empathy. When a young male is free to express himself as 'girly' or as 'manly' as he wants to, society eliminates another distraction and roadblock in his life to allow him to focus on more important things. When a young male is supported by his male peers instead of being ridiculed by them, only then can we be taking a step toward a stronger-bonded society and away from the hyper masculinity of the past."

What are qualities that a human who lives up to their full potential has?

_____
_____
_____
_____
_____
_____
_____
_____
_____

How close are you to being that human? What can you do to get there?

_____
_____
_____
_____
_____
_____
_____
_____

I want to be the best version of a human that I can possibly be. I don't care about being the 'perfect female' anymore - it's time consuming and the standards are ridiculous. And the male standards are too - a 'real man' isn't someone who degrades others. I am putting my focus into being the best human I possibly I can be, and I hope that we can all understand that it's much better to be an awesome human, than a 'real man' or 'ideal female'.

And other possible suggestions of what we can do??

_____
_____
_____
_____
_____

_____

_____

****

Changes We Need to Make

It is critical we change the definition of masculinity, because the consequences are evident. Boys and men deserve better. And now is the time. Let's change our larger culture and expectations of masculinity and look forward to a happier, safer world!

****

Reflection Questions

What did you learn during this chapter?

_____

_____

_____

How did this chapter make you feel? Were you surprised, upset, etc? Why?

_____

_____

_____

Do you think our current standard of masculinity needs to be changed? How so?

_____

_____

_____

Do you think that men should receive paternity leave?

_____

_____

_____

How have you seen the standard of masculinity affecting the guys in your life?

_____

_____

Will 'boys be boys'? Or, are boys a reflection of the socialization we teach them? Should the term 'boys will be boys' excuse someone for bad behavior?

MENTAL HEALTH

****
Introduction

NOTE: This section's opening quotes and questions are incorporated into the beginning of different sections.

Let me introduce to you the blunt reality of today:

Mental illness is extremely common, and many people are struggling on a daily basis with depression, anxiety, eating disorders, and more. **In fact, approximately one in five youth aged 13 to 18 will experience a severe mental disorder at some point during their life.** Additionally, we're coping with the pressures of today's society through dangerous outlets like self-harm, drug and alcohol abuse, and more.

Unfortunately, there's a lack of awareness surrounding mental illness. Sadly, in its place is a curtain of shame. And, to make matters worse, our extremely rigid male gender roles only encourage the shame. **The whole 'not talking about mental health thing', combined with our current male gender role, results in a country where few people with mental illness go through recovery.**

And, when those who are struggling refuse to get help, millions of incredible, capable people fall short of reaching their full potentials. Millions of smart, creative people don't contribute to society to the extent that they could have. **With each suicide and death by anorexia, the world loses someone who could have been a game changer...the world loses someone who could have found the cure to cancer, someone who could have been the next Oprah or Steve Jobs, or someone who could have solved world hunger. When we fail to get help, the world suffers as a natural consequence.**

Today, I am going to talk about mental illness. I aim to break the silence and shame and I hope that you will leave a bit more informed than you were before. Furthermore, this is a very basic chapter - I hope you recognize it to be the start of a conversation on mental illness - certainly not the end, as there is much more to be said. That being stated, this is a tough chapter and at some points, it may be triggering. If you need to take a break, **please do.**

So, with that, let's begin.

****

Eating Disorders Opening Quotes

"Please, please, please write about eating disorders. Go into the depth of them, don't allow people to see your book and glamorize starving yourself; show how horrible and vile they are. People need to see the truth - not just what they imagine perfection to be..." - Anonymous survey taker

"Before everyone started talking about thigh gaps, I had no idea what they were. Now, I have an obsession of looking at people's thighs and the gap in them and how spread apart their feet are. I imitate how they're standing and it makes me feel bad when my gap is smaller than theirs." - Anonymous survey taker

"I've battled an eating disorder since I was eleven years old. I'm still trying to recover but I feel I will never have a healthy body image or relationship with food." - Anonymous survey taker

"All my life, I have struggled with my weight. I was so pressured to be thin, even from when I was really young...I just remember being insecure about my weight and feeling fat. I have never, ever been happy with my weight. In the third grade, I started dieting. Weight watchers, calorie counting. Since all the 'perfect' people I saw were thin, I realized that to be loved, I had to become skinny. For four years, nothing worked. I would tell myself, 'Okay, today I will be healthy'. But, then I would come home from school and start snacking. And I wouldn't stop. Then after, I would feel mad at myself for eating, but then just eat again because I was angry. I just wanted to be thin. In the seventh grade, I stopped eating. It was the only 100% sure way I would be able to lose weight. *I went days without eating.* Along with this, came sadness and me feeling like I didn't belong...I felt no interest in doing anything. I started cutting myself. Crying myself to sleep because I felt I wasn't good enough. The cutting and skipping meals became an addiction. Every time I ate something, I felt sick. I started to crave the hunger and release of pain while cutting...I have been hospitalized for my depression, and it's been one hell of a journey. I'm getting better every day, but slowly. I won't tell you I haven't cut myself in the last few months, because I have. I won't tell you I

153

haven't skipped a meal, because I have. But, I am slowly realizing that my body deserves better. I deserve better. I realize now that I have people who love and care about me. There have been times where I can feel the pain again, and I almost give in. But I know I have friends who I can call, and they can tell me that I'm better than this. Because I am. And this what I want my story to show. You are better than this, and you are perfect. I know for all of you struggling, the last thing you want to hear is that it will get better, but it does. It truly, truly does." - Anonymous survey taker

"Women must claim anorexia as political damage done to us by a social order that considers our destruction insignificant because of what we are - less. We should identify it as Jews identify the death camps, as homosexuals identify AIDS: as a disgrace that is not our own, but that of an inhumane social order. Anorexia is a prison camp. One-fifth of well-educated American women are inmates. Susie Orbach compared anorexia to the hunger strikes or political prisoners, particularly the suffragists. But the time for metaphors is behind us. To be anorexic or bulimic is to be a political prisoner."
- The Beauty Myth

****
Eating Disorders Opening Question

What have you heard about eating disorders? Do you have any friends that have one, or have you ever experienced an eating disorder?

_____
_____
_____
_____
_____
_____

****
Let's Break It Down - Eating Disorder Edition

One of the most common mental illnesses that teenagers, and females in particular struggle with, is eating disorders. The National Eating Disorder Association, or NEDA, defines eating disorders as, "serious emotional and physical problems that can have life-threatening consequences". One of my friends speaks from the perspective of a person who has recovered from an eating disorder, and she personally defines them as "a psychological disorder where a person experiences abnormal or disturbed eating habits...Eating disorders are when you're so preoccupied with food that your body can't focus on anything else". **Eating disorders go beyond 'worrying about food'; they are an extreme and real disorder.** And according to the National Institute of Mental Health, eating disorders "frequently coexist with other illnesses such as depression, substance abuse, or anxiety disorders".

Though genetics play a role in the cause of eating disorders, the United States culture is encouraging an atmosphere where eating disorders can flourish. After all, we give girls a false and outstandingly narrow view of what a female should look like and convince them that they CAN attain the beauty standard, if they just work hard enough...

Furthermore, supermodels are more present than ever, thanks to social media. As I typed 'Victoria's Secret model' into the Google search engine to check one of their Instagram follower count and prove how immense their following is, the first thing that came up was 'Victoria's Secret model's diet'. Point in case to the fact that we are led to believe we can perhaps someday attain what they have....if we just starve ourselves and diet

In fact, I go to school with girls who put models as the background on their phone, and girls who tweet or Instagram pictures of models every once and awhile. I fully support them doing whatever makes them happy; it just goes to show that white, female **models are very present.** This extreme presence is a problem because of the enormous weight disparity. The average woman is 5'4 and weighs 140 pounds. The average model is 5'11 and weighs 117 pounds...Meaning that **most fashion models are thinner than 98% of American women.**

With all of this absurdity and intense pressure to conform, of course girls are struggling with their weight! Susie Orbach in Fat is a Feminist Issue writes, "This emphasis on presentation as the central aspect of a woman's existence makes her extremely self-conscious. It demands that she occupy herself with a self-image that others will find pleasing and attractive - an image that will immediately convey what kind of woman she is. **She must observe and evaluate herself, scrutinizing every detail of herself as though she were an outside judge.** She attempts to make herself in the image of womanhood presented by billboards, newspapers, magazines, and television". Eating disorders are, to an *extent*, a response to the ridiculous pressure society has placed upon us.

Perhaps because of this, eating disorder rates are soaring. One study proclaims that **eating disorders affect up to 24 million Americans and 70 million individuals worldwide.** And it's not just girls! An estimated 10 to 15% of people with anorexia or bulimia are male.

My own study, though not professionally done, found that:

- 58% of girls have not accepted their bodies for what it is
- 39% of girls have been affected by the thigh gap obsession
- 61% of girls have dieted because they didn't think they looked good enough
- **50% of girls are currently watching their weight, because they don't think they look good enough**
- 53% of girls have skipped a meal or not eaten because they thought they needed to look a certain way

There are many types of eating disorders, but there are three that are the most common. Though each of them are different, they all deal with food preoccupation. I'm going to *briefly* explain each of them below.

****

Anorexia

According to the National Institute of Mental Health, eating disorders all feature "serious disturbances in eating behavior and weight regulation".

Here are some characteristics of anorexia, taken from the National Eating Disorders Association website:

- Intense fear of weight gain, obsession with weight, and persistent behavior to prevent weight gain
- Dramatic weight loss
- Frequent comments about feeling "fat" or overweight despite weight loss
- Refusal to eat certain foods, progressing to restrictions against whole categories of food

- Denial of hunger
- Development of food rituals (e.g. eating foods in certain orders, excessive chewing, rearranging food on a plate)
- Consistent excuses to avoid mealtimes or situations involving food
- Excessive, rigid exercise regimen--despite weather, fatigue, illness, or injury, the need to "burn off" calories taken in
- Withdrawal from usual friends and activities
- No menstruation (in more extreme cases)

Of course, you don't need to fit into each and every last symptom in order to have anorexia. In hopes to understand anorexia, as I have never had to deal with it personally, I asked one of my friends to describe her experience with anorexia. Here is what she told me:

"I'm going to say that you can truly understand what it's like to be someone with an eating disorder until you've gone through the pain and agony of having one. **It's nothing easy, and it's not something that should be taken lightly.**

Let me start off by saying I was at a healthy weight; I was never medically considered 'overweight', yet I still somehow convinced myself I was the size of an elephant. It's sad the things people with anorexia can create about themselves.

You know that feeling when you first opened the double doors entering the high school for the first time as a freshman? It's supposed to be some great and amazing feeling, right? But for some of us it isn't. My eating disorder started in a similar way to most girls. I went through my freshman year in high school, looking at the seniors and never feeling like I could compare to their beauty. I felt that I HAD to be skinny to even maybe look like them one day. Looking back I know now that is not the case. But at the time, all I could ever imagine was being skinny. **Being skinny and imaging myself skinny started consuming all my time.** Imagining myself with what I perceived to be a better body would take over my day.

I started dating this boy my freshman year and he never made me feel bad about my body, but despite knowing how I felt, he never said anything to ease my insecurity. Although I know I should never have put this responsibility on him, I did. I looked to him to make me feel better about myself. He was six feet two inches, naturally skinny, nothing jiggled on him, and I was so envious of how he could eat whatever he wanted and nothing would change.

157

My sophomore year was when it all went really downhill. I was dating this other guy, and he was a senior and looking at colleges. He eventually decided that Arizona was going to be his new home (I lived in Massachusetts). That made me feel like I HAD to be skinny if I wanted to visit him - after all, how would I put on a bikini if I wasn't tiny? Right?

I'm wrong and I hope none of you ever feel that way. Looking back at it, I make myself mad. But regardless, towards the end of my sophomore year and the summer before he left I stopped eating. Yes, just like that, one day I was like "I need to get skinny RIGHT NOW" and that's how it all began. I stopped eating breakfast, then I stopped eating lunch, and at dinner I would tell my family 'I wasn't hungry' or 'I don't have an appetite'. They didn't suspect anything for a while. So I was getting away with it. My boyfriend had left for Arizona and that was hard on me but I always thought about how not eating would make it better. I started losing more and more weight, and I was so proud of the results of not eating. I dropped four jean sizes in a matter of weeks. And for some reason, everyone around me ignored it like it was okay.

This whole time I wasn't eating, I was denying I had a problem. I denied it to my closest friends, family members, and to anyone who asked how I lost weight, I came up with a lie on the spot. I was lying to myself about how bad I had got, and how quickly not eating consumed my life.

I was lucky. I had someone, a friend at the time, who loved me for me. He was an outstanding supporter. He noticed me getting smaller, and confronted me. No one had done this prior to him. Everyone had asked and I had lied. He went about it a totally different way and said 'You have a problem, don't tell me you don't, when I've watched you change, you NEED help' I looked back at him and couldn't think of anything to say, I just cried. He genuinely wanted to help me. I felt loved.

Admitting to having a problem was hard. Just saying the sentence 'I have a problem' took roughly ten minutes to say. But he made me feel special, and different, and beautiful. Beautiful was something I hadn't felt in a while. Getting help from him was hard. Eating again was hard, I cried during my first few meals. One day he sat me down and told me how much it hurt him that a beautiful girl like myself could do this to her body. He tried getting through to me that ALL body types are beautiful. That's when I realized what I was doing was hurting him. Me not eating was affecting someone else, too.

But I wanted to be skinny and I ignored the fact that it was hurting him for as long as I could. I had turned into some awful person I didn't want to be. **The only thing**

that could give me happiness for more than a few minutes was feeling hungry. I lied to him, saying that I was eating, sending pictures of food and saying I ate it (I never had eaten anything in those pictures). I never realized the stress I put on our friendship.

Eventually my boyfriend in Arizona had cheated on me with some girl at college and I figured it was probably because she was skinnier than me. Just when my life had sort of begun getting back on track, it back spiraled, I was back to not eating and being happy about it. This had really hurt my friendship with my best friend. He was so close to being like 'fine do whatever will make you happy, I tried' but something in him made him stick around. After a while he would sit with me at lunch, come over to my house for dinner, do anything so he could see me eating again. He would text me daily telling me he's never looked at someone more beautiful and that I was perfect the way I was. I never believed it. So I kept lying about my eating.

It wasn't until he threatened to tell my parents that I completely started eating again. One day he sat me down and said 'I can't express how beautiful you are to me, I can't express my love for you, and I can't continue watching you do this to yourself, so start eating or your parents will make you'. I cried for hours. I didn't know what to do, eating again seemed out of the picture. It had been months since I had eaten a full meal, and it seemed hopeless. And I felt like I had disappointed him so much because I convinced myself I was fat.

I was so sad that he was going to have to tell my parents, because I didn't want them to be mad at me for what I was doing. Truly, I was punishing myself because I felt I deserved it.

Well, I didn't deserve it and neither does anyone else. I eventually started getting professional help which is something I recommend to anyone who feels like they need to punish themselves by not eating..."

The first time I read her story, I cried. She is one of the most outgoing, friendly, and beautiful (inside and out) girls out there. I had no idea that she had gone through something so terrible. What makes me particularly sad is the fact that she didn't realize her worth, even when her friend did. Luckily, she is in a much better place. She has found a wonderful therapist and credits him to really helping her through that tough time. I'm so proud of her.

Anorexia is largely a response to society's demands. Fat is a Feminist Issue states, "Women are expected to be petite, demure, giving, passive, receptive in the home and, above all, attractive. Women are discouraged from being active, assertive, competitive, large, and above all attractive. To be unattractive is to not be a woman". **Anorexia is the perfect way to fulfill what a woman should be**, because the anorexic complies with the standard of beauty - the anorexic is dangerously thin, just like the majority of our media representatives. Furthermore, the anorexic quickly becomes passive and weak, just as we expect women to act, as they surrender to their disorder.

Anorexia, like most addictions, depends on the illusion of control. Teenagers usually lack total control - we are encouraged to please the media, our parents, our peers, school, the list goes on. I love being a teenager, and I am not complaining, but rather stating that often times *we search for some sense of control in a world where we feel we lack it, and addictions are the perfect way to feel as though you're in control.* **Anorexia is a cry for control over one's body**. Orbach writes, "They [anorexics] were attempting to gain control over their shapes and their physical needs. They felt their power in their ability to ignore their hunger." Anorexics feel powerful, because they believe they are in control of their body. Liz Funk, author of Supergirls Speak Out reiterates by talking about her own experience with anorexia, saying, "To me, how many calories I was eating was the equivalent of a sum that quantified for an adult his or her worth through a combination of his or her salary, likability, gender, race, hierarchy in the office, age, and sexual potency. It was my ultimate - and only - power". **Especially in a world where females lack a great deal of power, anorexia appears to give the female suffering from anorexia a sense of power and control over their bodies.**

****

Bulimia

What have you heard about bulimia? Do you have any friends who are bulimic, or have you ever experienced bulimia?

_____

_____

_____

_____

_____

Bulimia nervosa is the second eating disorder we're going to talk about. According to the NIMH, bulimics have "have recurrent and frequent episodes of eating unusually large amounts of food and feel a lack of control over these episodes. This binge eating is followed by behavior that compensates for the overeating such as forced vomiting, excessive use of laxatives or diuretics, fasting, excessive exercise, or a combination of these behaviors". Bulimia is a terrible cycle. **First, the bulimic uncontrollably eats an enormous amount of food. Then, to 'make up' for all of the eating, the bulimic will by purge (vomiting, laxatives, etc.), and cycle just keeps miserably repeating.**

As Mary Pipher, author of <u>Reviving Ophelia,</u> puts it, bulimia "starts out as a strategy to control weight, but soon it develops a life of its own. Life for bulimic women [and men] becomes a relentless preoccupation with eating, purging, and weight. Pleasure is replaced by despair, frenzy, and guilt. Like all addictions, bulimia is a compulsive, self-destructive and progressive disorder. **Bingeing and purging are the addictive behaviors; food is the narcotic**". Sadly a majority of bulimics are women. Here are a few characteristics of bulimia nervosa, which I referenced using the NEDA website:

- A feeling of being out of control during the binge-eating episodes
- Self-esteem overly related to body image
- Evidence of binge eating, including disappearance of large amounts of food in short periods of time or finding wrappers and containers indicating the consumption of large amounts of food
- Evidence of purging behaviors, including frequent trips to the bathroom after meals, signs and/or smells of vomiting, presence of wrappers or packages of laxatives or diuretics
- Excessive, rigid exercise regimen--despite weather, fatigue, illness, or injury, the compulsive need to 'burn off' calories taken in - compulsive exercise
- Creation of lifestyle schedules or rituals to make time for binge-and-purge sessions
- Withdrawal from usual friends and activities
- In general, behaviors and attitudes indicating that weight loss, dieting, and control of food are becoming primary concerns
- Abuse of laxatives, diuretics, diet pills
- Denial of hunger or drugs to induce vomiting

It is important to note that you cannot tell if a person is bulimic or not from simply looking at them. Those who have bulimia frequently have an 'average' weight. Devastatingly, bulimia is common.

It is also important to note that culture associates a great deal of guilt with eating, which could explain why some women purge. Women who eat too much food 'eat like a pig'. We also learn guilt through associating eating food as 'bad'.

As soon as I turned 16, I started working in a grocery store bakery, and worked there for a year and a half. I currently work in one restaurant and also one coffee/bakery shop. What always interests me while working in the food industry is how many women, especially in the first bakery, come and stare longingly at the bakery goods in the window, without buying anything. Time after time, I would ask them if they needed anything, and the responses were frequently the same. Women would state, 'Oh, I wish' or, 'No, it's too many calories' or something along those lines. What interested me even more was how women often justified themselves when they bought a bakery treat! They would literally explain to me why they were getting it, and would tell me how they were being 'bad', as if I was some kind of calorie police. I never had a man justify buying a bakery treat, and though some men would look longingly at the case, it was usually older men and when I would ask them if they wanted anything, they would decline due to health reasons. More often than not, women would use the words 'bad' or 'good' to describe themselves. When some women declined, they informed me they were 'being good today'. And when some women got a treat, they would guiltily smile at me and say that they were 'being bad'.

It shocks me time and time again how closely we associate eating with being bad, and not eating with being good. Though, with Urban Outfitters selling shirts that say 'Eat Less', I suppose I shouldn't be so surprised.

****

Binge Eating Disorder or 'Compulsive Eating'

Do you know anyone with a binge eating disorder, or have you or a friend ever experienced one?

_____

_____

_____

_____

Binge eating disorder or 'compulsive eating' is the third and final eating disorder we're going to briefly discuss. According to the National Eating Disorder Collaboration, Binge Eating Disorder is "is a serious mental illness characterised by regular episodes of binge eating". Binge eating disorder affects women slightly more than men, however men are still heavily affected by this.

Here are a few characteristics, according to the NEDA:

- Frequent episodes of consuming very large amount of food but without behaviors to prevent weight gain, such as self-induced vomiting
- A feeling of being out of control during the binge eating episodes
- Feelings of strong shame or guilt regarding the binge eating
- Indications that the binge eating is out of control, such as eating when not hungry, eating to the point of discomfort, or eating alone because of shame about the behavior

Those who have a binge eating disorder are sometimes overweight, contradicting the notion that you need to be skinny in order to have an eating disorder. With binge eating disorder, there is no purging, the person simply eats an excess of food they're not truly hungry for. Additionally, those who binge eat will typically divide food into 'good' and 'bad' type of food.

This is my best friend Maddie's story and her struggle with binge eating disorder:

"I've struggled with my body image my entire life and I just recently opened up and shared that I've been dealing with an eating disorder. The first time I ever felt poorly about my body was when I was in the second grade, eight years old. We had to do a project in math where we used our weight as the data. I hopped on the scale and I weighed 70 pounds, all my friends weighed low 60s and I felt immediately embarrassed. Everyone kept coming up and asking me how much I weighed, and I felt humiliated, like they were asking just to make fun of me. So I lied and told them a lower number. Eight years old and I had already been taught to feel ashamed of a number on a scale and unfortunately that's the way so many girls are taught to feel nowadays.

The negativity towards my body would not end in years to come, in fact it only got worse as I got older. Every year, the doctors would tell me I needed to lose weight. Ten years old and I was forced to 'diet' and watch what I ate, always feeling like what I was, was wrong and that I needed to change who I was in order to be 'right'. Most of these feelings were just brushed off though because they were just in my head and I was a child! When you're young, you don't dwell on things as much.

By the time I turned twelve, that had changed though. I was getting bullied on a daily basis for my weight. I remember waking up scared to go to school because my locker was right in between my two worst bullies. They would slam my locker shut every time I opened it and mutter words like 'tubby' and 'fatty' at me under their breath. They also sat on either side of me in English class (just my luck right?) and they would always tease me and irritate me and do anything they could to offend me or get on my nerves. I would never let it show how much they were hurting me. I would sit there straight faced and roll my eyes because that's what my mum always told me to do. She always told me I was so much better than them, so I should act like it. I acted like I was a queen, a defense mechanism that's stuck with me to this day.

Unfortunately, I couldn't go home to escape the bullying. I went home only to log on to Facebook and see status' written about me, calling me 'Sargent Tubs: The fattest girl in our homeroom' and receive messages from all the boys telling me I would never become successful with my YouTube account and I would never become a successful dancer because I was too fat for that. I spent my seventh grade year being tortured by a group of insecure boys, but I did a very good job of making it seem like they didn't bother me.

To this day, I don't know if they know what they did to me. They tattooed in my brain that what I was, was not good enough and it never was going to be. They made me scared of nearly every man or boy on the face of the earth. And for the next four years of my life, the only positive male figure in my life was to be my father. They made me believe I was disgusting, unable to be loved, hopeless. I started starving myself at age fourteen. I lost an unhealthy amount of weight, went to the doctors, and I asked them 'When will I be skinny enough to wear a bikini?', a question that haunts me. My mother and my doctor laughed and told me I should want to show of my beautiful body and that I could totally wear a bikini. I went home that night and broke down because no matter what everyone else saw, I still saw the same fat disgusting human being staring back at me in the mirror. I was at the lowest of lows.

This was when I started binging and over time, developed a binge eating disorder. If you don't know what that is, it's basically compulsive overeating due to stress and other strong emotions. It's uncontrollable and hard to explain to someone who hasn't experienced the feelings that I have or hasn't done it to themselves. It's a vicious cycle of feeling not good enough, eating to ease the pain, and hating yourself even more afterwards. It's a coping method and a very addicting one at that.

Day by day, I am still trying to get over this, but I have come a long way. Yes, I have bad body image days often and sometimes I feel like no boy is ever going to like me for who I am because my body is too much of a turn off. I've been fortunate to meet some boys who have proven to me that not all males in the world are evil and out to destroy me. I finally have more positive men in my life and it's something I'm very thankful for. Like I said, I still have bad days, though. Not every day can be a good one, that's just life. But over the years, I have learned a lot from dealing with an eating disorder and an extreme hate for the person staring back at me in the mirror.

Now, at age 17, I like who I am most days. I like the person staring back at me in the mirror and I don't harbor hatred in my heart towards the extra fat on my stomach (again, most days). It's gotten easier because somewhere along the way, I realized my weight didn't define me. No matter how many people told me I could never be a dancer because I was too fat, somehow I managed to land a CAREER as a choreographer at age 14 and win awards at age 16 and 17. No matter how many people told me I was too disgusting to ever have a lot of viewers willingly watch me on YouTube, somehow I managed to gain thousands of viewers and supporters who love me endlessly - no matter the size of my jeans. No matter how many times they told me I wasn't good enough, I somehow found a way to prove them wrong.

I realized my weight didn't hold me back from accomplishing things I wanted to and doing things far beyond what my bullies might accomplish in their entire lives. I've grown up with a bunch of positive body image role models- like Lady Gaga, constantly reminding me that I'm a superstar whether I've got a thigh gap and a flat stomach or not. The size of our bodies doesn't determine our futures, or anything in our lives for that matter. We've been programmed into believing that our worth is read to us in the numbers that blink on our scales, but that couldn't be more wrong. If I save a thousand starving children, I'm going to be a hero whether I was underweight or overweight. It's not going to matter! **Weight simply does not affect the greatness of action in our lives!** It just won't! Beauty does not have any set definition, you determine it for yourself. All body sizes are beautiful and we need to spend a bit more time appreciating that. Appreciating who we are and the body we have rather than hating ourselves for the things we're not.

You need to start treating yourself the way you would treat your little sister or your mother or your best friend. Would you ever tell them they weren't good enough because of a number on a scale? OF COURSE NOT! Because you love them because of who they are and how elegant and lovely the depths of their soul are, not because of how much they weigh. We need to realize that the same goes for ourselves! We need to stop neglecting ourselves from the same respect and love we give those around us.

An eating disorder does not define you. Sure, it's a bump in the road that makes things a bit harder. But nothing is impossible. *It is okay to have bad days*, just make sure to appreciate the good ones twice as much and always remember to say a lil compliment to the person looking back at you in the mirror because you deserve it. Let's make a change. Together, we can spread the message of positive body image and take out the unrealistic standards set for women and girls. Big or small, we are beautiful. Let's get rid of labels. Let's get rid of Fat and Skinny and replace them with words like Lovely and Captivating. There is not one version of beautiful, there are many. Let your version shine through, my loves, life is too short to spend it wishing you were something that you're not. You are absolutely wonderful and please don't you ever forget that."

Thoughts?

_____

_____

_____

_____

We are not sure completely as to why people suffer from eating disorders, but genetics, depression, and environment does seem to play a role. I wonder, if socialization to regard food as an emotional solution, is part of the 'why'...especially when it comes to binge eating disorders. Often times, we will encourage eating as a way of dealing with pain. I mean, how many times have we eaten something to 'eat our feelings away', or encouraged someone to eat a ton of chocolate, rather than feel the pain of a breakup or something traumatic? Reviving Ophelia suggests, that "**young women who eat compulsively have learned to use food as a drug that mediates their emotional pain**". **Compulsive eating is an addiction, and it's done to fill emptiness or**

emotion full with food. The book continues, saying, "Writer Susie Orbach distinguished between 'stomach hungry', which is genuine physical hunger, and 'mouth hungry', which is a hunger for something other than food - for attention, rest, stimulation, comfort, or love. Compulsive eaters are mouth hungry eaters. **All feelings are labeled as hungry.** Eating becomes the way to deal with all feelings. Compulsive eaters eat when they are tired, anxious, angry, lonely, bored, hurt, or confused". Like self-harm, binge-eating disorder is an addictive way of coping. For compulsive eaters, it is potentially difficult to separate their emotions from their eating habits.

And given the way we advertise food, I don't think it should be a surprise. Jean Kilbourne writes, "While men are encouraged to fall in love with their cars, women are more often invited to have a romance, indeed an erotic experience, with something even closer to home, something that truly does pump the valves of our hearts - the food we eat". If you've ever seen a chocolate commercial, you'll know exactly what I'm talking about. In these ads, women truly look as though they are involved in a deeply satisfying sexual experience. It's ridiculous, and the women appear to be substituting food for sexual intimacy. Can you imagine a man taking a bite of chocolate on television, then closing his eyes in pleasure?? It would be so weird!!

It really shouldn't be a surprise that we turn to food as a way to cope. After all, our eating patterns are once again partially about control. As Body Outlaws puts it, "Our bodies - and our convoluted relationships with them - tell the real story. In a world that offers women challenges along with choices, compromises along with control, our bodies may seem the only realm where we can control sovereignty. SO we focus our power there. We start with what we can control - sorta. Our bodies. Our hair. Our weight. Our breasts. Our clothes. When this control inevitably eludes us, our feelings of powerlessness solidify". We attempt to control something in our lives, through controlling our body. **Unfortunately, we lack all control as the eating disorder takes over.**

And now we move onto depression.

****

Opening Quotes

"Tried to kill myself twice. Still suffering with self-harm...depression, suicidal thoughts, anxiety, trust issues, and so much more." - Anonymous survey taker

"Because of all the bias I'm very insecure and I've self-harmed for almost a year." - Anonymous survey taker

****

Let's Break It Down - Depression Edition

What do you know about depression?

_____

_____

_____

_____

Right now, clinical depression is the leading cause of disability in the United States. The National Alliance on Mental Illness defines clinical depression as, "a mood state that goes well beyond temporarily feeling sad or blue. **It is a serious medical illness that affects one's thoughts, feelings, behavior, mood and physical health. Depression is a lifelong condition in which periods of wellness alternate with recurrences of illness**". Like the definition goes, depression isn't just being 'sad'. It's all consuming, happens for an extended period of times, and affects various aspects of a person's life.

Depression is currently a major issue for those of us trying to grow up. Kalman Heller, PhD from PsychCentral states, "It is estimated that about ten to fifteen percent of children/teens are depressed at any given time. Research indicates that one of every four adolescents will have an episode of major depression during high school with the average age of onset being 14 years!" And it's not just teenagers - Depression is a problem around the globe. The World Health Organization states that, "**Depression is a common mental disorder.** Globally, more than 350 million people of all ages suffer from depression".

Suicide affects white males and transgender or 'trans' individuals to the greatest extent. Sadly, white males have extremely high suicide rates. In addition, a huge number of trans individuals have attempted suicide - 46% of trans men have attempted, and 42% of trans women - that's nearly HALF of trans individuals! Moreover, suicide affects multiracial and American Indian or Alaska Native in the trans or gender-nonconforming community even worse, as well as those with lower levels of educational attainment and of course those with disabilities or are HIV positive.

The National Institute of Mental Health outlines the symptoms of depression. I have put some of them below:

- Difficulty concentrating, remembering details, and making decisions
- Fatigue and decreased energy
- Feelings of guilt, worthlessness, and/or helplessness
- Feelings of hopelessness and/or pessimism
- Insomnia, early morning wakefulness, or excessive sleeping
- Irritability, restlessness
- Loss of interest in activities or hobbies once pleasurable, including sex
- Loss of pleasure in life
- Overeating or appetite loss
- Persistent aches or pains, headaches, cramps, or digestive problems that do not ease even with treatment
- Persistent sad, anxious, or "empty" feelings
- Thoughts of suicide or suicide attempts

In most cases, in order for depression to be recognized from a medical standpoint, the person has to experience some of those symptoms for at least two weeks. And sadly, most depression goes on for much, much longer than two weeks.

There are many different kinds of depression. Here is a list of a few types. Rather than telling you, I encourage you to educate yourself, and write down a sentence or two about what you learned.

Major depression

_____

_____

Chronic depression

_____

_____

Bipolar depression

_____

_____

Seasonal depression (SAD or seasonal affective disorder)

_____

_____

Postpartum depression

_____

_____

Obviously, a few Google searches alone can't completely inform you of these different kinds of depression, but they can serve to be a beginning to your understanding.

****

The Depressed Experience

Most people will experience a period of unhappiness at some point in their lifetime, and I am no exception. There was a long period of time when I was very unhappy, and unsure as to why I felt so awful. When you're in a depressed state, you don't even know why you're unhappy most of the time. Sometimes a bad mood will strike and you're not sure what triggered it, and you're suddenly sobbing and you can't snap out of it. And every little thing suddenly becomes devastating, because of how awful your mindset is.

Leymah Gbowee summed up depression very well in her book <u>Mighty Be Our Powers</u> saying, "When you're depressed, you get trapped inside yourself and lose the energy to take the actions that might make you feel better. You hate yourself for that. You see the suffering of others but feel incapable of helping them, and that makes you hate yourself, too. The hate makes you sadder, the sadness makes you more helpless, the helplessness fills you with more self-hate".

The best description I have EVER seen of depression is by J.K. Rowling, who has suffered from the mental illness herself, "It's so difficult to describe depression to someone who's never been there, because it's not sadness. I know sadness. Sadness is to cry and to feel. But it's that cold absence of feeling - that really hollowed-out feeling."

She nailed it. When you're in a depressed state of mind, sometimes you aren't sad. Sadness is an emotion. And emotions are healthy and good and positive to feel - even the negative ones like sadness or anger, as long as it's not in excess. When you've reached the worst level of depression, you don't even feel anymore because your mind is so exhausted.

It's like you're in this mental fog that you just can't escape. And your mind is hazy and blurred thanks to the fog, but totally clear and grey and clean because there is just this accepted defeat where you don't feel anything. Your head is so messed up and the only thing that's clear is your mind is this terrible clarity of depression.

A depressed state is hard to fight with and easy to give in to. It's this internal struggle that never stops, no matter what time of day it is.

When you're feeling so low, and something happens, it won't even have a reaction on you. Nothing matters anymore. It's just so meaningless and you lose all hope. Because of this resolved emptiness, some individuals self-harm, often to feel something.

****

Let's Break It Down - Self Harm 101

To put it completely bluntly, self-harm is when a person physically takes pain out on themselves. It's important to know that **self-harm is a coping method**. Self-harm is used as a release, and it can be incredibly addictive, not to mention life threatening. Though self-harm occurs in varying levels, **it is important to know that all self-harm is serious and worth getting help for.**

Right now, we are going through a self-harm crisis. Though it is difficult to know how many people self-harm due to secrecy, estimates are higher than one would expect. **It is undeniable that self-harm is a problem and a growing problem.**

****

History and Self Harm

Interestingly enough, depression can be traced back throughout history - there is nothing new about depression. However, self-harm is a really interesting phenomenon.

In <u>Reviving Ophelia</u>, the author writes, "In my first ten years as a therapist, I never saw a client who mutilated herself. Now it's a frequent initial complaint of teenage girls." This book was published in 1991. One of my smart, older mentors told me that growing up, she had never so much as heard self-harm. However, as a current middle school principal, she is shocked to see it all the time. I am also shocked, but because I can't imagine growing up and not knowing anyone who self-harmed. I wanted to learn about the history of self-harm, and why it is such a frequent issue among individuals my own age, so I studied the history of it.

I found that self-harm is growing in rates higher than the world has ever seen. There is not an excess of information about the history of self-harm, however, it is recorded that self-harm was an issue during the sexually repressive Victorian Era. I didn't know any of this before researching this chapter, and I am absolutely fascinated, because it all clicks.

Much like today, this phenomenon of self-harm was most common in young females (though anyone, regardless of gender, ethnicity, etc. could be dealing with self-harm). During the Victorian age, American Doctors George Gould and Walter Pyle reported that (presumably white) girls all over Europe were puncturing themselves with sewing needles. The irony, of course, is that they're literally hurting themselves with instruments they are supposed to use to conform to their gender stereotype! They were called 'needle girls' - and here's the most interesting part:

The 'needle girls' were often regarded as 'hysteric' for their actions and **self-harm was attributed to hysteria.**

So, the problem wasn't the fact that women weren't allowed the same rights and privileges as men and were forced to conform to repressive standards...**The problem was just that women were too emotionally weak and hysterical.**

So why are we self-harming today, if it's so rare historically?

****
Self-Harm Is Largely Caused By Society

Now listen to this. **Before puberty, boys and girls are equally likely to develop depression. By age 15, however, girls are twice as likely as boys to have had a major depressive episode.**

All of this evidence leads me to believe that self-harm as a coping method is caused by society - a society that we actively contribute and participate in. Because self-harm is not very present historically, we can infer that there is nothing biologically inherent about it, and since it's happening (mostly) to a specific group of people, **I believe that this trend of self-harm has something to do uniquely with our culture and the way we treat females.** Or, more specifically, with the way we encourage females to internalize their pain during times of great pressure for unrealistic and unfair female conformity.

History seriously repeats itself. Different circumstances, **but both girls in the Victorian age and today have an unbelievable amount of pressure to conform to standards so high that it's impossible to win. Both times self-harm was used as a way to relieve internal pain and suffering.** And it's saddening, because though there's been an extreme amount of progress, we are in some ways facing a severe backlash that's brought us back so many years.

****
There Are Many Kinds of Mental Illnesses

We're dealing with a range of other disorders too. I would like you all to take some time to learn some basic facts about Anxiety, ADHD, and Bipolar disorder. Simply Google the name of the disorder and read about it. You may use the space below to record what you're learning.

Anxiety:

_____

_____

_____

_____

_____

_____

_____

_____

_____

_____

_____

_____

_____

_____

_____

_____

_____

_____

ADHD:

_____

_____

_____

_____

_____

_____

_____

_____

_____

_____

_____

_____

_____

_____

_____

_____

_____

_____

_____

_____

Bipolar disorder:

_____

_____

_____

_____

_____

_____

_____

_____

_____

_____

_____

_____

_____

_____

_____

_____

****

Addicted

All of this mental illness and pain reminds me of a quote from <u>Reviving Ophelia</u>. Pipher states, "Girls have four general ways in which they can react to the cultural pressures to abandon the self. They can conform, withdraw, be depressed or get angry...Of course, most girls react with some combination of the four general ways". I would like to add a fifth way that both boys and girls react with to the categories: Become addicted.

Addiction is defined by the American Society of Addiction Medicine as, "a primary, chronic disease of brain reward, motivation, memory and related circuitry...Addiction is characterized by inability to consistently abstain, impairment in behavioral control, craving, diminished recognition of significant problems with one's behaviors and interpersonal relationships, and a dysfunctional emotional response. Like other chronic diseases, addiction often involves cycles of relapse and remission. **Without treatment or engagement in recovery activities, addiction is progressive and can result in disability or premature death**". Essentially, addiction is a mental disease that toys with the brain by massively and relentlessly craving for some reward or substance. With addiction, there is a *near lack of control over behavior, an inability to clearly view consequences, and relapses are frequent.*

More recently, self-harm and eating disorders are being identified by professionals as something that can be addictive. Though there has not been a great deal of research on self-harm, some research does indicate that self-harm has the potential to be an addiction. For example, Jarin Kasper, of the National Eating Disorder Information Centre in Canada states, "Some professionals have linked the behaviour patterns seen in eating disorders to those commonly identified with substance abuse or addiction. The patterns common to both include: loss of control, preoccupation with the abused substance, use of the substance to cope with stress and negative feelings, secrecy about behaviour and maintenance of the behaviour despite harmful consequences. They see these patterns as definitive of addictions". **I am inclined to believe that eating disorders and self-harm are more than coping methods, and have the potential to be addictions, just like alcohol, marijuana, and prescription drugs can be.**

In high school, I see lots of people (regardless of gender, etc.) constantly self-medicating and using weed, alcohol, self-harm, sex, or other addictions to temporarily stop their unhappiness. Honestly, it's downright devastating. I've witnessed quite a few people, one especially that I really care about, lose nearly all motivation because they're so addicted. It is so heartbreaking to watch people who have enormous amounts of potential, get sucked into addiction, and then to watch their potential deteriorate. I hate it. I absolutely hate it.

Have you ever been addicted to something, or seen someone addicted? What is it like?

_____

_____

_____

_____

Quite frankly though, speaking as a teenager, it's easy to become addicted. Jean Kilbourne, advertising expert states, "Most addictions start as survival strategies - logical, creative, even brilliant strategies". At this point in the book, you've read the self-esteem statistics, you know how badly we are faring, and most likely, you've experienced some of the things I've talked about yourself. Right now, as I write, some of us are desperate for a way to cope with expectations, some of us need to escape from self-hatred (if only for a few hours), some of us are recovering from rape and, some of us are lonely and find that it's easier to form a relationship with a bottle than a person.

Sometimes I feel like screaming, 'Of *course* we're addicted - how could we not be?? We're looking for a way to cope in a world that thrusts us unprepared into a world of expectations!' - I really don't think it should be such surprise that teenagers are resorting to coping methods.

****

Advertising Plays a Role

And in a world where 2.05 billion dollars were spent on alcohol advertising in 2013 *alone*, **addicts are victims of circumstance in a system that encourages addiction.** After all, addicts are the ideal consumer. **It makes sense financially to encourage drug and alcohol dependence, because addicts will do nearly anything, including spending an absurd amount of money on products to cope.** Advertisements won't make us addicted, per say, but according to advertising expert Jean Kilbourne, they "promote abusive and abnormal attitudes about eating, drinking, and thinness. It thus provides fertile soil for these obsessions to take root in and creates a climate of denial in which these diseases flourish". Currently many businesses are fostering addiction for their advantage, despite the destruction of human potential. They're winning, and we're losing. *Because of this enormous pressure, we might be gaining profit...but we're losing both lives and human potential.* I just don't think the money is worth the harm it's causing. In order to move forward, we have got to stop glamorizing and advertising alcohol and drugs to kids and teenagers.

****

The Irony

The addictions we are resorting to are sometimes **coping methods. We have turned to drugs and alcohol, to eating away our feelings, and to self-harming, in order to deal with our pain, stress and emptiness. And this behavior holds us back.**

We've been tricked. Though we may be led to believe that alcohol solves all problems, that weed will bring us happiness, that eating disorders will make us beautiful, and that self-harm will ease our pain, unfortunately and truthfully, **addictions do the opposite.**

Untreated depression affects nearly everything. A National Survey from 2005-2006 found that "Approximately 80% of persons with depression reported some level of functional impairment because of their depression, and 27% reported serious difficulties in work and home life". Additionally, here's a VERY shortened list of things depression impacts: the relationships with people you love, your work, how you view yourself, sleeping patterns (you can oversleep or have insomnia), eating patterns & appetite, interest in sex, and your health, (since your immune system is more prone to illness).

Additionally, self-harm truly takes a toll on everything and everyone. It can cause people to withdraw from things they used to love and depression can separate people from others or things that they love.

Those who are depressed or self-harming aren't the only ones tricked. Those who suffer from eating disorders have also been tricked.

Anorexia may feel powerful, but to be an anorexic is be nearly powerless. Orbach writes, "This power to overcome hunger results in a contradiction because in her very attempt to be strong, the anorectic becomes so weak that she becomes less independent, more dependent. She needs more care and concern from others because of her weakened physical state". The anorexics that live face serious health complications. Here are a **few** of the problems anorexics face: Difficulty concentrating (feeling dull), dizziness, thinning of bones, brittle hair and nails, dry and yellowish skin, lanugo (or growth of hair all over the body), mild anemia, muscle wasting, weakness, severe constipation, low blood pressure or slowed breathing and pulse, heart damage, brain damage, multi-organ failure, constant coldness due to the body temperature drop, lethargy or feeling tired all the time, less desire for sex, and infertility.

There are many consequences associated with binge eating disorder and bulimia, as well.

Take a second to look up the consequences linked bulimia:

_____
_____
_____
_____

And now look up the consequences to binge-eating disorder:

_____
_____
_____
_____

Now, go to a computer and take a moment to research some of the consequences linked to drug addiction.

_____
_____
_____
_____

We've been tricked.

The great irony of addiction is that the person has absolutely no control over their addiction - they are being controlled by the very thing they believe they have control over. Everything about addictions are ironic, especially the belief you are in control of your addiction. Kilbourne writes, "All addictions depend on denial….It is seeing the evidence of one's addiction everywhere and still believing that one is 'in control'. **'I can quit anytime' is the self-deluding matra of the addict**" The problem with coping methods is that they are only a **temporary solution**. For example, weed may reduce pain for a few hours, but nothing can get better in the long term.

In fact, we've been tricked so badly that things get actually WORSE long term. This is because addictions hold us back. **Addictions are all consuming; they demand focus, energy, and commitment.** Kilbourne writes, "The great irony is that there is nothing more monotonous, more routine, more ultimately boring than being an addict. <u>The addict's world becomes more and more constricted, centered only on the drug or substance or activity</u>". **When you're addicted, your entire life revolves around keeping your addiction in check.**

That being stated, *addictions keep us all too tired and too busy to make any advances in society.* When you're addicted, all of your focus, energy, and commitment is spent on an addictive battle, *rather than on something truly profound and meaningful.* It's this horribly disgusting distraction that keeps everyone from reaching their full potentials - it's awful!

Jean Kilbourne, advertising expert, recognizes this and states, "For all the talk about freedom and liberation, **the truth is that addiction of any kind makes women more passive and far less likely to rebel in any meaningful way.** When people are drunk or stoned or high, they don't usually have the energy or the focus to make serious changes in their situation as individuals, let alone as a group". When I read this for the first time, I just sat there in a stunned silence. My mind was racing as I began to realize the enormity of the statement. <u>**As long as we are addicted, we will remain where we are….we will be unable to make necessary positive changes that will enable the betterment of all people.**</u>

Naomi Wolf wrote in <u>The Beauty Myth</u>, "**Starving people are notorious for a lack of organizational enthusiasm**", and she is so right. When I was struggling, I stayed quiet and was too busy dealing with my mind to have time to become passionate or live up to my full potential. We can't make conditions better for ourselves, and for the world as a whole, if we're close to death.

****

Anger and Emotion

Until we encourage females to feel anger, and we encourage males to feel emotion, we will remain addicted and continue to not seek help.

We deny females the right to anger, and we teach females to internalize their pain, so females typically take our frustration out on ourselves. On the other hand, we deny males the right to feel emotion, and we teach males to externalize their pain, so males typically take their frustration out on others or the world through what's considered criminal behavior. This is a dangerous game to play.

From a young age, girls are discouraged from feeling angry. Girls are always expected to 'play nice', and as females grow up, their anger is regarded as 'hysterical' and not very valid. In fact, anger in women is so rare, that it is feared. Orbach writes, **"Anger, as a legitimate emotion for many women, has no cultural validation"**. After all, an angry woman is 'unfeminine' and needs to 'calm down'.

Females - have you ever had an experience where your anger was not taken seriously? Or where you were regarded as hysterical, told to 'calm down', and treated in a patronizing way?

_____

_____

_____

_____

I know I have, and almost every female I know has a story like that. Victoria Brescoll, Professor at Yale's School of Management, recently did a study about anger in the workplace. She "concluded that people reward men who get angry but view angry women as incompetent and unworthy of status and power in the workplace". We are often uncomfortable when women express any kind of discontent, and we have a tendency to blame them for acting out of our expectations. On the other hand, men are denied the right to show emotion, and are actively discouraged from crying or feeling sadness.

Here's the problem with this phenomenon: When you deny women the right to be angry, you deny them the ability to identify sources of discontent, and consequently deny them the motivation for creating a world that is better for everyone. And when you deny men the permission to feel emotion, you deny them an opportunity to feel something that could eventually spark well needed change.

You see, it is anger and emotion that sparks my motivation for a better world. I am writing this book because I am **angry**. I am **emotional**. I am **sad** that so many girls think they can't do things because they aren't 'pretty enough'. I'm **devastated** by the fact that we teach little boys that masculinity is vulgarity, violence, and sex with an object. I am **upset** that I spent so many years of my life, sitting in class, holding my thighs up off my desk chair so that way they wouldn't look big. I am beyond **annoyed** that I once believed 'big' was unattractive. **I am angry. I am emotional. This frustration (and equal level of hope) is what keeps me motivated, what keeps me going, and is the reason why I do what I do.**

So, the fact that we teach individuals to channel their frustrations into different addictions, rather than something productive, is disturbing. Addictions hold us back, and perhaps we resort to addictions because we have been taught not to show anger or pain.

As Jean Kilbourne writes, "Addiction hinders a woman's search for equality and power in many ways, <u>not least by defusing the anger and frustration necessary to fuel it</u>". Orbach reiterates this statement, saying **"Whether we realize it or not we are being taught to accept silently a second-class citizenship. Secondary status is further compounded by having our anger denied us."** *When we devalue female anger, we devalue the very quality that sparks change.*

****

Change The Energy

Like so many others, I used to take my anger and pain out on myself. But today, I am taking my anger, emotion, energy, time, and commitment and channeling them in a different way.

Because of this and the sheer number of people that are dealing with addictions and mental illness, I would like to be clear that things like eating disorders, self-harm, and everything else are more than personal problems. They're full blown societal issues, and need to be regarded as such.

Imagine if everyone who is suffering from anxiety, bipolar disorder, a learning disorder, and more, realizes that the problem is not their illness, but the fact that they've been shamed into silence...And now imagine what would happen, if all of that pent up frustration, energy, and sheer ability was directed outwards into the world, for a positive cause and change! Can you imagine the power we would have?? Can you imagine the incredible things that would get done?? If we just redirected our energy! That would be amazing!!!

We have all been affected by the pressure society has placed on us, and you might be really upset with the way you've treated yourself or others. I know I am. But if you're going to be angry or sad or upset, don't be upset with yourself. **Be upset with the world and use that anger to get social change done. Emotion is a powerful, motivating force, so channel it to make the world a better place!**

I may be 17 and hopelessly naive about the way the world works, but I believe in a future where people take the emotions that kept them down and use them and turn them into social change. **I believe because I'm proof! I am proof that previously negative energy can be used change things for the better!** And I'm just one teenage single girl who is committed to change....the collective power we could have together is endlessly exciting.
So how do we begin?

****

The Game Plan

There are three key things we need to do, in order to turn this dream into a reality. We need to:

1. Help ourselves
2. Help others

3. Help the world

So, let's begin!

****

Help Yourself - Opening Quotes

"Everyone thinks of changing the world, but no one thinks of changing himself." - Leo Tolstoy

"Yesterday I was clever, so I wanted to change the world. Today I am wise, so I am changing myself." -Rumi

****

It's On Us

I think the majority of us can agree that we want lower rates of suicide and fewer people starving themselves because they believe they aren't 'good enough'.

So if we all have the same goal, how do we reduce the numbers of people struggling with eating disorders? The numbers of middle schoolers struggling with depression? The numbers of human beings who don't know they need help or refuse to get help?

Albert Einstein offers our solution: "The world as we have created it, is a process of our thinking. *It cannot be changed without changing our thinking*".

Culture won't change unless we do, because **our beliefs are what create culture.** <u>In order to change the world we live in, we need to help ourselves first.</u> Change *has* to start somewhere, and it needs to start with us....meaning, it needs to start with you.

You know who is capable enough to save the world?

You.

You're totally capable.

And I'll be the first person to believe in you.

The first way to make things better is to get help for yourself, if needed. **You can't reach your full potential if your thoughts are being consumed by stress, addiction, or difficulty.**

****

My Story

In the fall of 2012, I decided that I needed to take better care of myself. I wanted to stop being so cruel to myself.

At first, I tried to help myself without getting anyone else involved. This was unbearably difficult at times, and terribly lonely. I remember crying in the bathroom, struggling to keep my determination to stay strong.

And so, a few months later I broke down and admitted to myself that I needed professional help. Upon finally admitting this, I was horrified and absolutely terrified because this meant that I needed to tell a trusted adult. I didn't know how to tell someone, and I didn't know what the reactions would be like, and I didn't want anyone to think that it was their fault.

Between sobs, sitting at my kitchen table, I finally said out loud I needed help to my parents. Finally admitting that I needed help, admitting the secret I had been keeping for a while, took a lot of courage and I was a mess while doing so. But it was one of the best decisions I have ever made.

I really am proud of myself, because *I did it*. And you all can too. I'm not going to sugar coat it for you and say that getting help is easy. Usually, it's not. If you want to get better though, just remember: **Recovery is ALWAYS possible.**

****

The Importance of Getting Help

I tell this story because getting help is nothing to be ashamed of. In fact, it should be the new norm and I know that by sharing my story I can help decrease the stigma, shame, and silence surrounding getting help. If you choose to go into drug rehab, see a therapist, tell your parents about your anxiety, tell a teacher about your eating disorder, or take medication, I AM SO PROUD OF YOU! It takes so much courage to get help and a true kind of strength to admit that you're worth being saved.

Have you ever had a time when you've struggled with yourself or a circumstance? How did you handle it/what did you do?

_____

_____

_____

_____

_____

Have you ever gone to a guidance counselor or adult or therapist to talk about how you're feeling, or to voice a concern with the way you've been feeling? How would you feel reaching out for help?

_____

_____

_____

_____

_____

Do you think that there's a chance you could be dealing with something that's holding you back from reaching your full potential? Even something as simple as a friendship issue could do that.

_____

_____

_____

Growing up is full of experiences - some positive and some negative. If there's one thing to count on though, it's that *everyone will have their full share of lows – though it's important to note that the lows may significantly differ depending on your social identity.* In high school, my friends and I were all dealing with things such as: school, SAT stress, AP stress, friendship troubles, breakups, full blown eating disorders, suicidal friends, abuse, and sadly, the loss of friends or family. And

I was lucky...I wasn't worried about things like dropping out of school, whether or not I would get into college, gangs, or more. Honestly, growing up can be extremely overwhelming.

If there is one thing that I have learned over the course of my 18 years, it is that there are resources out there for you when it gets tough. Rely especially on guidance counselors - it's their job. In elementary and middle school, I maybe went to the guidance counselor two or three times total over friendship feuds that were starting to get out of control. I was uncomfortable with the thought of involving someone else in my issues, especially when I didn't consider them to be a big deal. Luckily, I changed my perspective in high school and I started to realize how absolutely amazing it was to have a guidance counselor as a resource. Over the course of high school, I've been to my guidance counselor maybe five or six times on nonacademic runs.

Who are a few people you can talk to? Really think about this, resources are important to have...

_____

_____

_____

Unfortunately, not all school systems are created equally and there are plenty of you out there that don't have fantastic guidance counselors and are lucky if you have one parent or guardian who you feel comfortable talking to. If this is the case, there are still resources - please, please, please use a computer to look up local help hotlines. If you don't own a computer, there are public libraries that ideally should have a computer to help you. Though the quality of resources may vary significantly (which is definitely an issue), there are ALWAYS resources to get help.

Reaching out and talking to a guidance counselor, parent, or professional when we get stressed or overwhelmed can be intimidating. Believe me - I know. **But it's the only way for things to get better, and the only way to reach some kind of solution.**

And I actually want to take a moment to add something in - I'm literally two weeks away from this being published and I'm 19 so this isn't really my 'high school voice' but this is way too important not to add - here it is: **I can't get help for you.** I seriously can't. I can't walk to guidance for you, I can't tell your parent for you, I can't take medication for you. All I can do is encourage you to get help, like I've done. **The rest is up to you, my friends. YOU are the only person that can get help for you, and you have GOT to take that responsibility seriously.**

After helping a friend, I asked her to write a segment on her experience with reaching out, and I think it's really relatable and helpful:

"I attended my first self-confidence workshop when I was a freshman. I looked up to Ashley and I trusted her with stories and things going on in my life that I didn't know how to deal with on my own, and I never really shared with anyone else.

When I was a sophomore I began to go through a rough time. My best friend was self-harming, depressed, and spiraling out of control. She stopped talking to all of our friends except for me. That caused a lot of tension between us, they thought I was choosing her over them, and I couldn't tell them why. It was so confusing and hard to deal with. My best friend couldn't even manage to get out of bed most days. She would cancel every plan on me, and to be totally honest, I was really frustrated and annoyed with her. It sounds selfish now, but I was so angry that she wouldn't even try to let me help her. I was completely helpless. That was what sent me over the edge to talk to somebody.

I was already dealing with a lot going on in my own life. My family would fight all the time and I would cry myself to sleep in my room every week, praying for them to stop. I didn't belong in my own family, there was so much going on in my head and I just wanted to run away and for everyone to stop being so mean. I also went through a depressing time myself as well. I was always sad and had really dark thoughts. I had no idea why I was sad, and so I tried to distract myself. I would hang out with a group of friends but that only made things worse. It felt like nobody even cared about me. I could have disappeared and nobody would have noticed. I didn't know how to snap out of it. It is a really lonely feeling, being in a group of people, and yet you feel so alone.

Another problem I dealt with (and am still working on) is I don't feel worthy of basic things. When I finally talked to a guidance counselor, I just remember feeling so selfish for sharing my problems when people have it so much worse then me. When I dated a boy in school, I felt like I was being stupid because I was so young and I didn't deserve to be loved or call someone my boyfriend. It is hard for me to let myself say things out loud like that, because I worry people will judge me and think of me as ungrateful or 'just a little kid'. I didn't realize until I saw the look on my guidance counselor's face that I was actually keeping really serious problems bottled up.

Finally, I couldn't take it anymore. I didn't know what to do and I really thought I was helpless in the situation. I emailed Ashley, who told me it was time to get help. I never would have made that step if it wasn't for her. I emailed a guidance counselor in my school that I trusted and felt comfortable talking to. I told her that I had a lot of things on my mind that I needed to talk about. She was so quick to respond and comforted me saying that she was more than happy to help. Sitting outside her office when the day came, I was a mix of nervous and relieved. I was so close to getting help and I could not believe I was there. It was hard at first to explain what I was feeling because there was so much pushed down deep inside me. But it all eventually came rushing out. When I was done she told me that sometimes just talking about something can make the situation so much easier, which proved to be 100% true...

If you ever have anything you can't deal with on your own, even if you don't think it is that serious, talk to somebody. It is the most freeing feeling in the world not to carry all the burden alone. Your problems could be so much more serious than mine were (or even just a small thing that bothers you and you want to get it off your chest), and you need to just take the step to get help, no matter how scary it may seem. The way Ashley believed in me to get help for myself, I believe in you."

I believe in you too. **That's two people standing behind you already.** We all have GOT to take care of ourselves emotionally, and I encourage all of you to have an open mind to reaching out when you're not doing your best.

If you think there's a chance you have depression, or an eating disorder, or a learning disability, or bipolar, or anxiety, or anything, it's important you recognize that **it is serious. Even if you're not sure what you have, the best thing to do would be to have a conversation with a trusted adult.** It never hurts to check it out - you have literally nothing to lose and only by speaking up can we expect to get better. We have such incredible resources and teachers and guidance counselors and I encourage you to use them.

Survival of the Prettiest   Ashley Olafsen

Ask to speak to your trusted resource in person, at a time that works for both of you. When you're able to talk, I would suggest using 'I feel' statements. I know that they're super lame, and we learned about them in guidance in like 3rd grade, but 'I feel statements' are incredibly effective. For example, you could say,

'Thanks so much for talking to me. This is really difficult for me to say, but I'm going to try. The past few months have been really hard for me. I feel low sometimes, and I'm not sure why. I feel really bad about myself, and I feel like I'm not good enough. I'm wondering if I could maybe talk to the Doctor, or maybe schedule an appointment with a therapist. I'm not sure what is going on, but something isn't right'.

And take it from there. **Sometimes, it might take a few tries to get you the proper help.** *That's okay. You can't give up.* As long as you get there in the end, it doesn't matter how it happens.

What can you say to a trusted resource?

_____

_____

_____

_____

In addition, mental illness can be confusing and difficult to understand. Your parents or guidance counselors or friends might not say the things that you want to hear - they have no idea what the right thing to say is! Remember that this is probably overwhelming for them too. If your parents and loved ones don't know how to respond or handle a situation, you can't blame them or give up because of them. **Don't ever be discouraged from a bad start... getting help is a process. I promise you'll get there in the end.** There are different solutions for different people, and if it's not working out, then it's not the right solution

****
The Way You Talk to Yourself

Another part of taking care of yourself is talking to yourself in a kind manner - We need to stop putting ourselves down. Self-destruction doesn't happen just in the physical sense. It happens with what we say to ourselves things like this:
'I don't deserve to live'

190

'Everyone hates me and I'm so annoying'

'Everyone would be so much better off without me'

'I'm so stupid'

It's so awful that we would allow a person to think those things. I hate to be so blunt, but words like that don't help someone who wants to get better. If you're surrounding yourself with negative self-talk, you're going to think poorly of yourself. Plain and simple. Once you get yourself into this apologetic, messy mindset where you're constantly telling yourself such terrible things, you're only contributing to your anguish.

It's time we all learned to speak about ourselves positively. Please don't apologize for your existence, or who you are, or what you do. Instead, start realizing when you're hurting yourself verbally and begin attempting to talk to yourself the way you would to someone you love. And in turn, you'll love yourself when you give yourself the love you deserve.

How do you talk about yourself?

_____

_____

_____

_____

****

Re-Evaluating Media

Another part of helping yourself means re-evaluating the kind of media you like or follow. Right now, go onto your instagram, vsco, whatever the popular media of the day is, and take a second to look at what kinds of things you're following. For example, on Tumblr, the blogs I follow are pictures/videos of quotes, food, and fashion. There are also humor and social justice posts. What kinds of media are you following?

Social Media Type: _____

What You're Seeing on Social Media:

_____

_____

Social Media Type: _____
What You're Seeing on Social Media:

_____

_____

Social Media Type: _____
What You're Seeing on Social Media:

_____

_____

Social Media Type: _____
What You're Seeing on Social Media:

_____

_____

Media has the power to shape attitudes and, consequently, the power to be incredibly unhealthy. **The social media I used to follow made it extremely difficult for me to take care of myself and to realize my self-worth.**

Glamorization is when a serious mental illness is turned into something beautiful, or desirable. Glamorization of mental illness happens when graphic images, texts, videos, and any kind of media form (including magazines and books) promote mental illness, rather than emphasizing the seriousness of the situation.

There is so much scary glamorization out there. There are websites where people can share self-harm tips, there are how-to videos, and *there are anorexia tip websites, which teach individuals about the best and most effective way to go without eating.* When you type in bulimia or anorexia and add a space, the second thing that pops up on Google is 'bulimia/anorexia tips'.

Glamorization is extremely public and accessible to anyone who wants to find it - including eight year old girls. The Internet has the potential to be a dark place for someone without good coping skills, because glamorization of mental illness can be outstandingly present, and consequently, unbelievably dangerous. **Social media can make mental illness and eating disorders inescapable.**

Sadly, *millions* of girls follow pro-eating disorder and self-harm accounts. By viewing negative messages **constantly throughout the day, posts like these become normalized.** When negative media is so easily available, it's easy to become surrounded by messed up ideas and I can attest to this. **Glamorization feeds into addictions, amplifies them, and assures the individual that they don't need to get help.** Instead, glamorization proposes not eating or self-harming as acceptable solutions. In fact, 38% of girls reported to me that tumblr actually 'triggered' them to self-harm.

Another reason why glamorization is so destructive is because of this whole being saved by someone else concept. **Glamorization often promotes the idea that some beautiful person, usually a boy, is going to come kiss your scars, convince you to eat again, and try to fix you.** The 'being saved' concept breaks my heart, because when you're really low, you'll believe anything. This concept really hurt me, because I waited for months for someone else to come pick me up. **I used this idea as a way to justify not doing anything to help myself, and decided that I was not capable enough of picking myself up. It's cruel to teach young girls something so unrealistic, something so unhelpful, and something so destructive.**

And finally, glamorized media is so awful because mental illness and eating disorders are hard enough as it is. Honestly, it sucks and is all consuming. The dark mindsets are so outstandingly hard to get out of. Glamorized images pull you farther and farther away from recovery at a time when you are at a desperate low. It keeps you stuck in a dangerous mindset and doesn't allow you to get out of it.

The social media you follow has the potential to seriously shape the way you view the world. In fact, it's so powerful that a study of college-age females identified a link between disordered eating and appearance-based social comparison on Facebook! Media really does make a difference.

Perhaps many of you have never been exposed to glamorization, prior to this chapter. But I bet that many of you have followed Instagram accounts of models or fitness motivation that has stressed you out and made you feel bad about your body. I personally unfollowed an account the other day, because I realized that I was feeling a lot of body shame from not having the 'perfect' body. Perhaps your social media has made you feel left out or hurt. I once deleted my twitter because I was tired of seeing all my friends tweet about being together, and I have considered on multiple occasions getting rid of my Snapchat for the same reason.

How does your social media affect you? Have you ever felt excluded, hurt, or like you weren't good enough based on the social media accounts you're following?

_____
_____
_____
_____
_____
_____
_____

The good news about media is that we get to choose what kinds of social media we want to see. I would suggest that if you are following any kind of glamorization or anything that makes you feel bad, **unfollow it and get the heck away from it**...I know from experience that if your media is incredibly negative, your outlook and attitude is going to reflect that. So I ask you - are you going to fill your social media up with pictures of photo shopped models that make you feel awful about your body? Or, are you going to fill your social media up with empowering stories and updates (because that's what I do and it's really amazing)?

What is your game plan for your social media?

_____
_____
_____
_____
_____

****

Get Help

I very strongly believe that no one should have to feel so helpless when there are solutions. And, there are unbelievably effective solutions for mental illness. The recovery rate is high!

Happiness is a choice. We might not get to choose if we have a mental illness, but we sure get to decide what we do with it. YOU need to make the decision to be happy, and to get help, because no one else can choose your happiness for you.

Please stop waiting for someone to show up...take matters into your own hands and get the help you need. If you are having suicidal thoughts, starving yourself, or even dealing with friend drama - THAT IS SERIOUS. **You are worth the help. You matter. You are loved.**

And you are not alone. You are never alone. Mental illness can be lonely, but please know that you are not the only one going through these tough things. I care and I want you to get better.

****

Looking Out For Each Other

We need to be on each other's teams, and we need to be on the lookout for everyone. We need to support each other, more than we ever have before. That being said, we need to know warning signs.

****

Warning Signs

As a response to that, my best friend Lexie created this concept. She broke warning signs into yellow flags, and red flags:

"Yellow flags are things you need to have a discussion with your friend about, and discuss options...Tell a trusted adult, parent, teacher, or doctor. Yellow flag characteristics are:
- Upset often
- Really low self confidence
- Withdrawing themselves from friends and activities
- Eating less or more
- Obsessing over appearances
- What they're posting/ retweeting on social media

Red Flags are things that you should immediately have a discussion with your friend about and get them help from a parent or guidance counselor. You can offer to go with them for support, or let them go on their own. If they don't want to go, *you must put it upon yourself to tell an adult. These red flags can be seriously damaging, or even fatal, if not paid attention to.* Red flag characteristics are:

- Having suicidal thoughts
- Seeing self-harm on their body
- Inducing vomiting or taking pills
- Skipping meals or starving themselves
- Substance abuse"

So maybe you have a friend who you suspect is going through an eating disorder or depression. Or, maybe even a friend who just seems to be acting differently and kind of down. What do you do? If there's a red flag, you have no time to waste - **go talk to a trusted adult, right now.** If you notice some yellow flags, read on and then take action immediately following.

****

A Note

Also, I want to make it incredibly clear that **helping someone else should never be your sole responsibility - mental illnesses require much more than one person can provide, and professionals need to be involved in all instances. It is unfair for you to become your friend/family member's therapist if you are not a professional, and that is not a burden you deserve to take on. Please, please, please get professional help in all instances.**

****

How to Discuss Your Concerns

Let's talk about discussing your concerns with a loved one. If you are worried about someone, have a conversation with them in a calm, quiet place. I would strongly recommend that the conversation is between only the two of you; extra people can make a difficult conversation even more scary and overwhelming.

I know that it is potentially uncomfortable to talk about mental illness, but you need to realize that a life could be at stake. **We cannot be silent about something so deadly, and something so important. We need to have these kinds of hard conversations.**

196

I also want to say that if you're unsure of what to do, or want to talk about your concern with someone, **please reach out to someone!**

I combined my own thoughts and information from the help service Samaritans to create a sample conversation.

If you suspect your friend is going through something, approach it tactfully and honestly. Start out with a general statement like "This is hard to say, but I care a lot about you, and I'm worried". Then, list reasons why you're worried….perhaps you're worried because they seem to have lost motivation, or are sleeping much more than they used to.

Once you have started talking, make it clear how much you care about them, and how you're asking because you want them to be better. The person you're confronting is most likely scared, so try and make them feel as comfortable and loved as possible. You also need to realize that everyone handles this kind of conversation differently, so respect whatever way they choose to handle it. If they fall silent or pause, that's okay. Give them some time….like I said, these kinds of things are scary to open up about. Don't press them for too much information, and allow them to say what they're comfortable with. If they are willing to talk to you, make sure that you thank them for being so brave and opening up. Give them all of your attention, and truly listen attentively, without interrupting, to what they have to say. Feel free to ask polite questions, so you can better understand their perspective. **Above all, be respectful.**

The Samaritans have a list of things not to do, and I have included it below. When listening to a friend, don't:

- Try to solve the person's problems
- Give advice that wasn't asked for
- Say that the person's actions or feelings are wrong or unimportant
- Tell the person about your own problems

It's also critically important for you to know people with mental illnesses can't just 'get over it'. You would never tell someone with a broken leg to 'get over it', and likewise you shouldn't say that to someone who has mental illness.

Additionally, it you MUST talk about getting professional help. Mental illness in any form cannot be cured by a friend. It is far more serious, far more devastating, and far more complicated than that. Ask them if they've ever considered getting help. Tell them that you really think it would be in their best interest, and talk about the different options. Ask them to think about who they can speak to about this, and figure out a game plan.

Have you ever helped a loved one before? How did it make you feel?

_____

_____

_____

Is there a loved one that you can help? How so?

_____

_____

_____

****

Tell Someone

Getting help is <u>non-negotiable</u>, and if your friend or loved one refuses to get help, **you need to tell someone - whether it's the police, your parents, their parents, your school; <u>someone needs to be notified.</u>** I asked one of my friends to write her experience, and I want you to take it to heart. She wrote as follows:

"A few years ago, one of my best friends was bullied really badly for a long period of time. She progressively became more and more upset, insecure, and anxious; the bullying truly took over her life. One day she called me sobbing telling me how much she hated her life and herself, and how much she wanted to die. This was the first time I had heard her, or anyone, say and truly mean those words. I was overcome with fear, guilt, and confusion. I calmed her down and told her everything was going to be okay. I made her pinky promise she wouldn't hurt herself. At the time, I felt like everything was under control, but I now realize I had only put a band-aid on a wound that required much more healing than a 14 year old girl was capable of providing. And this is something I have grown to accept and recognize in many cases I have heard that are similar to my/my friend's...

When somebody has suicidal thoughts or a mental illness, you can't just calm the person down and make them pinky swear it's going to be okay. It's much more complicated than that, and requires professional help. Being a friend and contributing to a support system is so important and helpful, but <u>you</u> alone cannot be someone's support system. It's not fair to you, or the person you are attempting to help, for you to try to solely take on something much bigger and scarier than even a best friend can handle.

Additionally, letting suicidal thoughts and depression go on for longer will only create even more damage... I quickly realized that our phone call hadn't changed or helped anything for her, it had only postponed the inevitable breakdown. When that time came, a few other friends were involved at that point. The decision to share this information with a trusted adult was something that I did not come to lightly. I felt as though I was betraying her for telling her secret. I feared losing her as a friend...But something a good friend recently told me, it is better to lose a friend than for a friend to lose their life.

I so often hear of young people being too scared to speak up for their friend or even themselves when they are in dangerous and life threatening situations. Whether it be suicidal thoughts, self-harm, an eating disorder, bullying, etc. etc. **speaking up is always the best, and honestly the only choice you have.** My friend ended up receiving help; a support system of parents, teachers, doctors, friends, and nothing but endless love. After all was said and done, my friend was grateful and happy that we had acted on the situation. We had shown her that people cared for her and wanted to see her get better, we wanted to see her live and thrive.

Despite my previous feelings of fear, guilt, and helplessness about the situation, I understood that I had made the right decision. **Getting help is always the right decision, and that has become apparent to me time and time again no matter what the circumstances are. Getting someone help is the best gift you can give a friend who is suffering.** So please do not ever feel guilty or feel like a bad friend for doing exactly that."

Quite literally, my friend saved this girl's life. After the teacher was told, the girl's parents started getting involved. The girl started going to therapy, and getting professional help. She's okay, and she lived through it. I can't even imagine what would happen, if my friend didn't tell a teacher, and I don't want to think about it. **Make sure that you get your friends help, if they are unwilling to help themselves.**

Also, let your loved one know that if they want, you can help them talk to a professional. If you feel capable, offer to take your friend to the guidance counselors, or offer to help them talk to their parents. Like I said, I've gone with friends to help them get help.

And finally, check up on them. Maybe your first conversation didn't go well and wasn't very productive. That's okay. You got them thinking about help, you were there for them, and you showed them you care. That's huge and you should be so proud of yourself for reaching out and being a good friend or family member. Regardless of their response, make sure to check up on them. Ask them how they're doing, and be there for them.

****

If Your Loved One is Getting Help...

If your loved one is getting help, the best thing you can do is remind them how much you care and support them. **It isn't your job to be a therapist.** You should be a friend or daughter or; you shouldn't be the person that they come to every hour of everyday, miserable. You shouldn't have to worry about their life every second, and you shouldn't have to worry what will happen if you don't pick up your phone one time. That's terrifying, and it's an awful position to be in. I've seen so many of my friends in this state, and it's so unfair to them. **Encouraging them to continue to get help is as much as you can do.**

****

Help the World

It is imperative that we **speak up about mental illness**. I understand that mental illness is a sensitive topic, *but it needs to be addressed for exactly that reason*. **If we continue to remain silent, people will continue to die.** That's just the reality of it. Anorexia has the highest death rates of any mental health condition, and on a global level, The World Health Organization states that every year *more than 800,000 people die from suicide.*

We can't continue like this.

Furthermore, the silence is completely foolish because so many of us have either been affected by mental illness, or we know someone who has been affected by mental illness. It doesn't even *make sense* to remain silent about something that is so common to society.

****

We Need to Change Something

What are the stereotypes you've heard about those with mental illness?

_____

_____

_____

Sometimes, those with mental illnesses are portrayed as dangerous, needy, abnormal, cowardly, stupid, selfish or crazy. There's even the notion that people who have mental illness are 'faking it' - despite the fact that we know mental illness is a very real kind of illness.

These untrue characterizations and generalizations restrict so many people from getting help. I'm willing to bet that often times, people don't even realize they have mental illness because they either don't know what it is, or the people they've seen depicted in the media that are mentally ill are different cases than theirs. **People are struggling as a result of this unhealthy perception, and we need EVERYONE to feel free to get the help they so rightly deserve.**

If we want things to get better, we have to change the way we talk about mental health.

We can do this by not shaming mental illness, and by having a positive and compassionate cultural response to people who are going through things out of their control.

****

Few Receive Help

Often times, people who are suffering convince themselves that what they have isn't serious, and doesn't need to be taken care by a professional. **Only 1 in 10 people suffering from anorexia nervosa receive treatment. Additionally, only**

about a third of those suffering from severe depression seek treatment from a mental health professional. One of my life goals is to change those numbers.

****

End the 'Attention Seeking' Stereotype

One way we can stop shaming is by contradicting the idea that people who have mental illness are 'just doing it for attention'. A common myth surrounding mental illness, is that the individual is 'attention seeking'. Truly, there could be nothing further from the truth. As you just saw above, people with mental illness rarely get the help they need. Sadly, a large reason why I didn't reach out for help sooner was because I was scared of being labeled as attention seeking. **I didn't want people to judge me, and I was so scared of labels that my fear kept me from getting help.**

It is critical we speak up and encourage those who need help to get the help they need. The particular phrase 'attention seeking' is one that I have heard used to describe many people who make their difficulties public, and I am ashamed to admit that I have used the phrase as well.

<u>This needs to end.</u> Regardless if the person is actually attention seeking or not, we need to stop using this phrase because people who are legitimate in their struggles hear what we say, and are scared to speak up and get the help they need. People who suffer from any kind of mental illness need to know that we won't reject them as attention seeking.

****

End Mental Illness Romanticization

It is also critical we stop romanticizing mental illness and various addictions, because it's having serious consequences. While sadness, like any other emotion is beautiful, there is NOTHING beautiful about being sad for a prolonged time. Depression is not, by any means, 'beautifully tragic' - it's straight up tragic. Similarly, smoking is not glamorous - it's deadly.

****

End Stereotypes

We also need to break stereotypes. One of the common stereotypes about mental illness is that 'normal' people can't be mentally ill. We think that only the troubled teenagers, or 'the outsiders', can suffer from a mental illness. Moreover, one of the common eating disorder stereotypes is that only skinny girls can have an eating disorder. In reality though, there's nothing physical that can identify who is dealing with mental illness and who isn't. Anyone can and do have mental illness!

Unfortunately, these stereotypes contribute to why so many people refuse to identify with mental illness and this needs to end.

****

End the Notion That Someone Will Save You

We also need to dispel the dangerous notion that someone will come save us. I found that 62% of females have dreamed of being saved by someone. It's so scary, because *62% of us are allowing something as important as our LIVES to depend on someone else's ability to save us*....And even worse, a lot of times, we don't even know who the hell we're waiting for. A girl from my survey wrote, "I didn't start self-harming until two years ago, around the time I joined tumblr. YES, I do think tumblr romanticizes sadness and depression in a big way. I remember thinking that someday one boy would come to get me. But, one day I had a reality check when I went too far and almost killed myself. Now, I realize that depression ain't a beauty, it's a nightmare...At least now I understand that nobody will ever come to save no boy, no girl, NOBODY". No one can save you but yourself.

This 'being saved by someone' infatuation (for many girls) may have started with princess movies, where the female is saved by her knight in shining armor. Yet, it has escalated to movie after movie where the female is nothing more than a helpless side chick. And, I am sick and tired of it. Feminism is about making *your* own choices. **I fully respect individuals who want to be taken care of by someone else,** however, the way we portray women is in the media is pathetic. I want more movies where girls are courageous and save themselves, and **I want girls to know that they CAN save**

themselves! Because you can save yourself. I saved myself by reaching out for professional help. You can do it too.

****

End the Blame

And finally, it's not okay to blame people who have mental illness or a disorder for what they have - it's not their fault.

Mental illness is separate from who the person is; it is an illness - AN ILLNESS - and not the person. To illustrate my point, in sports, when you fracture something, you are injured. What do you do when you're injured? It's so obvious that I feel weird asking it. Naturally, you go to the Doctor and get it checked out by a professional. Then, you do whatever the Doctor tells you, whether you need medicine, tests, etc., you make sure you follow their professional orders. That's how you get better.

Mental illness is the same way. Mental illness is the same as a physical injury - for both, it's important to reach out for help. **And if you don't reach out for help, whether it be a physical problem or mental one, it only gets worse.**

****

Take a Compassionate Approach to Mental Illness

In turn, **we need to discuss mental illness and disorders with correct information, understanding, compassion, and above all respect.** Imagine if we handled mental illness with understanding instead of shame.

What would happen? What would the world be like?

_____

_____

_____

Can you even imagine how much better the world would be? **Can you imagine how many lives would be saved, how many people would be happy?**

****

Encourage Boys Especially to Get Help

Additionally, we need to encourage everyone, especially boys, to get help. We also need to redefine what strength is. True strength is reaching out for help when you need it, and boys need to see that as the truth. Until we make these necessary changes, things will remain toxic and not get better.

****

You Can Make a Difference

You can help create a world where everyone is encouraged to speak up and get the help they need. **You just need to speak up.**

You might be overwhelmed and not sure how to use your voice. That's okay. If you care and if your heart has been emotional throughout this book, you've already begun. I care, and because I care, I've written this book. **Change starts with people who care, and then transforms with determined people who are committed to change.**

If you care, use your voice to speak up about things you care about. If you're not sure how, **a good starting point would be creating awareness.** I think that a large reason why we have such a messy approach in handling depression and eating disorders is because people simply don't know or understand them. If we were to spread awareness, or to take the time to help inform people about what mental illness is, I really think that we would be in a much better place. This entire book is dedicated to awareness of issues, and (hopefully) that awareness has made a difference in your life.

I have a few ideas of ways that you can speak up: You can make informational videos, give speeches, create posters with information and hang them up in your school, or email educators to ask them to put a segment into health class about mental illness and eating disorders. Or perhaps you can compose a tweet, a Facebook post, or even share a TEDx on mental health!

I really think that if everyone was better informed, more people would feel comfortable to come forward and get the help they need.

You have the power to speak up. I also cannot emphasize enough how much of an advantage social media is. Because it's so powerful, you have the ability to make whatever you do go viral,

We all have voices, and it's time to start speaking out against the stigmas. Other things you can do would include speaking up by sharing your story, what you've learned, or what you're trying to accomplish. You can publish your story in my newsletter, you can tweet, you can make a facebook post, you can make a blog dedicated to recovery.

Any other ideas of things you can do?

_____

_____

_____

_____

****

You Can Make a Difference Through Social Media

One extremely powerful thing I learned from social media is that **I wasn't alone in suffering. And you are not alone in your struggles, no matter what they may be.** Behind the hundreds of blogs I was following, there were individuals sharing my same low. And devastatingly enough, through my friends' tumblrs, I found out that my own friends too were equally as sad. This was shocking to me.

At first, it may seem like a relief to know that your struggle is not singular. But, a community like this one can become quickly dangerous. If members of the online community don't get help, they have the potential to trigger others.

However, that online community could just as easily be unbelievably helpful and supportive to each other. They have the potential to. **Social media can influence us to get help, and can even change our current social stigma regarding mental illness.** I have seen countless blogs dedicated to recovery out there, and we are making strides. All of those people could be recovering together, sending kind messages and reblogging recovery posts. One girl from my survey wrote, "While triggering images may be common, I've found far more valuable information on self-harm and a community of accepting people that push you to be your best and let you know that you are important. The culture of support is certainly present, and I've found it to be amazing. While the triggering tags and communities can be overwhelming, they're not all that's available". **There are alternatives to glamorization, and you have the power to create an encouraging, supportive space for people to share honestly.**

****

Yes We Can

The future is literally in our hands, and I hope you'll all join me, because it's time to change history, for the sake of betterment of the human society! I want to conclude with a quote from Margaret Mead:

"Never doubt that a small group of thoughtful, committed, citizens can change the world. Indeed, it is the only thing that ever has".

****

Final Thoughts

I remember one night a few months after I got help, when I was lying in bed, almost asleep but thinking about all of things I wanted to accomplish in my life. I shot up in the dark, sitting upright and alone; I had thought 'I never want to die'. I had SO many things that I wanted to do. I just didn't have the time to be bogged down by negativity! It's a laughable moment and a ridiculous statement, but I thought that exact thing and it shocked me. I never dreamed in a million years I would one day be able to feel such a sense of contentment and happiness. Since reaching out for help, things have gotten significantly better. I have gained such a deep appreciation for life and for everyone. It's a fantastic place to be, and I'm excited for my future. I never imagined I would ever feel this way. You don't know what's in store for you.

Keep going. **Hang in there for me, okay?**

****

Reflection Questions

Did anything stand out to you while reading this section?

_____

_____

_____

_____

Did anything surprise you? Why do you think it did?

_____

_____

_____

_____

Why is it important to talk about mental health? Why don't we usually talk about mental health?

_____

_____

_____

_____

What role does the media play in influencing things like eating disorders/self-harm, etc.? How should the media play a role in influencing things like eating disorders/self-harm, etc.?

_____

_____

_____

_____

How does it make you feel to talk about mental health? Why?

_____

_____

_____

_____

What are you going to do from here on out, regarding mental health?

_____

_____

_____

_____

SEXUALIZATION

****

Opening Quotes:

"Developing sense of oneself as a sexual being is an important task of adolescence, but sexualization may make this task even more difficult. Indeed, Tolman argued that in the current environment, teen girls are encouraged to look sexy, yet they know little about what it means to be sexual, to have sexual desires, and to make rational and responsible decisions about their pleasure and risk within intimate relationships that acknowledge their own desires." - Report of the APA Task Force on the Sexualization of Girls

"Cross culturally, unequal nakedness almost always expresses power relations: In modern jails, male prisoners are stripped in front of clothed prison guards; in the antebellum South, young black male slaves were naked while serving the clothed white masters at table. To live in a culture where women are routinely naked where men aren't is to learn inequality in little ways all day long." - Naomi Wolf, <u>The Beauty Myth</u>

"Nobody's surprised that girls aren't achieving all that they are able to achieve. Sexism is real. And when girls are thinking that their biggest value and their worth - what's most important and valid about them - is how they look, that's what they spend the most time thinking about and doing. And when boys are taught their birthright is taking action and adventure and making things happen and succeeding...then that's the road they're going to take. We aren't born with self-doubt, low self-esteem, eating disorders, self-hatred, pleasing, rape, molestation, violence against women - nope, we're not born with it. We're spoon fed it." - Kathy Najimy

****

Opening Questions:

What do you think a healthy sexuality is?

_____

_____

The World Health Organization defines *sexual health* as:
"Sexual health is a state of physical, mental and social well-being in relation to sexuality. **It requires a positive and respectful approach to sexuality and sexual relationships**, as well as the possibility of having pleasurable and safe sexual experiences, free of coercion, discrimination and violence."

Do you think most people have a positive experience with sexual health?

_____

_____

_____

_____

From who or what have you learned about sex, sexting, relationships, etc.?

_____

_____

_____

_____

How has sexualized media affected you or others around you?

_____

_____

_____

Do you think that there are different standards for different genders, in terms of being sexual?

_____

_____

_____

_____

What has your experience with kissing, sex, etc. been like? Positive? Negative?

_____

_____

_____

_____

_____

_____

_____

****

Introduction

It is time to talk honestly about sex, and the messages we, specifically children and teenagers, are absorbing. It is also time to talk about how these messages are affecting our way of thinking.

****

Sex is confusing

Mary Piper writes in <u>Reviving Ophelia</u>, "Sex is considered both a sacred act between two people united by God and the best way to sell suntan lotion". This line sums up why I, like so many kids and teenagers, have a difficult time understanding what to think when it comes to sex, sexuality, and sexualization.

At age 18, I am thoroughly and utterly confused. Previously, I have been a scared and overwhelmed 12 year old, as well as a sad and very stressed out 15 year old.

I have learned about what sex and being sexy means through the messages that media, friends, my parents, my school, my religion, and culture have sent me.

Let me tell you some of the messages that I have learned:

- You aren't sexy unless you're completely shaved, have a huge and toned butt, big boobs, a flat stomach, the list goes on.
- You ALWAYS have to look your best around boys, and you have to change the way you look for them.
- It's not classy to send nudes, and you should stay away from girls who take pictures of themselves and send it to boys - that's gross.
- There's a difference between sexy and skanky, and you have to be careful not to cross that line, but it's hard to figure out what the line is.
- Sex is a sacred gift shared between two married people; you should wait until marriage for sex.
- It's embarrassing to go into college a virgin, and being 18 years old and a virgin is weird and to be shamed.
- People want me to have a healthy sex life, but that I should wait until I'm older.
- Virginity is a very, very special thing and I should not give it away to boys - after all, all boys want is sex!
- Sex is for straight people only.
- Providing men with sex and blow jobs is the only thing a woman is good for.
- If I have sex, I'll be a total whore, slut, and absolutely disgusting. Girls should NOT have sex.
- If a boy gets hard and he doesn't have sex, he'll be in a lot of pain, so I really may as well have sex with him if I care about him.
- That the above statement isn't actually true, and that I shouldn't ever be pressured into sex.
- If I have sex, I need to get onto birth control and I need to take all these precautions, or else I could get sexually transmitted infections, pregnant, and --
- ---- Wait, what?? How can I get an sexually transmitted infection?? How do I get pregnant???????

Sex is confusing, overwhelming, and hard to figure out. Not to mention scary finding out potential consequences that often go untalked about.

Girls aren't the only ones confused or intimidated by sexual expectations. Regardless of gender or sexual orientation, sex can be confusing. I asked one of my friends to tell me some of the messages that he's learned as a male, and here's what he had to say:

- You should lose your virginity by the end of high school.
- The more girls you can hook up with, the better.
- The hotter the girls you have sex with, the better.
- Adolescent boy view of hot = large breasts and slim body.
- The only place girls should have hair is on their heads, and that hair should be luscious and blonde.
- Getting a blowjob is superior to getting a hand job.
- The larger the dick, the better the sex.

Do you notice a difference between the messages that girls learn versus boys?

_____

_____

_____

_____

The world of sex is confusing, contradictory, and straight up overwhelming. The world of sex isn't just confusing though - it's downright dangerous.

****

Here's Our Reality

Right now, we are in the midst of a crisis.

At age 18, I have five friends who have been raped. I have two friends who have been in abusive relationships - (let me remind you I'm in _high school_). As I go back to do a final edit, I am in college and the number of friends who have been in abusive relationships has risen greatly. I have two friends that I know of, whom have been molested. I have several friends who were in extremely unhealthy relationships. I have many friends who have been street harassed or sexually harassed. In fact, sexual harassment (being the object of a sexual joke, comments, gestures, being touched, grabbed, pinched, etc.) is a part of daily life for most girls. According to a 2001 study, 63% of girls report experiencing sexual harassment 'often' or 'occasionally'. Though research is limited, research also suggests that teenagers who aren't straight experience more harassment than their peers.

And these are only the instances that I am aware of....I have no doubt that more of my friends have experienced these things - they just haven't told me.

Sadly, the odds of having a healthy and happy experience with sex is not in our favor.

To begin with, 1 in 4 girls and 1 in 6 boys will be sexually abused before they turn 18 years old. **That means 25% of females are abused sexually as children.**

From there, things only get worse. **One in five women** and 1 in 71 men will be raped at some point in their lives. Rape affects different groups of people differently. For example, **American Indians are twice as likely to experience a rape/sexual assault compared to all races.** Additionally, rape rates are disproportionately high for inmates in prison.

It's also incredibly important to note that violence is not just a merely heterosexual problem. In fact, dating violence affects EVERYONE regardless of gender or sexuality - usually even more. For example, **46% lesbians and 75% bisexual women reported sexual violence during their lifetimes, while 40% gay men and 47% bisexual men reported sexual violence.**

Abuse rates aren't much better. Nearly 1.5 million high school students nationwide experience physical abuse from a dating partner in a single year. In fact, 1 in 10 high school students has been purposefully hit, slapped or physically hurt by a partner. In HIGH SCHOOL. It makes my heart so heavy, especially because I have seen it happen over and over again.

Physical abuse isn't the only kind. **In fact, one in three adolescent girls in the U.S. is a victim of physical, sexual, emotional or verbal abuse from a dating partner, a figure that far exceeds rates of other types of youth violence.** And that number only raises as females get older. Nearly half of dating college women report experiencing violent and abusive dating behaviors. Scarily, girls and young women face the most abuse - females between the ages of 16 and 24 experience the highest rate of intimate partner violence - almost triple the national average. It's also important to note that disabled individuals face abuse at much higher rates than able-bodied individuals.

The sheer number of individuals that have been affected in a negative way by rape, abuse, stalking, prostitution, molestation, and so much more is incredibly overwhelming. And deeply personal - almost everyone has been affected in some way by these issues, whether personally or through a friend or family member. **It's too many people.**

****

Silence During a Crisis

Despite the enormously personal impact that negative sexual behavior is having on our society, we rarely talk about sex in a meaningful way - or perhaps more importantly, what a healthy relationship looks like. Almost ever.

In fact, I have a few friends whose parents have not once, never even mentioned sex. Ever! And my friends aren't alone - we collectively have few meaningful conversations about sex with our parents. Seventeen Magazine and the Henry J. Kaiser Family Foundation discovered that among 15 to 17 year olds, only 61% of females and 42% of males had discussed with their parents 'how to know when you're ready to have sex'. And, even when kids are getting information from their parents, it might be inaccurate. One study found that parents often give incorrect information, and only semi-accurate facts regarding sex.

Schools aren't doing a much better job. In fact, only 24 states and the District of Columbia mandate sex education. **Furthermore, only 13 states require that sex education is medically accurate.**

The blunt truth is that there ARE a lot of parents who are unaware of the crisis we're in...After all, 81% of parents believe teen dating violence is not an issue or admit they don't know if it's an issue. **And sadly, many aren't giving their kids information about something that their children are exposed to constantly.**

****

Let Me Break This Down For You

Here's how it is:

Half of teenagers have had sex by age 17 (yes, parents, that's completely true). Nearly a quarter of teens have posted nude or semi-nude photos or videos of themselves, with nearly 11% of those teens being teen girls between the ages of 13 and 16. And many kids and teenagers are being raped, abused, molested, or so much more.

Yet, our parents and schools as a whole REFUSE TO TALK ABOUT SEX.

So if we're getting little to no information from our parents or our schools, where do we look for guidance on sex?

Well duh. **The internet.**

****

Sex Ed in 2015

Allow me to introduce the way we receive our sex education:

My parents gave me 'the talk' the summer before 5th grade. It was the first of many helpful talks that we had over the course of my middle/high school career.

But 5th grade wasn't really the first time I got 'the talk' - it was just the first time I got the talk from my parents. Truth be told, I have gotten the talk hundreds of times before my parents even breached the subject of sex with me.

Today, kids growing up get many talks. **Our media, friends, and larger culture are constantly giving us the talk, and we're almost *always* being sent messages about sex and what sex means.**

The harsh reality is the largest group of internet porn consumers are children aged 12 to 17. I kid you not.

Staggeringly, *51% of boys have viewed porn before they even turn 13. In fact, the average exposure of males to pornography is age 12.* And it's not just boys - 32% of females have viewed porn before the age of 13.

However, today's porn is not even close to our parents' porn. Today's porn is so much more graphic and dangerous; it's often violent and scary. Horrifyingly, **88% of top rated porn scenes contain aggressive acts.**

And it doesn't end there. Here are some of the things that kids are being exposed to:
- 15% of boys and 9% of girls have seen child pornography
- 32% of boys and 18% of girls have seen bestiality online - or a person having sex with an animal
- 39% of boys and 23% of girls have seen sexual bondage online - or tying up and restraining partner for erotic pleasure
- 83% of boys and 57% of girls have seen group sex online

This *is* the horrifying reality of today.

With the media easily accessible, porn is so easy to find. Porn is the advertisement on the side of the weather channel website, it's on our blog dashboard, and it's coming up as a suggested YouTube video. The U.S. Department of Justice has even stated, "Never before in the history of telecommunications media in the United States has so much indecent (and obscene) material been so easily accessible by so many minors in so many American homes with so few restrictions".

Truly, all it takes is a curious 9 year old boy to type 'boobs' into Google, and immediately, he's exposed to much more than he was ever hoping for...and it can only escalate from there.

And, we're spending a LOT of our time watching porn. **64% of college men and 18% of college women spend time online for Internet sex every week.**

Even if we're not watching porn directly though, we're still being exposed to messages about sex at increasingly young ages.

The Kaiser Family Foundation reports that **two out of every three television shows include sexual content.** And that's just TV - so much of our music is sexual in nature. In 2009, **92%** of the 174 songs that made it into the Top Ten contained one or more or phrases referencing sex. However, the vulgarity in music videos is almost unmatchable - the APA reports that **44 to 81 percent of music videos contains sexual imagery.**

Sex is everywhere. **And the reality is that we are largely learning our sex education through the media - which, as stated before, we spend an increasingly large amount of our time on.**

****

A Quick Clarification

I have spent and I'm going to spend a lot of time talking about the negatives of media on sex education. That being stated, I certainly want to acknowledge that the media CAN be and often is a great place for healthy, honest sex education! For example, there are so many positive resources out there, especially on YouTube that do a great job of educating on sexual health. Also, the internet is a great way for communities of marginalized people to come together so they feel less alone. Basically, what I'm trying to say is that I recognize that the internet can be a really positive place for sex education...though media certainly has negatives, it also has positives. Media itself is neutral - we determine how it's used.

****

The Problem

Here's the thing: If we watched porn occasionally, or saw a sexualized female once in a blue moon, there wouldn't be (much of) a problem. **Quite honestly, porn isn't the problem. Rather, the problem is the kind/content of common pornography, and the fact that our sex education is mostly and only porn.**

Furthermore, the problem is that the negative messages we are learning about sex are so reinforced, on a daily basis, as we are growing up and learning what to think about sex. **In fact, the current media is allowing a crisis to take place right in front of us.** Rather than teaching positive information about waiting until you and your partner are ready for sex, or teaching how to say no, **our media has, at the very least, created a climate where disrespect against females can thrive.** In fact, our incredibly sex saturated culture has created a climate where behaviors like rape, abuse, and more can truly prosper. And at a time when so many females and males are facing the consequences of rape, abuse, and more - we shouldn't be messing around like this.

****

Women Are Overly Sexualized

Right now, our sex education is hugely problematic because women are so often overly sexualized.

What do you think sexualization is?

_____

_____

The American Psychological Association states that sexualization occurs when any of the follow happen:

- a person's value comes only from his or her sexual appeal or behavior, to the exclusion of other characteristics;
- a person is held to a standard that equates physical attractiveness (narrowly defined) with being sexy;
- a person is sexually objectified - that is, made into a thing for others' sexual use, rather than seen as a person with the capacity for independent action and decision making; and/or
- sexuality is inappropriately imposed upon a person.

Unfortunately, I had to take out the original pictures I had in this part because of copyright reasons, but take a moment to Google 'examples of sexualized ads 2016' or whatever the year is. I really think you're going to be surprised.

In many advertisements, women are subject to sexualization. Their bodies are used to sell products, and **they are valued only for what they look and what they can perform sexually**. Disgustingly, the APA reports that studies find in advertisements, women often pose as decorative objects, and are displayed in ways that emphasize their bodies, body parts, facial features, and sexual readiness. As per usual, this is racialized.

Sadly, advertising isn't the only place where women are sexualized….movies and other media forms sexualize women as well. One study concluded, **"Together, the**

age and appearance findings reinforce that cinematic females are valued more than cinematic males for their looks, youthfulness and sexy demeanor". Time and time again, women exist in the media only to be looked at.

But the sexualization doesn't stop there. Music and music videos are just as bad, if not worse. Studies have found that female artists are more likely to be sexually objectified, are held to stricter appearance standards, and are more likely to demonstrate sexually alluring behavior in comparison to men. Furthermore, females are frequently portrayed in a sexy role or as a sex object in the games reinforcing gender stereotypes and potentially impacting attitudes towards women

In fact, sexualization is so common that the American Psychological Association found that nearly every form of media studied provided "ample evidence of the sexualization of women".

Sorry to be the bearer of bad news, but this is the reality of what 12 year olds are watching and learning.

****

Females Exist to Please Males with Sexual Favors

Here's the reality: Women are overly sexualized in our media, and many individuals are facing the consequences of our sex saturated & sexist culture. There are many consequences to this.

The first of many consequences is that some males become entitled, or rather believe that women 'owe' them sexual favors.

And before half of you freak out on me note that I truly and purposefully stated 'SOME' men rather than all men. Let me explain to you what I mean, because it is undeniable that some men do in fact believe this:

In 2014, a 22 year old man named Elliot Rodger went on a killing spree, murdering six people and injuring many more.

His reasoning for this killing spree was the supposed cruelness of women. According to him, no female had ever expressed interest in him.

So, this begs an important question: **WHY** did he do what he did??

And that is not a simple answer, and I am not going to attempt to answer it in full because I cannot do it justice. However, I think it's important we look at the role culture played in creating that murder. Elliot believed that it was embarrassing to be a 22 year old male virgin. And this embarrassment is something that we have largely created as a culture - like I talked about before, our expectations of men include that they are having lots of sex. And, because masculinity is power, and power is having lots of sex - Elliot most likely felt a sense of powerlessness. But in addition to our dangerous male gendered expectations, Elliot believed it was the **female's** fault for not being attracted to him.

Though he is one of the very, very, VERY few that actually murdered because he didn't get what he wanted sexually, it seems as though males not being able to handle rejection is trending. Of course, not ALL males have difficulty with rejection, but in high school at least, it seems like there are enough boys that believe girls *owe* them sex or sexual favors to make it a trend.

In Connecticut, a 16 year old girl was stabbed to death by a boy after she refused to attend junior prom with him. In 2014, a woman was shot and killed after refusing to give a man her phone number. That same year, a pregnant woman was slammed on the ground and stabbed after rejecting a man's advances.

Have you ever had an experience when someone lashed out at you for rejecting them?

_____

_____

_____

_____

Frustration at not being liked back is understandable - I spent so much of middle school and the first half of high school trying to figure out why I wasn't 'good enough' to be kissed, and frustrated at what I perceived to be wrong with me. **But what we have going on today is a little more than frustration...it's scary, it's mean, and it's life-threatening.**

And, it's learned - what in the world makes a person think that it's okay to murder people, to make threatening Facebook posts, to call another person names, because they didn't get what they wanted? What are we teaching boys, that makes them believe that girls owe them sex or sexual favors? And what are we teaching, that some boys have learned it's okay to be disrespectful when they are rejected?

Here's part of the answer: We're teaching boys that girls exist to provide sexual favors.

So many boys feel like they are entitled to sex or to nudes or to being liked back - simply because that's what they've learned. As a society and culture, we constantly thrust sexualized women and pornified women into the faces of growing boys. When we don't represent women in accurate ways, we teach growing boys that females are sex objects. When we don't see women represented as people with thoughts, emotions, and storylines - we teach boys to view females as objects, instead of people. **And instead we teach boys that girls EXIST TO PLEASE THEM. And more than that, boys learn that female bodies are FOR THEM and not for themselves.**

Porn especially sends the message that women exist to please men sexually. Dines writes how porn declares that women are "always ready for sex and are enthusiastic to do whatever men want, irrespective of how painful, humiliating, or harmful the act is. The word 'no' is glaringly absent from porn women's vocabulary. **These women seem eager to have their orifices stretched to full capacity and sometimes beyond, and indeed, the most bizarre and degrading the act, the greater the supposed sexual arousal for her".**

This is perhaps why some married men believe that they have a 'right' to have sex with their wives at any time they want, no matter what - the female is theirs. Furthermore, this is why a pregnant woman 'ruins' her body by having kids. After her body has clearly been used to have heterosexual sex, and she has been 'used' by a guy, her body has no more value and is consequently ruined.

Research backs this up. Fight the New Drug, a company dedicated to porn awareness, declares "Since porn often portrays women as nothing more than sex objects that need to be dominated, it's not surprising that porn users often start seeing real women that way as well. In one study of porn's effects, researchers broke participants up into three groups: to one they showed a high amount of pornography, one a medium amount, and the third a lower amount, and then followed with questions about what participants thought about women. **Results showed that the more porn a man was exposed to, the more likely he was to prefer that women be submissive and subordinate to men".**

Therefore, we strongly encourage the idea that females exist to please males and there is sometimes a backlash when females reject a male's advances.

****

Harassment

Our culture has created an atmosphere where harassment can thrive, as we frequently show boys that the female body is an object to be looked at and nothing more than a body.

For example, one study found that about 84% of shows contain at least one incident of sexual harassment. However, the incidents are regarded as humorous, teaching that sexual harassment isn't actually a serious problem. **We have created a culture that encourages harassment, and regards harassment as nothing more than a trivial joke.**

More than that, we're teaching boys that there's nothing wrong with commenting on a woman's body in an objectifying way.

A month ago, I was walking to a car with a group of my friends after we grabbed dinner, and a car drove by and whistled at us.

One time, my friend and I were swimming and some guys on a dock screamed at us to 'suck their d*cks'. We were 16 years old, didn't know how to respond, and laughed along at their demand.

Just this weekend, there was a man that kept trying to call my best friend and her middle school sister over to talk to him, because they had 'terrific asses' and when they declined, he took pictures of them from behind, as they ran away.

Yesterday, people in a car screamed out to my friends and I about our asses as we were walking back to our dorms.

As I go to back to edit this, I will note that this weekend (in my full coat and all!) my friend and I were honked.

As I go back to edit this again, I will note that yesterday a car drove by my male and female friend and I, and someone screamed to my male friend "YOU BETTER BE GETTING WITH THAT!"

As I go back to do a final edit, I would like to note that a few weeks ago I was walking to a friend's dorm in literally athletic shorts and wet hair with no makeup and was STILL yelled at on the side of the road.

At my first job, a man that worked in the section next to me would always call me beautiful, tell me I was very pretty, and comment on my eyes. I can understand how this may seem flattering, and I am sure that he meant this in a kind way - *but it does not feel that way. And I should not have to justify that.* As a 16 year old girl, I felt weird and kind of scared that a 40 something year old man was commenting on what I looked like - he was well over twice my age, old enough to be my father. I was scared by the attention I was getting and I felt uncomfortable, and I didn't know how to handle it.

I now work in a restaurant, and the other day I was hosting with another girl, and a man walked in and asked for a table outside. Both my friend and I responded enthusiastically and politely, saying 'Absolutely!' - He responded something along the lines of 'That's what I like to hear - I know it's going to be a great night when two girls say absolutely!'

UH, GROSS! BACK THE HECK UP! I was just doing my job, I don't need some 50 year old man to say that to me - that's disgusting!

Even today, as I was walking in the plaza where I work to pick up flowers for my job, some creepy old guy tried to start a conversation with me after checking me out.

One of my friends told me that on her first day of waitressing at a restaurant, her first table was a group of older men, and when it came time to order the first thing one of them said was, "I don't see you on the menu".

I could keep going on. These instances are so common when you're a female. And sadly, these instances are even more common if you're not straight or cisgender - statistics show that the queer, gender nonconforming, and transgender community face extremely high rates of harassment...much higher than straight, cisgender individuals.

Now, let me be clear - first and foremost, NOT ALL MEN do things like this. But, some do.

Second, you may not understand why I don't like having those bizarre extended conversations, or being winked at, or being cat called at. Let me tell you why: The reason why I don't like being called at, having bizarre conversations, etc. is because **it makes me feel uncomfortable.** When I'm trying to walk some place and there are strangers talking to me, I feel threatened and scared because I'm not totally in control of the situation and I could be unsafe. When I'm working and men consistently wink at me and try to hold weird conversations, I feel uncomfortable, because they are so much older than me. And even when they're close to my age, I still feel uncomfortable - I'm at work to get a job done, not to be checked out, stared up and down, and commented on. Furthermore, it doesn't feel like a compliment. I feel like I'm being objectified and I feel creeped out that I'm being noticed.

I am sure that some girls feel complimented by this kind of behavior - and that's great. But I have yet to firsthand meet a girl who is flattered by this kind of attention. And when I've had conversations with boys about this, most of them don't understand why girls don't take it as a compliment. And I think that makes sense - boys don't have to worry the same way that girls do about being raped by strangers, and most boys haven't grown up learning to fear what girls are capable of doing. **After all, boys are led to believe that females WANT to be commented on - they've learned that girls live for male appreciation and approval.** In reality though, it's not okay - not even in the slightest.

In this way, our culture strongly promotes an atmosphere where harassment is considered to be acceptable.

****

Violence Against Women

"It isn't really sex that's a problem, it's the persistent linkage of violence and girls' sexual objectification. Boys, though victims, are not sexualized victims in these films. And because of those portrayals of girls, straight boys are very likely sexually aroused when the violence occurs. So male sexual pleasure becomes identified with violence - a really disturbing connection" - The Lolita Effect

Another message we're learning is that violence, specifically violence against women, is okay and justifiable.

Before we begin, I want to make it clear that sexual violence affects everyone. That being stated, the purpose of this chapter is to focus on how culture encourages and promotes violence against women, while shaming them into silence.

As you learned about before, a great deal of our media turns females into objects to be looked at. Unfortunately, this is extremely dangerous to do because **turning someone into a thing is one of the first steps to justifying violence**. Jean Kilbourne writes, "**Turing a human being into a thing, an object, is almost always the first step toward justifying violence against that person. It is very difficult, perhaps impossible, to be violent to someone we think of as an equal, someone we have empathy with, but it's very easy to abuse a thing**". Reread that, because it's important. We have turned women into objects, which creates fertile soil for violence against women to grow in.

Violence against women is often present in music too. Scarily, the impact of vulgarity and music really does make an impact on how men view women. One study found that **"Male participants who heard misogynous song lyrics recalled more negative attributes of women and reported more feelings of vengeance than when they heard neutral song lyrics"**. This means that men who listen to songs that are disrespectful to women, will be more likely to hold that attitude themselves. This makes sense given that they are at the point where they are learning about how to treat other individuals. **So naturally, if they're learning how to treat people, and the music promotes derogatory behaviors, they will follow those behaviors.**

One study notes how rap music specifically is a way to keep women (especially women of color) in 'their place'...which would be at the very bottom of the social strata. The study described how music legitimizes the mistreatment and degradation of women. There is not enough research done on how music treats ALL kinds of women, but again, that says a lot more about the state of women than statistics probably could.

Video games also encourage aggression. Durham eloquently writes, "During adolescent identity formation, at a stage when sexuality and gender roles are beginning to be established, **the connection between female sexuality and violence is being set up in these game scenarios**". Therefore, *sexuality is linked to violence.*

Pornography specifically is a big perpetuator of violence against women. As stated before, there is an overwhelming amount of physical and verbal aggression directed towards females in pornography.

Imagine if animals (specifically your favorite dog or cat) were to be abused in videos and pornography. It would be horrifying - right?! A dog being slapped at - that's awful! We would never stand for such poor treatment! Now imagine that's a child being abused. It would be ABSOLUTELY APPALLING! Right!?

So why is it okay when we abuse females?

We teach boys that they need to be in control at all times, and ***pornography teaches that violence is a way to maintain control***. In 70% of occurrences, a man is the perpetrator of the aggression, and 94% of the time the act is directed towards a woman. **This reinforces the idea that men must be in control, and violence is a way to achieve so.**

Yet, what's really scary, is that one study found that **95% of the victims of aggression in the porn scenes studied either were neutral or responded with**

pleasure. As Fight the New Drugs puts it, **"**In other words, _in porn, women are getting beat up and they're smiling about it._" And more than just smiling - they're moaning in pleasure. In a majority of pornography, women have no sexual wishes of their own, and do whatever the viewer desires - no matter how dangerous and humiliating it may be, she acts as though she enjoys the sexual act, **consequently teaching anyone watching porn that women collectively ENJOY being raped and abused. Female silence is a common theme.**

There is usually very little communication depicted in sexual scenes, teaching that consent or a conversation isn't necessary. In order for a sexual act to NOT be rape, it must be consensual. **Consent is permission for something to happen** - and consent must be vocalized, sober, enthusiastic, and consent must be voluntary - the partner should NOT be pushed into saying yes. **It is important to know that silence is not consent - consent must be verbalized.**

Unfortunately, a majority of our media depicts sex or sexual scenes without any kind of conversation. **While we teach our males to act in increasingly violent ways, we teach our females to accept it silently.**

Furthermore, that we also know that when people start to watch dangerous and degrading sex acts, those acts become normalized. And, we know that people are more likely to try out behaviors if they think they're normal - even if they're not. **All of this means that people who are exposed to violent behaviors are more likely to try the violent acts out.**

Moreover, one analysis of 33 studies found that exposure to porn (including non-violent porn!!) increases aggressive behavior.

Scarily, studies show that after viewing pornography men are more likely to:
- report decreased empathy for rape victims
- report believing that a woman who dresses provocatively deserves to be raped
- report anger at women who flirt but then refuse to have sex
- report increased interest in coercing partners into unwanted sex acts

Unfortunately, we know that we trust porn and the media. Several recent studies have found that teenagers around the world report using porn to gain information about real life sex.

We are promoting a culture of violence to children and teenagers who are trying to understand the confusing world of sex. And we're buying into these messages.

****

Female Pleasure is Less Important

And the consequences don't end there. At a time when girls <u>need</u> to be assertive and <u>need</u> to speaking up for what they want, we hurt them by encouraging girls not to use their voices. Earlier, I wrote about entitlement and how we encourage the idea that females exist to please males with sexual favors. This section continues that theme, but now I will focus on how female pleasure is largely neglected by our culture.

There is something missing from a culture that constantly sexualizes females for straight males. And that something is female desire.

It seems like there's this very unequal trend **of girls giving and boys receiving**. I really haven't hooked up with lots of boys, but I've had a lot of friends who have hooked up with guys throughout high school. And in high school, it seems like whenever a girl kisses a guy, it's expected that she gives him oral as well. It doesn't seem common for the favor to be returned.

Of course, if this is what people want, **then that's great.** But, it seems that overwhelmingly, in heterosexual relationships, boys receive more than girls do.

Granted, the girls ARE usually choosing to give, though I am not sure how much of that is because they actually want to or if it's because of pressure/that's what expected.

But it seems to me like girls have learned to receive pleasure in giving males pleasure, rather than in indulging in their own desire.

One girl who took my survey wrote "When you asked me if I have ever felt powerful and my answer was yes, it made me realize that the times in my life that I've felt most powerful is when I am sexually active with a guy (whether I wanted to do things he did or not) and that is really sad. This book is going to be really important and you're an inspiration to me. I want to feel powerful for real things one day". I think lots of girls have become convinced that solely giving is sexually empowering, and though it may be for some girls, it certainly isn't something that all girls truly enjoy doing.

And sadly, with pretty much all sexual acts, there's quite a bit of irony….girls are usually shamed and have to pay a price with their reputation.

It's interesting, because girls in America have more freedom with relationships than they ever have before. Yet, most girls I know don't appear to be sexually empowered. Perhaps this is because **girls are very rarely asked to consider their own desires and what THEY want. In fact, American society spoon feeds us ideas that what girls want does not matter. Culture really teaches girls that the most important thing they can do is fulfill male desires - and that what they want is not important.**

The Lolita Effect puts it best saying, "It's difficult to see where emancipation comes in. The concept of a mutually pleasing relationship, in which both partners work to understand the needs of the other, is conspicuously absent from these media".

For example, this is even evident even within the base system ('I got to second base tonight!'), as the 'base system' is built on a boy's pleasure, rather than a girls. Additionally, the base system is overwhelmingly heteronormative.

In Yes Means Yes!, I read a really awesome story about a girl who had sex for the first time with a guy and the guy was a good person. The girl wasn't forced into anything, and they only moved forward when she gave consent. Furthermore, the pair talked about having sex and were really smart and used protection and though it wasn't super blissful, it didn't hurt too badly! And, they felt closer in the end! When I read this story, I thought 'damn, that's great - good for them'.

But then the story said that something monumental was missing from the story. I was surprised, because the scenario seemed pretty perfect to me. The book noted that the thing missing was the same thing missing from pretty much all experiences. Of course, that something is female desire. The book noted, "Nowhere do we see a strong, undeniable, sexual desire, deep, dizzy sexual pleasure, or earnest, equal sexual satisfaction on her part….We saw her say yes, but we never once saw her beg the question herself. We saw her say yes as the answer to someone else's desire, rather than as an affirmation of her own". Well, damn. When I first read that, I just sat in stunned silence.

Culture has encouraged the idea that male pleasure is so much more important than females. Studies report that sex depicted in porn movies generally focuses on men's sexual pleasure and orgasm, rather than equally that of women's.

Moreover, an APA report states that "One of the dominant themes about sexuality reported across these studies and across magazines is that presenting oneself as sexually desirable and thereby gaining the attention of men is and should be the focal goal for women". <u>The Lolita Effect</u> included an analysis of magazines, and stated simply that girls are "empowered to be informed consumers of boys".

Females are constantly being told what to do and how to look FOR STRAIGHT BOYS. Girls are almost never, ever encouraged to wear what they want to wear, or to do whatever the heck they want to do. As <u>The Lolita Effect</u> puts it, "These magazines are oddly anachronistic: they offer a pre-feminist vision of a girl's life, where girls require male admiration and attention and can gain it by learning to fulfill male pleasure in very traditional ways: by paying breathless attention to boys' needs and then offering services that provide for them". **Girls learn how to act and look desirable, yet are never encouraged to have their own desires.**

Teaching girls that they exist to please boys is so dangerous, BECAUSE SOME GIRLS BELIEVE IT. The APA report says, **"Girls and young women who more frequently consume or engage with main stream media content also offer stronger endorsement of sexual stereotypes that paint women as sexual objects".**

<u>**Moreover, teaching girls that they exist to please males results in not all females feeling confident enough to speak up when they are uncomfortable.**</u>

I have noticed that females often feel guilty saying no, and it's because we consistently teach them that boys' desires are more important than their own.

From personal experience, every time I've said no to a guy I've felt guilty inside and I worry that they are disappointed. I'm afraid of not being or doing enough for them. But why should I feel guilty or bad for making decisions that are right for me? Why should I feel guilty about doing what I want to do?

Have you ever felt bad or guilty about saying no, or doing something that you wanted to do?

_____

_____

_____

_____

How many of you have friends, who haven't broken up with someone, or who say yes to someone because they don't 'want to be mean'?? Or even have just felt guilty for saying no to something you didn't want to do? Have you or a friend ever experienced that?

_____

_____

I honestly can't even tell you how many of my friends have been worried about 'being mean' and 'hurting someone's feelings' when it comes to ending a relationship. It's terrific that girls want to be nice, but females collectively have learned that if they don't like someone, it's their fault, and they're *mean* for not giving into every wish.

However, why should a girl feel guilty for doing what she wants, rather than what her partner wants? **When girls feel guilty about saying no, it is because they have sadly learned that what their partner wants is more important than their own needs.** *Girls have literally learned that it is 'mean' to do what they want to do, instead of what someone else wants to do.*

What's sad, is that even females have bought into the notion that a woman not liking a person back is her fault. We have learned to have such little respect for what a female wants, that all that matters to us is what the man wants. We don't care that a girl doesn't want to grind, and we don't care if a girl doesn't want to go on a date - if a girl refuses to go on a date, she's in the wrong. She's a mean bitch.

Think about it. We are so confused by women wanting to do anything other than be with a guy, and really struggle with the concept of a single woman who doesn't want to get married or have kids. One girl wrote for my survey, "It seems that society considers it much more important for a female to have a boyfriend or husband than to have a passion or talent. Everyone should recognize that it is important to first be your own person and be happy with who you are, and second to find a significant other who you enjoy spending time with. Often, I receive the comment 'But you're so pretty, why are you single?' which makes no sense to me at all. There are so many reasons that a woman may choose not to be in a relationship, from needing to focus on her studies/career to just not having met the right person". **We have literally learned that females exist to please males, and are baffled when a female is doing okay on her own.**

Sadly, the simple truth is that when uncomfortable, girls with a more objectified view of their bodies have diminished sexual assertion, and are less likely

to speak up and say no. Perhaps it's because with so much sexualization present, girls are learning that sexualization is normal.

That being stated, the APA reports that "Women who feel more positively about and comfortable with their bodies are more comfortable with their own sexual feelings". **Girls who are more comfortable with their bodies are more likely to be sexually assertive - yet another reason why positive body image is so important.**

Perhaps, if girls were encouraged to value their own wants, needs, and desires, girls would understand that what they want is important. It is crucially important to teach girls how to be sexually assertive. EVERYONE needs to learn how to consider what they want.

****

Always the Female's Fault

This brings us to another message we're learning through the media and pornography: that the female is always at fault.

When Elliot Rodger murdered innocent bystanders, some twitter users blamed not Elliot, but, yes, you guessed it - women.

I saw twitter users say things along the lines of, 'all it would have taken was one of you sluts out there to take one for the team...' or even 'I understand Elliot Rodger - the friend zone can strip a man's power away'.

This is disturbing, and goes to prove that we are quite literally teaching the idea that if a woman doesn't like a man back - SHE'S in the wrong. **We so reinforce the idea that women exist for male pleasure, that when a woman doesn't like a man back, the backlash is extreme.**

Females being blamed for sexual advances are not unusual. Girls are frequently blamed for being raped. Instead of the rapist being at fault for raping, we have learned that girls *'get'* themselves raped...girls who dress provocatively are 'asking for it' and girls who go to study in a boy's dorm should have 'known better'. **When we say that females are 'asking for it', we are first teaching that communication and consent is not necessary, and we are teaching that something as ridiculous as clothing counts as a yes, which could not be more dangerous and further from the truth. We are also teaching that females should be given respect based on not who they are as people, but rather on how they look and dress.** Additionally, saying that a girl was 'asking for it', depending on what she was wearing only reinforces the idea that women only dress and exist to please men.

When we constantly show females as existing only to please males, females are going to be blamed for unwanted and unasked for sexual activity.

****

Harmful Messages

Therefore, the messages we're learning about sex are not just harmful, but outright dangerous. **Teaching that girls are objects has dangerous real life consequences.** Unfortunately, sexualization usually leads to self-objectification which comes with its own set of consequences. This section, we're going to learn about self-objectification and the consequences that go along with it.

****

What Self-Objectification Is

Self-objectification is basically when people learn to view themselves based on how others would see them, instead of measuring their self-worth by their own personal self-perceptions. It's important to note that anyone can self-objectify, regardless of gender.

If you can believe it, from middle school to sophomore year, I spent my class time assessing how I looked to everyone else. I was constantly distracting myself from class to monitor my posture. For example, freshman year, I literally thought to myself, 'What would a perfect girl look like while sitting?' And then, I would readjust my body, expression, and hair to imitate the way a perfect girl might look. I cared so much about how my body looked, that I would sit on the edge of my seat and lift up my thighs, so they were barely touching the seat, all because I was embarrassed about how they expanded when I sat down. I wouldn't allow my legs to cross, because I was ashamed of the non-toned skin on my legs. I didn't want anyone to look at me, and I was afraid of judgment about my body.

And, if we're being really honest, I still get self-conscious sometimes. Sometimes in class, I'll catch myself thinking about how I look and how I should look. It's not every day, like it was before, but every once in a while I'll feel a little bit of shame about my body and I'll try to display it in a more attractive way.

Why in the world would I feel that way? Why would I care so exceedingly much about my body that I would spend class time moving around, in order to make my body look better? Have you ever felt that way? Why do you think someone would feel that way?

_____

_____

_____

_____

Media plays a role in encouraging self-objectification. The APA reports that "These studies have generally found that after men are exposed to sexualized content, their behavior toward women is more sexualized, and they treat women like sexual objects".

****

Body Shame and Anxiety

Self-objectification is linked to dozens of deeply troubling issues. For example, when girls self-objectify, they constantly monitor their body. *And, it's a fact that near constant monitoring of appearance leads to increased shame about one's body!* And, this leads to a multitude of other problems...

Sexualization is linked to:
- Body shame
- Eating disorders
- Depression
- Restrained Eating
- Smoking
- Low self-esteem
- Risky sexual behaviors
- Diminished cognitive ability (aka sexualization makes girls less smart!!!)

****

The Consequences of Pornography

I want to make it clear - porn isn't necessarily an issue...at least, it doesn't have to be. But, the fact that pornography is typically so aggressive IS an issue. Additionally, the fact that so many kids and teenagers are looking to pornography for sex education IS a significant problem. I'm not anti-porn...I'm just anti-aggressive-porn-for-sex-education.

Believe it or not, there are even more consequences to current pornography than the ones we've discussed. The segments below will elaborate on the kinds of consequences that a porn-filled sex education leads to.

****

A Lack of Proper Sex Education

The reality is that men are more than **543% more likely to look at porn than women**. When boys learn a majority of their sex education through pornography and the media, there tends to be a lot left out. One of my friends noted some important things that we should know about boys and the sex education they're receiving.

Here's part of what he said:

- "I would guess that most boys probably receive a basic sexual education from their parents and sex education health classes, but at least in my experience both personally and through talking with other guys, these educations tend to cover the broad issues without necessarily discussing more moral issues surrounding sex or even the specific mechanics of sex. (For instance, while the term 'consent' was mentioned a lot in high school health classes, I don't know if I learned what consent truly meant until college orientation when they explained that it meant 'enthusiastic, verbal agreement from both parties')

Just as important, here are things boys rarely learn and are probably afraid to ask:

- They rarely learn anything about female sexuality (wait, females derive sexual pleasure in ways besides giving blowjobs?!)

- They don't learn about ejaculation and the differences between sperm/semen and how that relates to pregnancy
- They don't learn about the actual prevalence of different types of sex (i.e., oral vs. anal vs. vaginal)
- They don't learn that breast size varies by body type
- They don't learn what a "normal" penis size is
- For that matter, they don't learn that size is irrelevant to sexual pleasure"

Additionally, sex education largely leaves out what a healthy relationship looks like. The incredible site 'Fight the New Drug' comments, "For teens, it gets even scarier. Many teens never have the chance to learn what a healthy relationship is like before porn starts teaching them its version -which is typically filled with violence, domination, infidelity, and abuse. Since most people aren't too excited about the idea of being in an abusive relationship, teens that have gotten their sex ed from porn often find that they struggle to connect with real romantic partners and that they don't know how to be turned on by anything other than images on a screen. As biologist Gary Wilson said, "Using porn is more than just training for the wrong sport. It's replacing these guys' ability to play the sport they really want to learn".

I found Wilson's thoughts and the reality of the situation to be very eye opening, and quite frankly, terrifying. We shouldn't be taking all of this lightly. There's a lot that our current form of sex education leaves out. And that doesn't even begin to cover it. Most sex education is certainly not going over sexuality or sex education for the queer community.

****

Porn Has No Consequences

In most of our media, consequences of sex are not addressed - it's not like anyone becoming pregnant or contracting a sexually transmitted infection is shown in our media. In fact, one study found that despite over 74% of television shows including sexual content, only 14% of shows actually reference the consequences and responsibility that comes with sex.

****

Porn is Racist

Additionally, pornography as a whole is racist. Dines notes that different races and ethnicities are sexualized in different ways. With black women, the 'booty' is the focus and many porn videos are titled after the black butt - an object to be acted on and nothing more in porn. Black women are depicted as aggressive and mouthy, with an attitude. On the other hand, Asian women are depicted as essentially perfect sex objects and are portrayed as "naive, obedient, petite, cute, and innocent" who will do anything. It's racist for men too, as Asian men are portrayed as asexual.

As Dines puts it, "As a woman of color, the porn performer embodies two subordinate categories, such as Asian f***bucket, black ho, or Latina slut. All past and present racist stereotypes are dredged up and thrown in her face while she is being orally, anally, and vaginally penetrated by any number of men".

And it's not just porn - our media is too. Yes Means Yes notes "You can't watch MTV or VH1 or countless other shows and videos without seeing a black woman who is dancing in almost no clothing and for the purpose of the male gaze. They are props in the story being told - not speaking, just shaking". **People of color are more than props - they are people and deserve to be treated as such.**

****

The Contradiction

Despite all of these consequences, we still refuse to talk about sex in a meaningful way. Durham puts it clearly, "The bottom line: We live in an increasingly sex-saturated society, while lacking the ability to talk about children and sex in measure or meaningful ways."

So instead of learning about sex from truthful and reliable sources like our teachers, our parents, etc. - we're getting our sex education from pornography and the media.

Today, the harsh reality is that we *are* learning about sex - whether our parents want us to or not. And we're learning a lot more than just what sex is - we're being exposed to messages about what sex means, what it means to be sexy, and what is expected sexually. We are learning what relationships should be like, and we are learning what kind of behaviors are acceptable or not. **It sucks, but we live in an incredibly sex saturated culture, that is exacerbated a million times by our media.**

Throw horny and unaware teenagers into that mix of extremely contradictory opinions, and you have a problem.

Let me tell you something completely truthfully: We kids and teenagers are learning our opinions on sex, virginity, rape, and so much more based on what the media and pornography is telling us.

I go to high school and I see this and I see how it's affecting our attitudes and it's really making a difference and it's absolutely horrifying!!!!!

And of course, if our parents choose to talk to us or our schools do, we learn from them too - but the messages of the media is much more persistent. Furthermore, we may learn from our friends - but you have to keep in mind, our friends opinions are also being shaped by the media's.

I know that this is an uncomfortable reality, but it IS the reality. We can't keep pretending that sex doesn't exist. We need to confront it honestly and head on - because the way that we are taught how to think about sex is having serious, real life implications on kids and teenagers today. We are absorbing these messages about sex, and they're affecting us in a dangerously negative way.

****

A Message

Here is a message to parents, our school systems, and our government:

There is so much pressure to be doing so much at such a young age. You honestly can't even imagine what it's like. Kids are learning about sex and so much more either from the media and their friends - straight up, I learned an explicit sexual term on the bus to my 8th grade DC school trip during Mad Libs. Everyone has a similar story where they learned something in a context they probably shouldn't have. **Truly, the pressure is there, and lots of kids are engaging in sexual activity - that's just the reality of it.**

We kids and teenagers of all sexualities and genders need to understand sex, the consequences of sex, and we need to understand how to protect ourselves. Furthermore, we need to understand what a healthy relationship is vs. an unhealthy relationship.

Now, that being stated, **I fully respect abstinence and those who wish to remain abstinent until marriage.** Yet, we can still learn about relationships, sex, and sexuality while still presenting information about abstinence as a valid choice to make.

Quite frankly, the consequences of sex are too large to not take into account. It's time we started having open and honest conversations about sex.

****

Pregnancy, STIs, and Sex Education

The United States has one of the **highest rates of teen pregnancy and births in the western industrialized world**, *making this problem something that has to do uniquely with our culture, and our sex education tactics.* Once again, teen pregnancy rates differ based on race and ethnicity.

Believe it or not, more than half of all people will have a sexually transmitted infection, or STI, in their lifetime. That's a huge number!

Side Note: You should all call up your doctors and ask to get tested for STIs – it is super easy and super important.

I understand that the simple solution to teen pregnancy, STIs & more is just not to have sex. I get that! But the thing is, that's just not going to happen for 100% of our population and it's absolutely foolish to expect teenagers to not have sex after what we teach them in the media!! **As dire as unintended teen pregnancy and STIs are, we could lower those rates through a comprehensive sex education program.**

****

Support a Comprehensive Sex Education Program

The reason why you should support a comprehensive sex education program, other than the fact that the consequences are so severe, is because we kids/teenagers NEED to hear truth amidst the confusing and overwhelming plethora of messages we hear for seven and a half hours every day.

The things we learn about sex are hugely inconsistent, and our current sex education is not working as a result of that.

Seriously. We just need to know some facts. We need to know how to make good decisions. **We need to be told that it's okay not to do something if you don't want to. And we need to be told that WE are in control of what happens to our bodies, and that WE can speak up if we are uncomfortable.**

You just read nearly 30 pages worth of consequences due to the way we're currently talking about sex. Sex education, and talking about sex in an informative and honest and open way CAN COUNTER THAT!

And, talking about rape and what abuse is versus what a healthy relationship is will help kids be able to identify rape and abuse, so that way they or their friends can avoid being in an unhealthy situation.

Above all else, kids and teenagers need to become empowered to make good, smart sexual decisions, and that can't be done without learning about sex and the issues surrounding it.

Please, I urge you, to consider your views on learning about sex in schools. We get SO MANY MESSAGES from the media on what we should be doing or how we should act, and it is imperative we hear the truth. **It is downright dangerous and irresponsible to ignore the fact that we are learning so many negative and scary details about what relationships should look like, and sex education programs can help that.**

We start learning about the effects of cigarette smoking when we are young in our health classes. No one says that learning about the consequences of smoking will 'make us want to smoke' or 'give us ideas'. So why do we say that about sex education?

I know that some people may be against this, because they think it encourages sex. Coming from a student perspective, I respectfully disagree. Sex education isn't pressuring anyone to have sex, and sex education certainly isn't telling us students that it's okay to have premarital sex - quite frankly, *our culture and media are already doing that.*

If you don't talk about sex - your kids and students are going to be get all of their messages from porn, sexualization, the media, and their friends. **I am telling you like it is, from the perspective of a person who is actually growing up with the sex saturated media and who (as I write this section) is in high school. Whether you like it or not, your kids are learning about sex through the media and porn. And, as you just learned, that is one of the dumbest ideas in the entire world.** Because once again, Durham states, "In many ways we aren't doing a good job of differentiating healthy sexuality from damaging and exploitative sexuality".

So please, *consider* how beneficial a comprehensive sex education system will be.

****

Note on Sex Education

I also want to make a few things clear about sex education:

1. When I say that we need a good sex education system, I mean that we need to have a sex education system that is diverse and accurate. **Sex education needs to be inclusive of all genders and sexualities in order to be effective.**
2. Sex education SHOULD INCLUDE AND SUPPORT ABSTINENCE. When I say I staunchly support sex education, that doesn't mean I'm necessarily advocating for sex before marriage. It simply means that I think students should be educated on ALL OPTIONS. In this day and age, we need something much better than an abstinence only program. This doesn't mean that we can't propose abstinence as a great alternative.

****

Sex Education Works

I'm assuming most of us want fewer unintended pregnancies and less STIs being passed around, and we have a solution that works! And that solution is comprehensive sex education!

One study found that teens who receive comprehensive sex education were 50 percent less likely to experience pregnancy - as opposed to those who had received abstinence-only education. There are many studies like this - science has proven that comprehensive sex education is effective, and abstinence-only sex education is ineffective.

I'd like to conclude by saying sex education doesn't encourage teenagers to have sex. Our media, culture, and society does. Sex education simply educates us on something that we have to deal with on a daily basis.

****

We Need to Talk About Sex

In order to begin to combat all of the sad consequences I talked about earlier, **we need to *actually address* sex and sexualization.**

This means we need to openly discuss and talk about sex. We need to change around our ideals, so that crude strip teases of women on television and objectification in ads are uncomfortable, and having honest conversations about sex can be the norm.

****

We Need to Change the Way We Talk About Sex

Moreover, we need to change the way we talk about sex. Right now, we talk about sex as though it is some kind of transaction between men and women only...which is completely untrue - most individuals of most sexualities engage in sexual behaviors. In the words of Yes Means Yes!, "women 'give it up', men 'get some'". The very language that we use to describe sex contributes to common gender stereotypes for men and women. I am constantly hearing boys be praised for 'getting some', as well as 'hitting that up', or 'banging' someone. All of those terms describe GETTING something, or casually associate sex with violence. On the other hand, my friends who are female 'lose' their virginity, they 'give it up', and can 'never get it back' once they have sex. When we talk about females having sex, we talk about it in terms of them losing something. **And these phrases reflect some truth - females who do choose to have sex will often lose respect, whereas males who have sex will gain respect.**

Allow me to introduce to you all something called the double standard. **The double standard is basically a concept that explains how girls get shamed for being sexual, whereas boys are encouraged to be sexual.** Essentially, with the double standard, we view boys and girls differently for doing the same act. For example, recently, one of my friends had sex for the first time with her boyfriend. Her boyfriend got high-fives, but she got yelled at by a friend.

There are many problems with the double standard. One of them is obviously the fact that females are unfairly shamed for doing the same exact thing as males. Another problem is how the double standard always portrays boys as sexually ready and aggressive, and in reality, that is TOTALLY not true at all. The double standard

243

contributes to the idea that boys can't get raped or sexually abused, which is false. Furthermore, this makes it hard for boys to say no to something - as they fear that they'll be considered gay, or in our society less of a man, if they say no to sex or even kissing. **Boys should be able to say no to what they don't want to do.**

In order for things to get better, we need to change the way we talk about sex. We need to talk about sex as an experience that people share, rather than as a transaction. Furthermore, we need to end the double standard.

****

We Need to Change the Media

Simply put, we need accurate and inclusive narratives. We need to view females as sexually empowered, and males as respectful of boundaries. And more than that, we need to represent *all* kinds of people.

****

We Need to Redefine Sexy

Currently, our media views only a certain kind of woman as sexy. And 'sexy' is exclusive, racist, and unappreciative of differences. In other words, **we deny the ability to be 'sexy' to millions of girls.**

This is because we have created a kind of exclusive sexuality that needs to be bought. Durham wrote, "For girls, the myth implies, it's necessary to attain the ideals in order to be sexual. **There's no hint that sexuality is an inherent human trait, that both people and animals are de facto sexual, and that sexuality expresses itself in multiple and many-dimensional ways. No: sexiness must be bough**t".

In reality though, **sexuality does not need to be bought. Sexy and sexuality and sexiness are inherent in *all* of us.** When I understood this, I was stunned.

In <u>Female Chauvinist Pigs,</u> Levy puts it this way, "If we were to acknowledge that sexuality is personal and unique, it would become unwieldy. Making sexiness into something simple, quantifiable makes it easier to explain and to market. If you remove the human factor from sex and make it about stuff - big fake boobs, bleached blonde hair, long nails, poles, thongs - then you can sell it. Suddenly, sex requires shopping; you need plastic surgery, peroxide, a manicure, a mall. **What is really out of commercial control is that you still can't bottle attraction**". She continues to say,

244

"Somehow, people have been figuring out how to have sex since the beginning of time. **It is not something that needs to be taught and sold, because we have our own desires to guide us**". This realization means that *anyone* can be sexy....brown, black, white, curly hair or straight hair - ANYONE can be sexy **because sexiness and sexuality is something that everyone possesses.** We just happen to have a very slim definition of sexuality, but we're all inherently sexy and sexual beings.

I hope you walk away from reading this section realizing that **you can be sexy, without conforming to society's standard of sexy.** How do you feel sexy? When do you feel sexy?

_____

_____

_____

We need to redefine what it means to be sexy, and have a wider acceptance of what sexy means. By working off a new definition of sexy, we can challenge the status quo and start to fix these problems.

How will you PERSONALLY define sexy? What is sexy in your eyes?

_____

_____

_____

_____

_____

****

Abuse, Rape, & Sexual Assault

At this point, I would like to briefly discuss rape, abuse, and sexual assault as we **desperately need to break the silence**...As per usual, this chapter is intended to be a starting point to the conversation. And once again, if any of this is too much for you – do what you need to do. It's okay.

The dictionary definition of rape is "unlawful sexual intercourse or any other sexual penetration of the vagina, anus, or mouth of another person, with or without force, by a sex organ, other body part, or foreign object, without the consent of the victim". In other words, rape is some form of sex without consent. **It is important to note that consent must be voluntary, enthusiastic, and sober. It is also important to note that every single one of you deserves a happy and healthy and most especially consensual experience with intimacy.**

I feel that no matter what I write, my words will fail and will be deeply inadequate, as I have thankfully never had such a negative experience. However, I still want to at least try to offer some words to those who have been raped: What happened to you is not, by any means, your fault. No, you were not asking for it. You did nothing to deserve it. It's important that you know that you are not alone, and that so many of us stand behind you and support you (even if it doesn't feel that). You are incredible and deserve the whole world and I will stand behind you.

Additionally, if you feel ready, get help and speak out. Sally Armstrong, author of <u>Uprising</u>, wrote "Rape has always been a silent crime. The victim doesn't want to admit what happened to her lest she be dismissed or rejected. The rest of the world would prefer to either believe rape doesn't happen or stick to the foolish idea that silence is the best response".

Don't let rape be a silent crime. You may feel like your voice has been stolen for you, but your voice is right there ready for you, whenever you are, to reclaim it.

I want to say more, but I know that my words my will fall short of what they should...

As for abuse, my goal is simply to have you identify the different kinds, so that way you can learn to prevent abuse from happening. I have had way too many friends in abusive relationships, and perhaps it could have been avoided with more of an education.

There are typically six different kinds of abuse that we talk about. I would like you all to go onto loveisrespect.org and I want you to write down five characteristics of each abuse, and then what to do if you or a friend are in that position.

Physical Abuse

Characteristics -

1.

2.

3.

4.

5.

What to Do -

_____

_____

_____

Emotional/Verbal Abuse
Characteristics -
1.
2.
3.
4.
5.
What to Do -

_____

_____

_____

Sexual Abuse
Characteristics -
1.
2.
3.
4.
5.
What to Do -

_____

_____

_____

Financial Abuse
Characteristics -
1.
2.
3.
4.

5.

What to Do -

_____

_____

_____

Digital Abuse

Characteristics -

1.

2.

3.

4.

5.

What to Do -

_____

_____

_____

Stalking

Characteristics -

1.

2.

3.

4.

5.

What to Do -

_____

_____

_____

Here are some other symptoms of abusive relationships, paraphrased from Queen Bees and Wannabes:

NOTE: 'They' refers to the person being abused

- They apologize for their abusers behavior
- They're stressed out constantly
- They isolate themselves from friends or what they previously loved
- They're unsure how to make decisions (abusers make the victims feel foolish and dumb about their choices, so victims can check with their abuser for decisions)
- They change their appearance or behavior (because their abuser asked them to)
- They have injuries they can't explain or don't match up with their explanation
- They believe controlling, jealous behavior is what love is
- They try to be the 'perfect' girlfriend or boyfriend or friend, and are scared as to what will happen if they aren't

At this point, I want to share with you my friend's story on abuse, to help you gain a greater perspective:

"I was in a 10 month relationship with a boy that controlled, manipulated, and hurt me. I spent my entire senior year staying in, cutting away close friends because I wasn't allowed to see or talk to certain people. All this started because I was trying to help.

I thought I would never forgive him for making me feel as stupid as I did. For a long time, I looked back and thought, 'Jeez, how dumb can you be about guys? You should have seen this coming, you should have realized'. But the truth is, relationships like mine can happen to anyone. It's happened to people around me, it's probably happening to someone right now, all I can do, is try to stop it from happening again. I hope my story will help you learn from my mistakes, and stop yourself or a friend from going through this.

Let me start by giving you some insight to what I'm like. I like to be the friend that people go to for help or advice. I have always had full confidence and belief in myself. I love helping people, but sometimes, I would feel like I was left with no one to talk to for advice. I was the type of person that kept everything in, and often took it out on myself. Then, last summer, I met a boy that paid all his attention on me. With him, I was so in love with the idea that I had someone to talk to for the first time. We would talk all day with no interruption. He was so smart and I valued his insight.

When he opened up to me, I learned he was extremely depressed and suicidal. There were nights I spent begging him to live for a little longer, that things would get better. While I helped him, he helped me. I had been self-harming since 7th grade, and he helped me stop that summer. He always liked to remark that my friends had known I self-harmed for years, but yet, he was the only one that got me to stop. That's when he put the idea in my head that I needed him. He left for college that fall, but we stayed together because he told me I was the only thing that kept his life worth living.

Let's take a second. I'd known him for a month or so, and now I was the only reason he was living. This is when I was starting to realize the depth of our relationship was a bit different to him than it was to me. The problem that these type of people and relationships have, is that they don't know how to love. Their love is based on control. He controlled me.

Night conversations bounced around from accusations about me flirting and cheating on him, to how I never gave him enough time, to how hard college was and how I wasn't any help. None of that was true. I had deleted every guy's number, talked to him all day every day, and wrote all his English and Spanish papers. Our fights lasted hours, and I wasn't allowed to sleep until I'd said what he wanted me to say. Somehow, nothing I did was ever enough.

He'd always twist things to be completely wrong. When I changed my profile picture to one just of me, he thought it was because I didn't want other guys knowing we were dating. When I wouldn't give him all my passwords, he accused me of hiding messages from other guys. When I wasn't texting back fast enough, he concluded that I was flirting with someone in class. IN CLASS. Obviously I was flirting, God forbid I tried to focus and learn in SCHOOL. He tried to tell me what colleges I could and couldn't apply to. He'd tell me I needed to lose more weight, and send me pictures of models as examples of what I should look like. I did everything wrong, and he was always right.

He started affecting my core self. I'd been the most confident person I knew for forever. Now, I found myself doubting everything about myself. I switched back and forth from being anorexic and bulimic. I stayed up until 3 am every night to make sure I'd get A's in all of my AP classes. I was physically exhausted and sick constantly because I had convinced myself I wasn't good enough and needed to be better. My confidence finally broke when I didn't get into my dream school. He was there with me while I cried and cried. I thought maybe he'd give me some encouraging words. Instead, all he said was, 'Now you can go to my school, and we'll be together all the time'.

He had injected himself as such a crucial role in my life, when really, he did nothing for me. All he did was take from me. Took my time, my confidence, and for the most part, my happiness. You would think that if a relationship made you upset more than it did happy, you'd end it right away. But it wasn't that easy. I was aware that I wasn't the person I knew myself as. I didn't hang out with my friends, I entered and left school as quickly as possible each day, and I found myself exhausted from dealing with his constant accusations and issues. But I couldn't get out. Unhealthy relationships seem to lock you in, and make you feel like you can't leave. Whether it's emotional or physical, abuse is a monster that binds you to someone.

This is where it gets a little scary. When I would try to explain how I felt, he'd turn dark. I'd try to explain how I felt the relationship was uneven. Instead of legitimizing my position, he'd threaten me. He'd say that if I broke up with him, he'd kill himself and it would be my fault. At the time, I hadn't know that this was considered abuse, but it is! One in three teenage girls are involved in an abusive relationship, but only 33% will ever tell anyone because they don't realize that even without physical harm, a relationship can be abusive. Emotional abuse is when someone uses words or threats to make you do something, or feel a certain way.

His constant threats kept me feeling that I would be responsible if anything were to happen to him. I was the only person who knew the depth of his depression, so of course it would be my fault if anything happened. I would have been the cause of his suicide and have blood on my hands the rest of my life. Can you imagine having that thought weighing on you for 10 months?

When he would come home for breaks, those conversations got a bit more extreme. As powerful as his angry texts or phone calls could be, his physical strength was much greater. Instead of threatening, he would grab me. He would hold my wrists, hard. One night, we were arguing, but his parents weren't home, so it escalated and got loud. He got so angry he threw me into the corner of a table. A sharp corner. That hit gave me my fourth concussion, and I had to end my athletic career.

It's not uncommon for relationships to progress like this. **When the effect of strong words wears off, physical steps in.** Anything that helps them maintain their control and lock you in. Of course, every time he left a bruise, he apologized profusely. How I was the best thing in his life, and he would never forgive himself for what he did to me. He'd wallow so deep that I actually felt bad for him. ME! I felt bad for HIM for hurting ME!

There was one night I told him I needed a week break, that my friends were going through a lot, and I needed to be with them. He told me how selfish that was of me. How he had done everything for me, how could I just drop him in a second? He told me he wish he didn't do so much for me. He told me he wished I still cut myself.

251

That text was the moment I fell out of love with him. I mean sky dived out of love. Nothing left. It was also the moment I grew dead terrified of him.

His anger had no limits, and I couldn't imagine what degree he'd get to if I officially broke up with him. After he said that, I told him not to talk to me until he got home in a week. That weekend, I went out with my friends for the first time all senior year. When he saw me in Snapchat stories, he texted me telling me he hated me for lying to him, and that tonight was the night he would die. He told me he stole acid from the chem labs and was drinking it. He'd finish it by midnight if I didn't leave and call him. Terrified, but still trying to keep my head out of his manipulation, I did the best thing I could think of, I called his mom. I called her at 11:30 pm, and told her that her son was drinking acid to kill himself. Imagine my surprise when she told me she had just been on the phone with him 5 minutes ago, and that he said he was in bed watching Netflix. I knew his threats were mainly empty, but this was a flat out, manipulative lie.

This led to one of my scariest moments of high school — I asked for help. My friends didn't know anything that had been going on — he'd threaten me if I told my friends anything. Heart pounding, I went to guidance. I sat down in the guidance office and tried my best to act contained. I'd went in planning on asking her for advice on getting him help for his depression, but I ended up crying. I mean ugly cry. Telling her the story of my senior year. The threats, the fights, and the constant responsibility I felt for him and his life. What became of that day was better than anything I could have imagined.

We called his mom to come into guidance. I had to explain to her how depressed her son was, and how I wanted to break up with him, but needed the security that he would be surrounded with people to deal with his problems. Mainly, I needed reassurance that whatever he did, I wouldn't feel the responsibility on my shoulders. It felt really good to finally tell someone. Later that week, I opened up to my friends and told them everything.

After I had a supervised 15 min discussion with him, I told him he couldn't talk to me in anyway, that we needed a lot of time apart. The next day, I woke up to 20 missed calls from him and pages of messages telling me how horrible of a person and waste of time I was. I blocked his number, Facebook, Instagram, Snapchat, even LinkedIn! Throughout the next week, I would see him driving through my neighborhood or sitting outside my house- watching me. After some police help and intervention, he stayed clear. From then on, I only heard of him from my guy friends talking about how bad he was into drugs, or how horrible his acne was.

Each day, I wake up and remind myself that I am free of him. Honestly, I feel free; I feel light. Physically I'm healthier and happier. None of that would have been possible if I didn't take the step to get help. I could say, none of that would have happened if I didn't get myself involved in that type of relationship, but I can't focus on that. That's not the point to focus on. Instead, I focus on what I learned, how much stronger I am, and the new responsibility I feel. The responsibility to stop other people from going through this.

Relationships, romantic or friendly, should never leave you feeling a responsibility for the other. You are responsible for yourself only. These types of manipulation and control sneak up on you. The beginning is amazing. He made me so happy and confident, but by the end of my senior year, I had been isolated from all my friends and looked over my shoulder everywhere I went, scared that he would be following me.

With the interference of your feelings toward someone, it's hard to recognize an imbalance in the relationship, which is why keeping other people aware of your relationship details is crucial. This is true for the other end. A relationship doesn't mean your friend should stop hanging out or doing the things they love. If you notice a friend becoming engulfed by a relationship, check in, don't assume they're ditching you because they want to. Friends should be there to give reality checks. Don't be scared to give an intervention.

Remember that staying true to yourself shouldn't be hard to do in a relationship. You're supposed to like each other for who you are, so if you feel that someone is trying to change you, don't let them. Be the person you want to be, and eventually, someone just like you will come around too. Be with someone who raises you higher, not someone who weighs you down.

And if you can remember anything from me speaking, remember this: Ask for help. The guidance office, your parents, your friends, are all there to help you. I know the feeling of being in a crowded room and feeling so alone. Whatever it is, whatever you're dealing with, don't do it alone. People are amazing and there is such great strength in numbers. Never let yourself feel alone.

We seem so young and protected from these sorts of relationships, but they're more common at our age than you think. I'm not here to scare you and tell you to stay away from relationships. I hope to do the opposite actually. Now that you all know my story, I want all of you to find people that you constantly feel equally supported and loved by. Don't get into a cycle of hurting then apologizing. We all deserve to live our lives without chains or responsibilities that hold us back from doing what we need to for ourselves. You should always remember your worth and importance in this world, and you should never let anyone else define it for you."

Queen Bees and Wannabes lists reasons why people stay in abusive relationships. Here are some of the reasons, paraphrased:

- They want privacy - the abuser will normally urge the victim to stay silent...or else
- They thrive on intensity - an abusive relationship feels like a drug and there are highs
- They feel special - the abuser will convince the victim that they are the only person who understands
- They're ashamed - they could be scared of their parents response, they could feel foolish for 'letting it happen', or they could be too stubborn to admit it
- They're inexperienced - they might not realize that it isn't normal
- They feel helpless - they might not be sure where to turn, and they could be worried that their abuser will hurt themselves or someone or something
- They feel it's normal - maybe they've seen it in their family and don't feel that they deserve better

If you have ever been in an abusive relationship, friendship, anything - you need to know that what has happened to you is NOT your fault.

I now want you to go onto the 'Get Help' tab of loveisrespect.org and take some time to explore there. Write down 15 things you've learned while exploring various parts of the tab - from 'help a friend' to 'get help for yourself'.

1.
2.
3.
4.
5.
6.
7.

8.

9.

10.

11.

12.

13.

14.

15.

It is so important to talk to your friends about their friendships and relationships, because an open dialogue could potentially allow a friend to get the help they need. Kilbourne notes that one of the most powerful antidotes to destructive cultural messages is close female friendship, yet girls are encouraged to sacrifice their relationships and to engage in a meaningless competition. If we reject competition, and work together, perhaps violence can be prevented.

If you think that you were or may be in an unhealthy relatlonship, *get help*. Tell a parent or guidance counselor or teacher or someone. There are national hotlines also available and plenty of phone numbers you can call. **You shouldn't have to suffer through an abusive relationship. You deserve so much better.**

****

Sexual Assault

According to The United States Department of Justice, "Sexual assault is any type of sexual contact or behavior that occurs without the explicit consent of the recipient. Falling under the definition of sexual assault are sexual activities as forced sexual intercourse, forcible sodomy, child molestation, incest, fondling, and attempted rape". Horrifyingly, it's incredibly common. One of my friends was recently sexually assaulted. Here are some of the things she wishes she had known:

"YOU DID NOTHING WRONG!

I was blamed for something someone else did, as countless others have, as I'm betting many of you have to. But I wanl you to know, you did nothing. When friends and family said that to me I thought, 'Other victims didn't do anything to deserve it. But

I did'. But I'm realizing now that I didn't do anything and neither did any of you. Sadly most times the victim is blamed for whatever reason. Many girls when reporting assault are asked 'What were you wearing when this happened?' A lot of people in my school commented on my outfits saying that I was a tease and that I deserved whatever came to me...Wear whatever the heck you want because it should not affect if you get assaulted or not. Frankly it shouldn't happen at all.

SPEAK UP FOR YOURSELF

Speaking up for yourself is one of the strongest things you can do. Just the words 'This happened to me at the hands of this person' will save yourself from this happening to you again and protect other women and girls from this happening to them too. Just uttering those few words can show people that you will not put up with it and there will be consequences to their actions. If someone won't listen, find someone else. I know it will be hard but you shouldn't feel ashamed...Many people will say terrible things about you and try to intimidate you not to tell. But that's their way of silencing you so it can happen again. Please don't let them take away your voice.

YOU ARE NOT WEAK TO NEED TIME TO HEAL!

Whatever happened to you is a huge deal! There is no way you are overreacting by asking for help. Or for pushing for charges to be pressed or a restraining order to be put on them. Also, there isn't a time limit on fear. I'm not going to tell you that you'll get over this or, that this is just a minor setback. I'm gonna tell you that there are people who care. You don't have to pretend to be strong and act like it doesn't matter. I know it does. I've been there. Admitting that what happened to you matters is the strongest thing you could do.

SEE SOMETHING SAY SOMETHING!

When it happened to me, I have no doubt someone saw. But they didn't know how to react. I wouldn't know either. But if you see something like this, do something. Maybe it's urging the victim to tell someone, or maybe it's telling an authority figure yourself, whether it's a police officer or teacher. Remember, this is an illegal act.

There are also a few ways to know if someone has been sexually assaulted. They might become distant, depressed or anxious. They may also seem always on edge as if someone was about to attack them. If you see these signs in a friend, try talking to them but don't push it. They will talk when they're ready. In the meantime, be a shoulder they can cry on; someone who is there for them no matter what.

NO MEANS NO

There are no excuses for not respecting someone's voice. No means no.

If this has happened to you or does happen to you, talk to someone. People care about you and want to help. I don't want to see any of you struggle with this more than you have to".

****

Lessons the Fairytales Left Out

At this point, I really want to talk to you all about healthy relationships vs. unhealthy relationships, as well as just general lessons I've learned about liking people, relationships, and more...because let's be real, the fairytales leave out quite a bit

The goal of this chapter is to say things that I think teenagers need to know. Like, for example: Having sexual desires is part of growing up and being a teenager. It's normal. There isn't anything inherently wrong with that and we shouldn't be so ashamed or scared of our sexuality. We all need to learn to respect the fact we have sexual desires (and sexual frustrations too lol).

I also really want to get you thinking about your own moral codes and what you're okay with and not okay with. I want you to really learn about yourself and figure out what **you** specifically believe in - don't feel like you have to agree with me on anything or everything!

And another thing: You don't need to create full opinions right on the spot. You're free to change your opinion at any time. Just because you write it down doesn't mean that it's set in stone.

We are allowed to change too. Even if we've allowed ourselves to be treated poorly in the past, we can still change how we let ourselves be treated. It is never too late to change and it is always okay to grow and develop into the people we wish to be.

****

Story Time

When I was in high school, I fell hard for a guy. At the time, he was everything that I wanted to be. He was charismatic, he was involved in everything, he was charming, and just unstoppable - I was really none of these things at the time, but I wanted to be. When he started talking to me, I could not believe my luck. I wasn't used to male attention, especially not from an older guy, and this boy made me feel really special. He texted me every single day, he kept the conversation going when there was nothing to say, and really made time for me. And then, things started to get worse and worse and worse.

I'm going to tell you characteristics of unhealthy relationships. I'm telling you these because I want you to avoid making the mistake I did, and I want you to get out of unhealthy relationships....whether it is abuse or manipulation or whatever it is, I want you to know how to recognize it. So here are unhealthy characteristics and these can apply to relationships, friendships, anything...it's worth noting that I never even dated this person, nor was I ever intimate with them.

So here are some characteristics of unhealthy relationships:

One: They make you feel guilty...for everything.
This guy would always tell me that I wasn't doing enough for him, and always made me feel guilty about how I was. He told me that I didn't put in enough time for him, that I never texted him, that I never gave him enough attention - essentially that anything I did would never and could never be good enough.. And despite the fact that I WAS texting first, that I WAS giving up my time, and so much more, I believed him.

You deserve someone who loves you and appreciates you for you, rather than someone who makes you feel inadequate and on edge.

Two: They make you responsible for their emotions, AND BLAME YOU FOR THEIR BEHAVIOR.
No matter what I did, it always seemed to be my fault. ALWAYS. One time, he wouldn't even look at me. He told me that he was really upset with me. After pleading with him for forever, he finally told me that he was angry because I didn't text him back the

night before. I pulled out my phone to show him that I did text him back, but I had deleted all of my messages, so I couldn't show him proof. So I told him that he should check his phone and he refused to. When he finally agreed to check his phone I couldn't believe it - there wasn't a message from me. But I had really texted him back and so I kept trying to tell him, yet he didn't believe me and told me that I always lied to him and that I never did anything for him. He kept making me feel so guilty...after this going on for quite some time, and me practically crying because I felt so bad, he told me that I had actually texted him back, but he just deleted the message to look like I didn't. And then somehow, I don't remember what he said, but he twisted it back so that way it was somehow my fault again. I have so many instances of small things being over exaggerated, followed by me being blamed for it.

You all deserve someone who treats you with respect and doesn't turn every little thing into a big, dramatic issue - only to blame you for it.

Three: They become jealous and possessive.
This boy always wanted to be my 'favorite' and was jealous of one boy that I was close to. Sometimes, he would actually FAKE CRY to me over it.

A lot of time, we think that jealousy is cute - and in small doses, it can be - sometimes. But overall, possessiveness and jealousy is not cute - it's a sign of abuse when someone wants you all to themselves and they don't let you make other friends or become close to other guys. And honestly, that's sort of behavior is a sign of insecurity and it's a little pathetic.

Four: They make threats.
One time, he texted me angrily and informed me that he was going to ignore me, but he wouldn't tell me why. After an hour of me sitting there completely panicked, practically in tears because I had messed up with him yet AGAIN, he told me that he was upset because I never 'liked' his social media post. I tried to explain to him that I wasn't even home, and that my phone didn't get internet, so there was no way I could have seen it. He told me he knew I didn't care about him and that it was always excuses with me.

Let's bring this back into perspective. I didn't even have wifi on my phone, so there's no way I could have checked social media. Needless to say, there's no way I could have pressed 'like' on his SOCIAL MEDIA POST. He had no right to be angry with me. But at the time this was a huge, stressful event.

He went on to give me a hard time and say he was never going to speak to me again - a frequent threat he would deliver. I almost lost it at this point. As per usual, he claimed it was all my fault and I never did anything for him.

I was lucky. He was always threatening to never talk to me again. I've had friends where people have threatened to kill themselves if they're broken up with. That's terrifying and ridiculously unfair - **that's not love.**

When you love someone, or even remotely care about them, you don't threaten them. Ever. Period. Threats have no place in love.

Five: They will briefly change their way when you're about to leave.
On the few occasions I resisted him, he turned his act around and was very kind towards me. And then, I would remember how kind he was in the beginning, and I would think 'I can't stop liking him - he's still really nice sometimes'. SOMETIMES. It's a vicious cycle.

Here's the story: It was the last day of school. I was laying in my bed, almost ready to go to sleep. I hadn't spoken to him in probably over a month. All of a sudden, I get a text message from him. And in the text message, for the FIRST TIME EVER (LITERALLY EVER!!!!), was an apology. He NEVER apologized and NEVER owned up to anything - it was ALWAYS MY FAULT. And for the first time, he owned up to treating me poorly and he said he was sorry. I forgave him right away because I am a big believer in forgiveness.

So a few weeks go by and I don't see him. And then, we were both invited to hang out by a mutual friend. This was the first time I was seeing him since the apology and I was ready to move on and be friends. I go over to him and he's with two or three other people and I say hello. **He doesn't even look at me.** I try saying hello a second time, because maybe he just didn't hear me, but nothing! He refuses to even acknowledge my presence. I stand there in stunned silence for two or three minutes and he just completely ignores me, won't even look at me. And then I backed away. I've seen him on several occasions since, but that's the end of it.

You get the point. It's important to know that abuse is a CYCLE of bad and good...In the beginning, it might feel like the relationship is 90 percent good and 10 percent bad. However, after a few months it might feel 50/50. If the relationship continues, it's most likely going to get even worse. **Truly, this cycle is what DEFINES abuse or unhealthy relationships...**abuse is a CYCLE that goes back and forth and THIS is what I believe separates unhealthy relationships from healthy relationships.

And you all deserve better. You deserve someone who's great 100 percent of the time (or honestly 95 percent of the time...we all make small mistake sometimes). Regardless, you certainly deserve better than someone who is on and off and on and off and on and off.

Here are some other unhealthy characteristics:
- **They force you to do things.**
- **They put you down, instead of bringing you up.**
- **They makes you doubt yourself.**
- **They're always one-upping you. If you had a bad day at work, their day was worse.**
- **They diminish your feelings and make you feel like are overreacting.**
- **They refuse to explain themselves, and often claim 'you wouldn't understand'.**

The more I talk to friends of mine about my experience, the more friends I have that I learn have had the same experience, just in varying levels. What happened to me isn't singular - lots of girls go through this, and most girls go through it much worse. In a way, I'm lucky because it never escalated or developed into a really scary or life-threatening level...Lots of people with unhealthy relationships aren't so lucky.

The good news is that I really grew from the experience, and now I don't take anything from anyone. So I want to tell you some things that I learned, and I hope that you can learn from me.

****

Depend On Yourself for Happiness

Have you ever depended on someone else for your happiness? We can rely on anyone for happiness; it doesn't just have to be the person we're infatuated with, it can also be a friend or family member.

This boy became my happiness. I hate to say it, but he was everything to me and I allowed myself to be dependent on him.

Like I said, in the beginning this worked out great, but as he started to withdraw and blame me and as things went wrong, I became an absolute mess. When he was angry with, me, I couldn't sleep, I couldn't eat. I felt so sick all the time and I felt so guilty - even though I didn't do ANYTHING wrong!! My emotions and happiness depended directly on where he stood with me.

Looking back, I hate that I allowed him to have complete control over me and my emotions. I hate that I allowed him to take up such a big part of my story when he is so utterly undeserving. Truly, it isn't fair for anyone to be responsible for my happiness, because the responsibility should be my own. It is SO dangerous to allow someone else to be in control of your happiness - if you let someone else take control of your happiness, you're letting them take control of you.

So be in control of your own happiness. NEVER rely on someone else. It's okay to get happiness from friends and lovers - we *should* be getting a lot of happiness from them - but there's a difference between gaining happiness and depending on them for happiness.

What are some things that you can do to make yourself happy? Some of the things can include people, but it's a good idea to learn a few ways to make yourself happy when you're alone too.

Here are a few things that I can do to make myself happy:
- I can read Harry Potter for the millionth time
- I can blast Les Mis and sing along
- I can bake crepes with my sisters
- I can write letters to people in my life to make sure they know I love them

What about you?

_____

_____

_____

_____

When are you happiest? For me, I have figured out that I'm always happiest when a) I'm creating. That means when I'm working on this book or researching, because I am so passionate. I'm just so happy to spend time by myself, listening to amazing music, engaged in a project. Or, b) When I'm at events like school football games, grad parties, school events, Relay for Life, basically events that everyone goes to. I can see all of my friends from many different groups and of varying ages! And nothing makes me happier than being surrounded by everyone that I love! Or, c) When I'm working with people on big ideas and exciting plans. I love the energy that surrounds the possibility of the future.

If you can, identify when you're happiest. And if you don't know, that's okay too. You can leave it blank and think about it for a while.

_____

_____

_____

It's important to evaluate your happiness, and to be happy on your own. I have learned to depend on myself for happiness and, truthfully, I have never been happier :) It took me some time to get here, but it is amazing being in control of your own mood and having the capability to change it around! I look back, and I was so such a different person, unhappy and sad. Now, I can't stop glowing. I learned that happiness is a choice. And I choose to be happy.

****

We Are Not Broken

I also learned that I don't need anyone to complete me - **I am already complete**.

As a culture, we have this idea that we can't be complete unless we're with someone. We have this idea that there's someone out there who is our 'missing puzzle piece' and they will 'complete us'. Growing up, I felt like I needed a boyfriend in order for my life to be perfect. I didn't realize that my love life could be perfect when I was single too, and I didn't realize that I could be happy alone.

It's obviously okay to want to date and have someone special, but it's important to recognize that we don't **need** someone to complete us. YES, relationships can be terrific, but single can be too!

****

Don't Change Yourself for Anyone

"I found out that when I had a boyfriend, I felt pressured to fit in with his friends, look good and be how he wanted me to be. I was constantly worried I wasn't good enough for him…" - Anonymous survey taker

The number of times that the word pressure came up in the 1,600 responses I received while conducting my survey for this book was insane. I so feel that. When I liked this guy, I wasn't dressing for myself or even being myself - I was constantly on edge trying to play that part that **he** needed in his life. But if we're constantly trying to play the part and be who someone else wants us to be, we're stuck. Because if they do fall for us, they're not really falling for **us**, because that's not who we are. **You should never have to pretend for anyone.**

On the other hand, if we pretend to be someone else, we could miss out on someone that's perfect for us, and wants us exactly as we are!! So then we're missing out on such a great opportunity!

Also, you guys are all beyond awesome. Don't worry - you're worthy of being loved :) There are people out there that are going to fall for your sparkling personalities, if you just reveal them and put who you actually are out there. It's scary, but the rewards are so SO much greater than you can imagine. And if someone doesn't fall for who you really are, you don't need them in your life. If they prefer the pretend you over the real you, they're SOOOOOOO missing out.

****

Know Your Standards

I also hope that you will take a moment to consider your standards, or what you want out of a relationship/hookup/whatever, if you were to ever be with someone. Everyone should have their own set of high standards. I say their own, because each person's list of standards should be different.

Make your standards as high as you possibly can, because you deserve it. I hope when you compare this list to your current relationship, if you have one, that your set of standards will closely match.

So set them. Really think about them and what kind of person you want to be with, if you so choose to be with a person.

My high standards	Your high standards
I want him to be passionate about something.	
I want him to be really thoughtful and I want him to show me that he cares.	
I want to have intellectually stimulating conversations and I want someone who challenges me to think in new ways.	
I want someone who's smart. Not necessarily 4.0 GPA smart, though that would be awesome, but there are many kinds of smart.	
Someone who really, really treats me with respect. Someone who can respect me and everything that I do.	
Someone who I'm sexually attracted to	

because that's important for a relationship.	
I want to be with a guy who is open and honest with me. If he can't communicate with me and is always playing games, that's not going to work.	
Loyalty.	
Someone who is reliable and dependable.	
And after going back and editing this, I'm putting in that I need a guy who fully accepts what I love to do and who I am...he needs to embrace my passion and every part of me.	

We all deserve to have our standards lived up to, and I seriously encourage you all to figure them out, and then to not give up on them. **Don't compromise what you want just to fit in, or to look cool, or whatever. You are so much stronger than that, and you deserve more.**

****

Take Things at Your Own Pace

You should **never** be afraid to take things at your own pace. Just because all of your friends have had their first kiss, had sex, or done more than you sexually doesn't mean that you need to. Do things on your own terms and when you want, with who you want.

****

What Do You Want?

I had an epiphany a month or two ago: I realized that I am so wholeheartedly happy and proud of myself, because I have been thinking about the decisions I've been making thoroughly, and I've been making the best possible decisions for myself! My decisions aren't always what everyone else would consider to be the 'right' choice, but I'm making the right choice for me. And I am so proud of myself!

For example, I gave up doing theater senior year of high school. I wanted to focus more on workshops and speeches and take what I do to the next level, and I needed more time to do it. It was a hard choice, because I've been involved in theater since I was in 7th grade, but it was the right one for me. This is a small example, but I've carried this kind of attitude into my romantic/sexual life, and I make smart decisions that are best for me.

In this section of the book, I want you to think about what is currently right for you. So, what do you want? Do you want to kiss others for fun? Do you want a significant other? Do you want to just focus on yourself? What is it that you want romantically or intimately right now?

_____

_____

_____

_____

If you can't think of what you want right now, that's okay. It's okay not to know as well :)

****

Do Things for You

Now that you know what you want, make sure that you're doing (or not doing) things for YOU.

One girl in my survey wrote, "The majority of things that I do is to impress guys and I hate it about myself". She's not alone. So often, I see people doing things not because they want to, but because they want to be liked by others. Or maybe because they're encouraged, or even forced to.

Whatever you do, you should do for yourself (or for God). Whether it's our clothing choices or who we hang out with or what we're doing or not doing, we should be doing it for ourselves.

Something that I've thought a lot about is what 'sexual power' is. Here's what I have concluded: **True sexual power, sexual empowerment, and sexual liberation**

comes from making decisions that work for you. NOT FROM CONFORMING TO WHAT OTHER PEOPLE SUPPOSEDLY WANT. It's about consent. It's about making sure that you are totally and wholeheartedly ready for sex, or any kind of intimate moment - whether it's holding hands, a kiss, or anything else. It's all about understanding yourself as a sexual being, and learning about what you specifically like. It's about all parties involved feeling comfortable and safe, and absolutely no violence. It's about finding what makes you happy, and learning how to respect yourself and your decisions. Self-respect simply means making decisions that you really like. THAT'S WHAT SEXUAL POWER IS. SEXUAL POWER IS DOING WHAT MAKES YOU FEEL HAPPY AND SAFE AND COMFORTABLE. FOR YOU.

This also means that we need to say no to things we don't like - **because you all have the right to say no to what you don't want. Let me be clear and say that it is NOT your responsibility to do anything you don't want to do. You NEVER have to send a person your nudes or give oral sex, even if you're in a relationship with them. If you are uncomfortable or being pressured or you feel uncomfortable - you don't have to go through with it. You can stop. You don't have to do ANYTHING if you don't want to. You NEVER owe anyone anything.** If someone tells you 'come on, you owe me' and you don't want to, don't do it. I have been in positions where I have said, 'no I don't feel comfortable with that', or 'no, I don't want to' and you can say that too. And if they tell you please or say that you're teasing them, just say no again. I know that it can be totally scary and weird especially when you want the person to like you. I promise you, guys I know, I'm a teenager too!! But, I've done it and so can you. It's okay to say no. Instead of worrying about hurting your partner's feelings, <u>care about your own and don't do things that you don't want to do.</u> Recognize your own emotions as valid and say no.

Of course, you also have the right to say yes to what you do want. If you want to kiss someone, that's totally awesome! What matters is that you're choosing actively to be intimate with someone - you are part of the decision. Say yes to what makes you happy and comfortable.

****

This Will Take Time

Finally, we need to realize that becoming an informative, honest culture that talks about sex isn't going to happen overnight. **But I do very, very firmly believe that all of this is possible, if we first acknowledge that what we have isn't working. And once we do that, we can speak up and use our voices. If we persevere, and stand up to sexualization when we see it, we will see positive change.**

EMPOWERMENT

****

Opening Quote

"Your voice matters. And it can create change. But that's only if you share it with others. Change starts with one person being brave enough, believing that change is possible" - Kat Lazo

****

Opening Questions

At this point in the book, we've covered how:

1. Gendered expectations are restricting everyone, and we are dealing with a huge array of problems - including insecurity, eating disorders, gossiping, and more - as a result of the terrific pressure. In order for the world to live up to its full potential, *we need to grow up learning that we are more than what our gendered expectations dictate.*
2. The shame and stigmas surrounding mental illness are having serious consequences on today's society, and we are refusing to get the help we need. In order for the world to live up to its full potential, *we need to treat mental illness with compassion and seriousness.*
3. Our contradictory attitude about sex - where we refuse to acknowledge sex in a meaningful way, leaving kids to learn about sex from porn and our ever present sex saturated culture - isn't working. In order for the world to live up to it's full potential, *we need to address sex in an honest, direct, mature and respectful way.*

What are the big lessons you've learned while reading this book?

_____

_____

_____

_____

_____

_____

What did you learn or what section surprised you the most and why?

_____

_____

_____

_____

_____

_____

How did you feel while reading this book? Why? Were you expecting to feel this way?

_____

_____

_____

_____

If you could go back and tell a younger version of yourself something, what would it be?

_____

_____

_____

_____

_____

_____

What changes in your life are you going to make after reading this book?

_____

_____

_____

_____

_____

_____

What is going to be the most difficult change to make and why?

_____

_____

_____

_____

_____

_____

How can you use what you've learned to make yourself a better leader or person?

_____

_____

_____

_____

_____

_____

Did any of the information you learned or any part of the book make you feel angry? Why?

_____

_____

_____

_____

_____

_____

****

I Need Your Help

As I go back to edit this, it is 12:48 am on February 1st, 2014. I am currently crying, and I have just finished writing my prayers in my journal. I need to tell you a story.

Last October, I was blessed enough to give a speech at an education and technology conference. I was the first speaker/event of the entire day, and over 1,000 educators were present for my talk on the power of social media.

Wherever I walked that day, people would recognize me and stop to talk. So many educators stopped to ask if I could come speak at their school. The entire day was surreal and I won't ever forget how proud and happy I felt. But there was one thing that especially stood out to me.

A lot of educators asked me if I would speak to their 6th grade. Each time, I declined saying, 'I work with 7th graders and up...I don't really work with 6th graders because some of the content is a bit mature etc.' - One time, while going through the spiel, a Principal cut me off, and looked me dead in the eye. 'Ashley', he said. '*All of my 6th graders are self-harming*'.

I felt like my entire heart sink to the ground, and I stood there numbly trying to comprehend. It hit me so clearly. When I imagine 6th graders dealing with the emotional anguish of self-harm, I feel like my heart is going to crack open. They're so young and so little and innocent to be dealing with so much pain. No one deserves to struggle with self-harm. After a pause, he continued, 'It starts young'.

As he told me this, my mind was racing, my heart was pounding, and I will never forget the words I thought to myself. As I stared blankly at the Principal, a voice inside me whimpered, '*I can't do this alone*'.

I can't do this alone.

I. Need. Help.

I need **YOUR** help.

Sometimes I get so sad, and I'm so overwhelmed because there's just SO many things that need to be done. The world needs help. There are people who are being abused, our criminal justice system is broken, the school system is failing those who come from low income families and people of color, there are people starving to death, and we teach hate instead of love - the list goes on and on.

I want to fix all of these problems, and I want to change the world. I want to speak at every high school and middle school in America, **but that isn't enough!** There are colleges and elementary schools that need to be spoken to! And parents and grandparents! I dream of becoming a Principal and working with kids, or going into education policy. I dream of opening up schools and mentoring women to help them succeed. I dream of creating my own self confidence/awareness summer camp and I dream of a world in which everyone is free to live up to their full potentials. And I'm not just going to dream it. I'm going to do it. Because I'm Ashley Olafsen and I turn my dreams into realities.

But I can't do this on my own. Though I may want to leave a positive impact on every single struggling 7th grade, realistically, I can't get to all of them. That doesn't mean I won't try - hell, I'm going to try - but this job is too big for me to do alone.

I. Need. Your. Help.

I am capable of changing the world for better, and I am capable of influencing culture. But I can't create an entire culture shift by myself. In order for a culture shift to happen, I need more people.

I. Need. You.

****

And I Really Do Need YOU

I really, really believe that God blesses every single one of us with special gifts, talents, and skills. Even if you don't believe in God, it's undeniable that every single one of us brings a LOT to the table. And I believe that if we are authentically ourselves and play to our strengths, incredible things will happen.

Take a moment to think about your skills and talents, and what you bring to the table. What skills/talents/strengths do you have? What would your friends say about you?

_____

_____

_____

_____

_____

_____

Something that I recently learned is not to deny the person that you are, because the world needs exactly YOU and your talents, in your fullest form.

For example, if I denied my ambition and if I cared more about what people thought of me, I wouldn't be co-running a summer program - I would be too busy conforming to female stereotypes. If I denied my ambition, I would not have written this book - I would have been too busy dieting to fit in instead. If I denied my ambition, I would not have inspired countless girls to speak up and reach their full potentials - I would have been too caught up in reading articles on the tips and tricks to getting male approval.

You can't deny what your talent or gift is, and you can't deny what makes you unique because THAT is what makes you special and THOSE are your greatest strengths.

And I really do need you. I shared my story, and quite honestly the world needs much more than just my story. As I said before, there are so many gaps that need to be filled in. And so, the world needs your story. What you have to say and how you feel is valuable and deserves to be shared.

So today I want to ask you all to do something difficult: I want you to make a commitment to be yourself in your fullest version...whoever that person may be. Take a moment to consider who you would be if you were in your fullest, or rather best, form....

Who would you be? How would you be acting differently from where you are now?

_____

_____

_____

_____

****

Agreeing Isn't Enough

It's great that you read this book (seriously, it really is - you made it through a book and in this day and age, that's an impressive feat) but if you remain quiet, nothing is going to change. **You may agree with every single thing I said in this book, but if you don't speak up or take some kind of action, nothing will change.** I mean that. Right now, agreeing isn't enough. **You need to speak up. Silence does not create change - silence fuels current circumstances.**

We enter this world with two things. The first is time. And the second is a voice. It's up to us to utilize both.

How will you use your time?

_____

_____

_____

_____

_____

How will you use your voice?

_____

_____

_____

_____

_____

****

The Power of Social Media

My friends - we cannot afford to let this kind of degrading, limiting culture continue...too many lives are being lost, and too much potential is being destroyed. We cannot be silent any longer - we must do something. So...how can you all play a role in transforming the world for the better?

Well, making the world a better place in the 21st century is made easy (or easier) because we have access to this awesome thing called social media! Ever heard of it?

Trick question. OF COURSE YOU HAVE!!!!!! BECAUSE PRACTICALLY EVERYONE HAS ACCESS TO IT!! That's what makes it so powerful and amazing!!

I would like you all to consider for a moment the sheer enormity and influence of social media. The word 'selfie' is now part of the Oxford English Dictionary. The President of the United States has a Twitter account. Videos go viral every day. Yet these three small realities don't even begin to cover the impact. Millions and MILLIONS of people are able to connect because of social media.

The fact that there is a platform that can connect a majority of the world is, in the simplest of terms, powerful. You can use this platform to speak up and make a difference.

In the epilogue of the groundbreaking feminist book <u>Backlash</u>, Faludi states, "The important question to ask about the current backlash then, is not *whether* women are resisting, but how effectively. " This book was published in 1991. Today, we can answer the question differently than 1991 because of social media. We can answer 'very effectively', because we have the power to organize through a common meeting point - social media.

Social media allows for accessibility that has never been possible before, and makes spreading ideas easier than ever. And because we have the power to spread our ideas, we have the power to change minds, and the power to transform the way the world works! **We have that power!**

In the past, this power has been abused, and we kids and teenagers are testament to that statement. In fact, the media's influence is so incredibly dramatic, that a few years ago, there was an island off of Australia, called Viti Levu where 'You've gained weight' was a compliment. In 1995, they began introducing this island to television. **Within three years, the standard of beauty dramatically flipped - the media's influence is *that* pervasive.** Before, induced vomiting was nearly non-existent at 3%. But within **three years, 15% of girls were forcing themselves to vomit.** Before television, girls had tried to put on weight, but with three years times, **69 percent of females had dieted. Technology has the power to spread ideas, and those ideas are powerful enough to be detrimental.**

However, **if technology can spread ideas that create so many huge problems, it can spread ideas that create a solution.** We have, at our disposal, the greatest tool to exist. Or the greatest weapon, used to destroy self-esteem and bully others. It's up to us to choose how we're going to use such a powerful tool.

How will you use social media to make a powerful and positive difference in the world?

_____

_____

_____

_____

_____

****

Imagine If We Used Social Media Positively

Sixty-four percent of online teens ages 12-17 have participated in one or more among a wide range of content-creating activities on the internet. That's a lot of people! Now imagine if the ideas people were spreading were body positive, gender equal, and without stereotypes. Imagine that the ideas promoted self-acceptance, discouraged petty competition, and were empowering.

Just imagine! If even 5% of those pieces of content shared promoted these positive ideals! This dream of mine, where people use social media to spread ideas like the ones I mentioned above is not merely idealistic. I know it's possible, because I see it every day.

At this point, I would like to invite you to join the MOVEment. MOVE is a company that I designed with my best friend, Lexie Phipps. MOVE stands for Motivate. Overcome. Value. Empower. **You are all invited to join the never stopping MOVEment.** Tweet out why you're joining and let the world know that you're a MOVE member!

****

How I've Joined the MOVEment

Let me tell you about the two main ways that I have used social media to join the MOVEment.

The first way I have joined the MOVEment is through educating myself. I have used the internet to read or watch articles, TED talks, YouTube videos, websites, and more. You can use social media to learn - that's what I did! And I did all of this while in high school, so there's literally no reason why you can't do it too.

The second way I've joined the MOVEment is by creating and as a natural result, sharing my work. I have created and shared speeches, YouTube videos, tweets, articles, and much more all over my social media.

And to further create and spread ideas, I've also made my own weekly email newsletter. Anyone can sign up, from anywhere around the world. If you haven't already, check out my website ashleyolafsen.com and make sure to sign up!

Finally, I have an Instagram, a twitter, and a YouTube channel. Make sure to follow me. Accounts are all by the name of @ashleyolafsen.

You can share your work through social media. And even if you don't use social media to create, you can still use social media to share videos, articles, artwork, written pieces, and more that other people have created.

The coolest thing about the power of social media is that single voices can be amplified and heard all around the world.

But it so important to realize that the only way a single voice can rise up is if that voice is backed up by other, strong voices. **We all contribute to ideas by sharing them, liking them, favoriting them - in turn promoting them. YOU have the power to determine if something goes viral or not. YOU have that power. YOU have a social responsibility to like and share what you see on social media. I mean that! It really is a social responsibility!** Share that FaceBook link! Retweet that tweet! Honestly, just do it!

****

Hashtags

Once again, I'd like to remind you to use the hashtags #SurvivalofthePrettiest and #jointheMOVEment. Make sure to post your favorite quotes, lessons learned, and more :) I'll be frequently checking these tags and there's a good chance I'll see it and favorite/like/share/include what you post in my newsletter!

****

How Will You Use Your Voice?

And now, you need to think about how you SPECIFICALLY are going to use your voice. And then how you're going to use social media as your tool to promote and share those ideas. I sincerely hope that you will inform me of your progress through the hashtag, and I look forward to publishing your work in my newsletter.

I want to invite you to brainstorm with me for a few minutes...I want to ask you to envision a perfect world - a world that prioritizes the ideals I outlined in this book. What is this world like? For example, I envision a world where 'those who are dealing with mental illness reach out for help easily' and a world where 'girls can sit in class and pay attention to the lesson - rather than the ways their thighs look on the chair' and a world where 'boys can be a virgin without being shamed or mocked'.

So, set a timer for 5 minutes and **describe to me in detail this incredible world.**

_____

_____

_____

_____

_____

_____

_____

_____

_____

_____

_____

_____

_____

_____

_____

_____

_____

_____

_____

_____

_____

_____

_____

_____

_____

_____

_____

_____

_____

_____

_____

Time's up! Shake out your hand and get ready! Because now, we need to figure out how to get to that perfect world. Set the timer for another five minutes. I want you to take this time to think about the things you enjoy doing and the skills you have, or rather your personal strengths. To get you started, I'll provide examples by writing down three of my answers, and you can check the box if it applies to you. Then, you can start making your own list. Ready? :)

Things You Enjoy Doing:
( ) Public speaking/theater
( ) Putting together outfits and makeup
( ) Writing

_____

_____

_____

_____

_____

_____

_____

_____

_____

_____

Skills You Have/Personal Strengths:
( ) I am good at organizing/planning and creating events
( ) I am very honest
( ) I dream big, without many boundaries

_____

_____

_____

_____

_____

_____

_____

_____
_____
_____

Time's up again! :) Now, ask a friend or family member or someone you're close with to write down some of your strengths/reasons why you're awesome. There are lots of things that make you capable and awesome, and it will be helpful to have another perspective, or another person identify your strengths!

_____
_____
_____
_____
_____
_____
_____
_____
_____
_____

What sections of the book affected you the most? What issues are you most passionate about?

_____
_____
_____
_____
_____
_____
_____
_____

And now, I have another question for you. Set that timer for 7 minutes this time. You ready? This is a loaded question: **How can you take those skills and strengths, and use them to make the world a better place? How can YOU use the traits and abilities you**

have to make a positive difference? How can we reach that perfect world? What can YOU do to turn that world into a reality?

      In my survey, I asked you if you had passion. Eighty percent of you responded that yes, you do have passion. You can use your passion to speak up. I am passionate about creating. Figure out what makes your heart sing, and use that to create real change.

Set the timer for 10 minutes this time. Start brainstorming ideas on how to connect your passions and strengths to make a positive difference!

Go!! :)

_____
_____
_____
_____
_____
_____
_____
_____

If you didn't come up with much - that's okay. Sometimes, ideas take time...Lots of mine have taken months to develop - Just keep thinking. And maybe think about what makes you angry, and how you can fix that. Or think about what issue you wish had been different when you were younger. **Now, it's up to you to take action on your ideas.**

****

Conclusion

Courtney E. Martin described an experience she had in her book <u>Perfect Girls, Starving Daughters</u>, "I look up from my ink and angst right as Carol Gilligan looks up from her notes on the lectern. Starting straight into the faces of her audience with determined steely eyes, she says, 'The seemingly impossible task is to tell a new story'. These words still echo inside me today". Courtney's story "began with anger. As I started taking account of all the friends whose passion and intellect were being wasted on their weight, as I forced myself to be honest about my own wasted time and energy, I got pissed. I felt duped". With that anger, Courtney wrote a book, writes articles frequently, speaks often, and blogs. **I tell my story by writing this book and speaking out frequently.**

In 1963, Betty Friedan questioned, "Who knows what women can be when they are finally free to become themselves? Who knows what women's intelligence will contribute when it can be nourished without denying love?"

In 1990, Naomi Wolf questioned, "How might women act beyond the myth? Who can say?"

It is 2016, and I, Ashley Olafsen at 19 years old, question, "Who knows who we can become when we are free from limiting gendered expectations, mental health stigmas, and confusing messages about sex and relationships? Who knows what kind of powerful impact we can have on the world, when we can reach our full potentials?"

My friends, I expect an answer. And in turn, I will leave you with a piece of advice and one more question.

My advice: Don't waste your time conforming to expectations that don't suit you. **Instead, use your energy to fight for positive social change. Don't waste your time and energy being upset, angry, or sad.** This is a heavy book, and there's a lot to be upset over. But getting *only* upset is 100% wasted and misdirected energy. You need to use that emotion for good. Nancy Pelosi once wrote about how there's a saying among her political friends which is, 'Organize, don't agonize'. This is one of my life mottos - don't get upset or worked up - DO SOMETHING PRODUCTIVE ABOUT IT!! **Take your frustration and use it to change the world!! Organize, don't agonize!!**
And my two questions: First, what is the new story you are going to tell? And second, how are you going to use your voice?

References

Abbey-Lambertz, K. (2014, October 07). Woman Shot, Killed After Saying No To A Man's Advances, Detroit Police Say. Retrieved

   June 11, 2016, from http://www.huffingtonpost.com/2014/10/07/mary-spears-killed-detroit_n_5945518.html

About Teen Pregnancy. (2016, April 26). Retrieved June 16, 2016, from http://www.cdc.gov/teenpregnancy/about/

Adams, T., & Fuller, D. (2006). The Words Have Changed But the Ideology Remains the Same: Misogynistic Lyrics in Rap Music.

   Journal of Black Studies, 36(6), 938-957. Retrieved from http://www.jstor.org/stable/40034353

Adichie, C. N. (n.d.). *The danger of a single story.* Speech presented at TEDGlobal 2009. Retrieved June 05, 2016, from

   https://www.ted.com/talks/chimamanda_adichie_the_danger_of_a_single_story?language=en

Adichie, C. N. (n.d.). *We Should All Be Feminists.* Speech presented at TEDxEuston. Retrieved May 31, 2016, from

   https://www.youtube.com/watch?v=hg3umXU_qWc

Alcohol industry: U.S. ad spend by medium 2013 | Statistic. (n.d.). Retrieved July 13, 2016, from

   http://www.statista.com/statistics/245318/advertising-spending-of-the-alcohol-industry-in-the-us-by-medium/

Allen, M., Emmers, T., Gebhardt, L., and Giery, M. A. (1995). Exposure to Pornography and Acceptance of the Rape Myth. Journal

   of Communication 45, 1: 5–26.

American Psychological Association, Task Force on the Sexualization of Girls. (2007). Report of the APA Task Force on the

   Sexualization of Girls. Retrieved from http://www.apa.org/pi/women/programs/girls/report-full.pdf

American Society of Addiction Medicine. (n.d.). Retrieved July 13, 2016, from http://www.asam.org/quality-practice/definition-of-

   addiction

Ana Bridges, Robert Wosnitzer, Chyng Sun, and Rachael Liberman, "Aggression and sexual behavior in best-selling pornography

   videos: A content analysis update," Violence Against Women 16 (Oct. 2010): 1065-1085.

Anorexia Nervosa | National Eating Disorders Association. (n.d.). Retrieved June 21, 2016, from

   http://www.nationaleatingdisorders.org/anorexia-nervosa

Any Disorder Among Children. (n.d.) Retrieved June 21, 2016, from http://www.nimh.nih.gov/health/statistics/prevalence/any-disorder-

   among-children.shtml

A quote by Albert Einstein. (n.d.). Retrieved July 21, 2016, from https://www.goodreads.com/quotes/1799-the-world-as-we-

   have-created-it-is-a-process

A quote by Leo Tolstoy. (n.d.). Retrieved July 21, 2016, from https://www.goodreads.com/quotes/12841-everyone-thinks-of-

   changing-the-world-but-no-one-thinks

A quote by Margaret Mead. (n.d.). Retrieved July 22, 2016, from https://www.goodreads.com/quotes/1071-never-doubt-that-a-small-

   group-of-thoughtful-committed-citizens

Barlett, C. P., Vowels, C. L., & Saucier, D. A. (2008). META–ANALYSES OF THE EFFECTS OF MEDIA IMAGES ON MEN'S

   BODY–IMAGE CONCERNS. *Journal of Social and Clinical Psychology, 27*(3), 279-310. doi:10.1521/jscp.2007.26.issue-6

Beasley, B., & Standley, T. C. (2002). Shirts vs. Skins: Clothing as an Indicator of Gender Role Stereotyping in Video Games. *Mass Communication and Society,5*(3), 279-293. doi:10.1207/s15327825mcs0503_3

Beauvoir, S. ., Borde, C., & Malovany-Chevallier, S. (2010). *The second sex*. New York: Alfred A. Knopf.

Bennett, S. (2010, September 16). This just in: The measure of a female candidate isn't in her measurements. Retrieved June 03, 2016, from http://www.nameitchangeit.org/blog/entry/measure-of-a-female-candidate

Berger, J. (n.d.). A quote from Ways of Seeing. Retrieved June 14, 2016, from https://www.goodreads.com/quotes/380575-a-woman-must-continually-watch-herself-she-is-almost-continually

Binge Eating Disorder | National Eating Disorders Association. (n.d.). Retrieved June 21, 2016, from http://www.nationaleatingdisorders.org/binge-eating-disorder

Black, M. C., Basile, K. C., Breiding, M. J., Smith, S .G., Walters, M. L., Merrick, M. T., ... Stevens, M. R. (2011). The National Intimate Partner and Sexual Violence Survey: 2010 summary report. Retrieved from the Centers for Disease Control and Prevention, National Center for Injury Prevention and Control: http://www.cdc.gov/ViolencePrevention/pdf/NISVS_Report2010-a.pdf

Bleidorn, W., Arslan, R. C., Denissen, J. J. A., Rentfrow, P. J., Gebauer, J. E., Potter, J., & Gosling, S. D. (2015, December 21). Age and Gender Differences in Self-Esteem—A Cross-Cultural Window. Journal of Personality and Social Psychology. Advance online publication. http:// dx.doi.org/10.1037/pspp0000078

Bulimia Nervosa | National Eating Disorders Association. (n.d.). Retrieved June 21, 2016, from http://www.nationaleatingdisorders.org/bulimia-nervosa

C., U., & N. (2002, May). Adolescent Brain Development - ACT for Youth. Retrieved January 9, 2016, from http://www.actforyouth.net/resources/rf/rf_brain_0502.pdf

Carlat, D.J. Camargo. Review of Bulimia in Males. American Journal of Psychiatry, 154, 1997

Center of Excellence for Eating Disorders. (n.d.). Retrieved June 21, 2016, from https://www.med.unc.edu/psych/eatingdisorders/Learn More/about-eating-disorders/statistics

Centers for Disease Control and Prevention, "Physical Dating Violence Among High School Students—United States, 2003," Morbidity and Mortality Weekly Report, May 19, 2006, Vol. 55, No. 19.

Cherry, K. (2016, April 26). Maslow's Hierarchy of Needs: What Motivates Behavior? Retrieved May 28, 2016, from https://www.verywell.com/hierarchy-of-needs-2795947

Children, Teens, Media, and Body Image | Common Sense Media. (n.d.). Retrieved June 03, 2016, from https://www.commonsensemedia.org/research/children-teens-media-and-body-image

Chiara Sabina, Janis Wolak, and David Finkelhor, "The nature and dynamics of Internet pornography exposure for youth," *CyberPsychology and Behavior* 11 (2008): 691-693.

Cindy Crawford quote. (n.d.). Retrieved June 04, 2016, from http://www.brainyquote.com/quotes/quotes/c/cindycrawf140664.html

Cliff Pinckard, Northeast Ohio Media Group. (2014, April 04). New York Mets' Dan Murphy criticized for missing games for child's

   birth; team backs decision (poll) (video). Retrieved June 06, 2016, from

   http://www.cleveland.com/tribe/index.ssf/2014/04/new_york_mets_dan_murphy_criti.html

Collins M.E. (1991) Body figure and preferences among pre-adolescent children. International Journal of Eating Disorders, 199-208.

commissioned by the American Association of University Women ; researched by Harris/Scholastic Research. (1993). Hostile

   hallways : the AAUW survey on sexual harassment in America's schools. Washington, D.C. :AAUW Educational

   Foundation,

Communication: A Series of National Surveys of Teens about Sex. Menlo Park, CA: Henry J. Kaiser Family Foundation, 2002.

Comprehensive Sex Education: Research and Results. (2009, September). Retrieved June 16, 2016, from

   http://www.advocatesforyouth.org/publications/1487#ref

Coyle, D. (2009). *The talent code: Greatness isn't born: It's grown, here's how.* New York: Bantam Books.

Custodial Mothers and Fathers and Their Child Support: 2009. (n.d.). Retrieved June 6, 2016, from

   http://www.census.gov/prod/2011pubs/p60-240.pdf

Department of Justice, Office of Justice Programs, Bureau of Justice Statistics, American Indians and Crime, 1992-2002 (2004).

Department of Justice, Bureau of Justice and Statistics, Intimate Partner Violence in the United States, 1993-2004. Dec. 2006.

Department of Justice, Office of Justice Programs, Bureau of Justice Statistics, Sexual Victimization in Prisons and Jails Reported by

   Inmates, 2011-2012 (2013).

Depression. (n.d.). Retrieved June 21, 2016, from https://www.nimh.nih.gov/health/topics/depression/index.shtml

Depression. (2016, April). Retrieved June 21, 2016, from http://www.who.int/mediacentre/factsheets/fs369/en/

Dickey, J. (2014, November 13). Taylor Swift on 1989, Spotify, Her Next Tour and Female Role Models. Retrieved June 04, 2016, from

   http://time.com/3578249/taylor-swift-interview/

Dines, G. (2010). *Pornland: How porn has hijacked our sexuality.* Boston: Beacon Press.

Dittmar, H., Halliwell, E., & Ive, S. (2006). "Does Barbie make girls want to be thin? The effect of experimental exposure to images of

   dolls on the body image of 5- to 8-year-old girls": Correction to Dittmar, Halliwell, and Ive (2006).*Developmental

   Psychology, 42*(6), 1258-1258. doi:10.1037/0012-1649.42.6.1258

Does Our Looks-Obsessed Culture Want to Stare at an Aging Woman? - The Rush Limbaugh Show. (2007, December 17). Retrieved

   June 03, 2016, from

   http://www.rushlimbaugh.com/daily/2007/12/17/does_our_looks_obsessed_culture_want_to_stare_at_an_aging_woman6

Douglas, S. J. (1994). *Where the girls are: Growing up female with the mass media.* New York: Times Books.

Durham, M. G. (2008). *The Lolita effect: The media sexualization of young girls and what we can do about it.* Woodstock, NY:

   Overlook Press.

Dweck, C. S. (2006). *Mindset: The new psychology of success.* New York: Random House.

Eating Disorders: About More Than Food. (n.d.). Retrieved June 21, 2016, from

> https://www.nimh.nih.gov/health/publications/eating-disorders-new-trifold/index.shtml

Edut, O. (2003). *Body outlaws: Rewriting the rules of beauty and body image*. Emeryville, CA: Seal Press.

Eisenberg ME et al., Parents' beliefs about condoms and oral contraceptives: Are they medically accurate? *Perspectives on Sexual*

> *and Reproductive Health*, 2004, 36(2):50–57.

Eliot, L. (2009). *Pink brain, blue brain: How small differences grow into troublesome gaps--and what we can do about it*. Boston:

> Houghton Mifflin Harcourt.

Elizabeth M. Morgan, "Association between young adults' use of sexually explicit materials and their sexual preferences, behaviors,

> and satisfaction," Journal of Sex Research 48 (2011): 520–530.

Facts and Figures. (2013). Retrieved June 12, 2016, from http://stoppornculture.org/about/about-the-issue/facts-and-figures-2/

Faludi, S. (1991). *Backlash: The undeclared war against American women*. New York: Crown.

Field, A. E. (2013, November 4). Prospective Associations of Male Physique Concerns. Retrieved June 06, 2016, from

> http://archpedi.jamanetwork.com/article.aspx?articleid=1766495

Fine, C. (2014, April 05). Science Doesn't Support a Gender Divide for Toys. Retrieved June 06, 2016, from

> http://www.slate.com/articles/health_and_science/new_scientist/2014/04/girl_and_boy_toys_childhood_preferences_
> for_gendered_toys_are_not_innate.html

Finer LB and Philbin JM, Sexual initiation, contraceptive use, and pregnancy among young adolescents, *Pediatrics*, 2013,

> 131(5):886–891.

Finkelhor, D., Hotaling, G., Lewis, I. A., & Smith, C. (1990). Sexual abuse in a national survey of adult men and women:

> Prevalence, characteristics and risk factors. Child Abuse & Neglect 14, 19-28. doi.10.1016/0145-2134(90)90077-7

Fischer, P., & Greitemeyer, T. (2006). Music and Aggression: The Impact of Sexual-Aggressive Song Lyrics on Aggression-Related

> Thoughts, Emotions, and Behavior Toward the Same and the Opposite Sex. *Personality and Social Psychology Bulletin,*
> *32*(9), 1165-1176. doi:10.1177/0146167206288670

Frick, A. (2008, September 05). CNBC host praises Palin for 'putting a skirt on': 'I want her laying next to me in bed.'. Retrieved June

> 03, 2016, from http://thinkprogress.org/politics/2008/09/05/28702/cnbc-host-praises-palin-for-putting-a-skirt-on-i-want-her-
> laying-next-to-me-in-bed/

Friedan, B. (1963). *The feminine mystique*. New York: W.W. Norton.

Friedman, J., & Valenti, J. (n.d.). *Yes means yes!: Visions of female sexual power & a world without rape*.

Funk, L. (2009). *Supergirls speak out: Inside the secret crisis of overachieving girls*. New York: Simon & Schuster.

Gbowee, L., & Mithers, C. L. (2011). *Mighty be our powers: How sisterhood, prayer, and sex changed a nation at war: A*

> *memoir*. New York: Beast.

Goode, E. (1999, May 20). Study Finds TV Alters Fiji Girls' View of Body. Retrieved June 17, 2016, from

http://www.nytimes.com/1999/05/20/world/study-finds-tv-alters-fiji-girls-view-of-body.html

Grandoni, D. (2011, September 30). 92% of Top Ten Billboard Songs Are About Sex. Retrieved June 11, 2016, from

http://www.thewire.com/entertainment/2011/09/92-top-ten-billboard-songs-are-about-sex/43182/

Grant, Jaime M., Lisa A. Mottet, Justin Tanis, Jack Harrison, Jody L. Herman, and Mara Keisling. Injustice at Every Turn: A Report of

the National Transgender Discrimination Survey. Washington: National Center for Transgender Equality and National Gay

and Lesbian Task Force, 2011.

Grunbaum JA, Kann L, Kinchen S, et al. 2004. Youth Risk Behavior Surveillance—United States, 2003. Morbidity and Mortality

Weekly Report. 53(SS02); 1-96. Available at http://www.cdc.gov/mmwr/preview/mmwrhtml/ss5302a1.htm.

Haas, A. P., Ph.D., Rodgers, P. L., Ph.D., & Herman, J. L., Ph.D. (2014, January). Suicide Attempts Among Transgender and Gender

Non-Conforming Adults: FINDINGS OF THE NATIONAL TRANSGENDER DISCRIMINATION SURVEY. Retrieved

June 21, 2016, from http://williamsinstitute.law.ucla.edu/wp-content/uploads/AFSP-Williams-Suicide-Report-Final.pdf

Haberman, M. (2010, September 20). Reid calls Gillibrand the 'hottest' member at fundraiser - Maggie Haberman. Retrieved June 03,

2016, from

http://www.politico.com/blogs/maggiehaberman/0910/Reid_calls_Gillibrand_the_hottest_member_at_fundraiser_.htmlf

Haddix, M. P. (2007). *Uprising*. New York: Simon & Schuster Books for Young Readers.

Health Consequences of Eating Disorders | National Eating Disorders Association. (n.d.). Retrieved July 13, 2016, from

https://www.nationaleatingdisorders.org/health-consequences-eating-disorders

Heller, K., PhD. (2012, October 15). Depression in Teens and Children | Psych Central. Retrieved June 21, 2016, from

http://psychcentral.com/lib/depression-in-teens-and-children/

Heslam, J. (2010). Radio Producer on Hot Seat for Referring to GOP Candidate's 'Tight Little Butt' | Fox News. Retrieved June 03,

2016, from http://www.foxnews.com/politics/2010/09/21/radio-producer-hot-seat-referring-gop-candidates-tight-little-

butt.html

Hoek and van Hoeken, 2003. Review of the prevalence and incidence of eating disorders. International Journal of Eating Disorders,

386-396.

https://twitter.com/potus

Hyde, J. S. (2005). The Gender Similarities Hypothesis. *American Psychologist,60*(6), 581-592. doi:10.1037/0003-066x.60.6.581

Internet Statistics | GuardChild. (n.d.). Retrieved June 10, 2016, from http://www.guardchild.com/statistics/

Jacobs, A. (2006, October 31). Scarlett Johansson Is the Sexiest Woman Alive, 2006. Retrieved June 03, 2016, from

http://www.esquire.com/entertainment/interviews/a367/scarlett-johansson-pics/

Jalees, T., & Majid, H. (2009). Impact of 'Ideal Models' Being Portrayed by Media on YoungFemales. Paradigm (Institute of

Management Technology), 13 (1), 11-19.

Jasper, K., Ph.D. (1989). Are Eating Disorders Addictions? Retrieved July 13, 2016, from http://nedic.ca/sites/default/files/files/Are

> Eating Disorders Addictions.pdf

Johnson, S. B., Blum, R. W., & Giedd, J. N. (2009). Adolescent Maturity and the Brain: The Promise and Pitfalls of Neuroscience

> Research in Adolescent Health Policy. *Journal of Adolescent Health, 45*(3), 216-221. doi:10.1016/j.jadohealth.2009.05.016

Juskalian, R. (2010, December 16). HOW TEEN EXPERIENCES AFFECT YOUR BRAIN FOR LIFE. Retrieved January 09, 2016,

> from http://www.newsweek.com/how-teen-experiences-affect-your-brain-life-69099

Kaiser Family Foundation, H. J. (2005). *Sex on TV 4* (Rep.). Retrieved June 11, 2016, from Kaiser Family Foundation website:

> https://kaiserfamilyfoundation.files.wordpress.com/2013/01/sex-on-tv-4-executive-summary.pdf

Karnasiewicz, S. (2005, November 03). Teens launch "girlcott" against Abercrombie. Retrieved June 03, 2016, from

> http://www.salon.com/2005/11/03/girlcott/

Katersky, A., & Newcomb, A. (2014, April 25). Conn. High School Student Stabbed to Death Over Apparent Prom Date Rejection.

> Retrieved June 11, 2016, from http://abcnews.go.com/US/conn-high-school-student-stabbed-death-apparent-
>
> prom/story?id=23470009

Kilbourne, J. (2000). *Can't buy my love: How advertising changes the way we think and feel.* Free Press.

Kohler et al. "Abstinence-only and Comprehensive Sex Education and the Initiation of Sexual Activity and Teen Pregnancy."

> *Journal of Adolescent Health*, 42(4): 344-351.

Koutsky L. (1997). Epidemiology of genital human papillomavirus infection. American Journal of Medicine, 102(5A), 3-8.

Kurth CL, Krahn DD, Nairn K & Drewnowski A: The severity of dieting and bingeing behaviors in college women: Interview validation

> of survey data. Journal of Psychiatric Research. 1995; 29(3):211-25.

Lamb, S., & Brown, L. M. (2006). *Packaging girlhood: Rescuing our daughters from marketers' schemes.* New York: St. Martin's Press.

Lazo, K. (2016, June 17). *Feminism Isn't Dead, Its Gone Viral.* Speech presented at TEDxNavesink, Monmouth County, NJ.

Lenhart, A., Madden, M., Smith, A., & Macgill, A. (2007, December 19). Teens and Social Media. Retrieved June 17, 2016, from

> http://www.pewinternet.org/2007/12/19/teens-and-social-media/

Lenker, M. (2015, August 01). 5 Times J.K. Rowling Got Real About Depression. Retrieved July 08, 2016, from

> https://themighty.com/2015/08/5-times-j-k-rowling-got-real-about-depression/

Levy, A. (2005). *Female chauvinist pigs: Women and the rise of raunch culture.* New York: Free Press.

Listen, Ask, Get Help - Helping the Suicidal. (n.d.). Retrieved July 21, 2016, from http://samaritanshope.org/get-help/helping-suicidal/

LM, Irwin CE & Scully S: Disordered eating characteristics in girls: A survey of middle class children. Journal of the American

> Dietetic Association. 1992.

Lyons, G. (2010, September 22). Forget the tea party, what about the crumpets? Retrieved June 03, 2016, from

> http://www.salon.com/2010/09/23/gene_lyons_tea_party/

Magaldi, K. (2015, June 25). Why Do People Self-Harm? It's More Complicated Than You Think. Retrieved July 08, 2016, from

http://www.medicaldaily.com/self-harm-rise-teens-and-needing-attention-has-nothing-do-it-339974

Mann, M., Hosman, C. M., Schaalma, H. P., & De Vries, N. K. (2004). Self-esteem in a broad-spectrum approach for mental health

promotion. *Health Education Research, 19*(4), 357-372. doi:10.1093/her/cyg041

Martin, C. E. (2007). *Perfect girls, starving daughters: The frightening new normalcy of hating your body.* New York: Free Press.

McCabe, J., Fairchild, E., Grauerholz, L., Pescosolido, B. A., & Tope, D. (n.d.). Gender in Twentieth-Century Children's Books.

Retrieved June 06, 2016, from http://gas.sagepub.com/content/25/2/197.abstract

McLeod, S. A. (2014). Maslow's Hierarchy of Needs. Retrieved from www.simplypsychology.org/maslow.html

Mellin LM, Irwin CE & Scully S: Disordered eating characteristics in girls: A survey of middle class children. Journal of the

American Dietetic Association. 1992; 92:851-53.

Mental Health, N. (2015). Child Depression and Adolescent Depression. *Psych Central*. Retrieved on July 8, 2016 from

http://psychcentral.com/lib/child-depression-and-adolescent-depression/

Michael Leahy, *Porn University: What College Students Are Really Saying About Sex on Campus* (Chicago: Northfield Publishing,

2009).

Moore, J., Kendrick, A., Astin, S., Wilson, R., DeVine, A., Camp, A., Snow, B., ... Universal Studios Home Entertainment (Film).

(2012). *Pitch perfect*. Universal City, CA: Universal Studios.

Morago, G. (2014, October 29). New creams go neck-and-neck to sculpt your neck, decolletage. Retrieved June 03, 2016, from

http://www.houstonchronicle.com/news/article/New-creams-go-neck-and-neck-to-sculpt-your-neck-5856042.php#photo-

7069135

Mustich, E. (2013, July 16). 'The Mask You Live In': Jennifer Siebel Newsom Documentary Will Examine Masculinity (VIDEO).

Retrieved June 06, 2016, from http://www.huffingtonpost.com/2013/07/16/the-mask-you-live-in-jennifer-siebel-newsom-

masculinity_n_3599812.html

NEMADE, R., Ph.D., STAATS REISS, N., Ph.D., & DOMBECK, M., Ph.D. (2007, September 19). Historical Understandings Of

Depression. Retrieved July 08, 2016, from https://www.mentalhelp.net/articles/historical-understandings-of-depression/

Northup, T., & Liebler, C. M. (2010). The Good, the Bad, and the Beautiful. *Journal of Children and Media, 4*(3), 265-282.

doi:10.1080/17482798.2010.496917

Odell, A. (2010, June 04). Urban Outfitters Stopped Selling Its 'Eat Less' Shirt Online. Retrieved June 21, 2016, from

http://nymag.com/thecut/2010/06/urban_outfitters_stopped_selli.html

Orbach, S. (1978). *Fat is a feminist issue: The anti-diet guide to permanent weight loss.* New York: Paddington Press.

Orenstein, P. (2011). *Cinderella ate my daughter: Dispatches from the front lines of the new girlie-girl culture.* New York, NY:

HarperCollins.

Ozer EM, Brindis CD, Millstein SG, et al. America's adolescents: Are they healthy? San Francisco: University of California, School
    of Medicine; 1998.

Part of Giuliana Rancic's Zendaya Joke Was Edited Out, Says Source. (2015, March 04). Retrieved June 03, 2016, from
    http://www.people.com/article/giuliana-rancic-fashion-police-comment-edited-zendaya-dreadlocks

Pelosi, N., & Hearth, A. H. (2008). *Know your power: A message to America's daughters.* New York: Doubleday.

Petri, A. (2014, April 8). 'Don't risk dudeness'? Veet's new ad hair-removal is a throwback dud. Retrieved June 03, 2016, from
    https://www.washingtonpost.com/blogs/compost/wp/2014/04/08/dont-risk-dudeness-veets-new-ad-hair-removal-is-a-
    throwback-dud/

Pipher, M. B. (1994). *Reviving Ophelia: Saving the selves of adolescent girls.* New York: Putnam.

Plastic Surgery Procedural Statistics. (2014). Retrieved June 03, 2016, from http://plasticsurgery.org/news/plastic-surgery-
    statistics/2014-statistics.html

Pomona Valley. (n.d.). Retrieved June 21, 2016, from http://namipv.org/depression/

Porn Kills Love. (2014, August 8). Retrieved June 11, 2016, from http://fightthenewdrug.org/porn-kills-love/

Porn Leads to Violence. (n.d.). Retrieved June 12, 2016, from http://fightthenewdrug.org/porn-leads-to-violence/

Porn Ruins Your Sex Life. (2014, August 8). Retrieved June 16, 2016, from http://fightthenewdrug.org/porn-ruins-your-sex-life/

Pratt LA, Brody DJ. Depression in the U.S. household population, 2009–2012. NCHS data brief, no 172. Hyattsville, MD:
    National Center for Health Statistics. 2014.

Pratt, L. A., Ph.D., & Brody, D. J., M.P.H. (2010, January 19). Depression in the United States Household Population, 2005-2006.
    Retrieved July 13, 2016, from http://www.cdc.gov/nchs/products/databriefs/db07.htm

Rape. (n.d.). Retrieved June 17, 2016, from http://www.dictionary.com/browse/rape

Research Informs & Empowers - See Jane. (n.d.). Retrieved June 07, 2016, from http://seejane.org/research-informs-empowers/

ReducingStereotypeThreat.org. (n.d.). Retrieved June 05, 2016, from http://www.reducingstereotypethreat.org/definition.html

RESULTS OF 2015 UNIVERSITY OF MICHIGAN CAMPUS CLIMATE SURVEY ON SEXUAL MISCONDUCT. (n.d.).
    Retrieved June 7, 2016, from https://publicaffairs.vpcomm.umich.edu/wp-content/uploads/sites/19/2015/04/Complete-
    survey-results.pdf

Revenue of the cosmetic industry in the U.S. 2002-2016 | Forecast. (n.d.). Retrieved June 03, 2016, from
    http://www.statista.com/statistics/243742/revenue-of-the-cosmetic-industry-in-the-us/

Ridcout, V. J., Foehr, U. G., & Roberts, D. F. (2010). *Generation M2: Media in the lives of 8- to 18-year-olds.* Menlo Park, CA: Henry
    J. Kaiser Family Foundation.

Rodger, E. (2014, April 23). Life is so unfair because girls dont want me. Retrieved June 11, 2016, from
    https://www.youtube.com/watch?v=7KP62TE1prs

Salk, R. H., & Engeln-Maddox, R. (2011). "If You're Fat, Then I'm Humongous!": Frequency, Content, and Impact of Fat Talk Among

    College Women. *Psychology of Women Quarterly, 35*(1), 18-28. doi:10.1177/0361684310384107

Santa Cruz, J. (2014, March 10). Body-Image Pressure Increasingly Affects Boys. Retrieved June 06, 2016, from

    http://www.theatlantic.com/health/archive/2014/03/body-image-pressure-increasingly-affects-boys/283897/

Schnall, M. (2013). *What will it take to make a woman president?: Conversations about women, leadership and power.* Berkeley, CA:

    Seal Press.

Schor, J. (2004). *Born to buy: The commercialized child and the new consumer culture.* New York: Scribner.

Sciolino, E. (2000, December 18). THE 43rd PRESIDENT: WOMAN IN THE NEWS; Compulsion To Achieve -- Condoleezza Rice.

    Retrieved June 03, 2016, from http://www.nytimes.com/2000/12/18/us/the-43rd-president-woman-in-the-news-compulsion-

    to-achieve-condoleezza-rice.html?pagewanted=all

Selfie. (n.d.). Retrieved June 17, 2016, from http://www.oxforddictionaries.com/us/definition/american_english/selfie

Sex and HIV Education. (2016). Retrieved June 10, 2016, from https://www.guttmacher.org/state-policy/explore/sex-and-hiv-education

Sexual Assault. (2016, April 1). Retrieved June 17, 2016, from https://www.justice.gov/ovw/sexual-assault

Sexual health. (n.d.). Retrieved June 07, 2016, from http://www.who.int/topics/sexual_health/en/

Slass, L., & Porter, N. (2001). *Progress or no room at the top?: The role of women in telecommunications, broadcast, cable and e-*

    companies. Philadelphia, PA: Annenberg Public Policy Center.

Smith, S. L., & Choueiti, M. (2010). Gender Disparity On Screen and Behind the Camera in Family Films; The Executive Report.

    Retrieved June 4, 2016, from http://seejane.org/wp-content/uploads/full-study-gender-disparity-in-family-films-v2.pdf

Smith, S. L., & Cook, C. A. (n.d.). Gender Stereotypes: An Analysis of Popular Films and TV. Retrieved June 4, 2016, from

    http://seejane.org/wp-content/uploads/GDIGM_Gender_Stereotypes.pdf

Somarriba, M. R. (2014, March 17). Sexism and Sports Illustrated - Acculturated. Retrieved June 03, 2016, from

    http://acculturated.com/sexism-and-sports-illustrated/

Spencer, S. J., Steele, C. M., & Quinn, D. M. (n.d.). Stereotype Threat and Women's Math Performance. Retrieved June 5, 2016, from

    http://www.leedsbeckett.ac.uk/carnegie/learning_resources/LAW_PGCHE/SteeleandQuinnStereotypeThreat.pdf

Steggals, P. (2015). *Making sense of self-harm: The cultural meaning and social context of non-suicidal self-injury.*

Stone, D., Patton, B., & Heen, S. (1999). *Difficult conversations: How to discuss what matters most.* New York, NY: Viking.

Suicide data. (n.d.). Retrieved July 22, 2016, from http://www.who.int/mental_health/prevention/suicide/suicideprevent/en/

Suicide Statistics - AFSP. (n.d.). Retrieved June 06, 2016, from https://afsp.org/about-suicide/suicide-statistics/

Sullivan, P. (1995). American Journal of Psychiatry, 152 (7), 10731074.

The Renfrew Center Foundation for Eating Disorders, "Eating Disorders 101 Guide: A Summary of Issues, Statistics and

    Resources," published September 2002, revised October 2003, http://www.renfrew.org.

The Samaritans of Bristol County - About Suicide. (n.d.). Retrieved July 22, 2016, from http://www.samaritans-

bristolcounty.org/suicide.html

The U.S. Weight Loss Market: 2015 Status Report & Forecast. (2015, January). Retrieved June 03, 2016, from

https://www.bharatbook.com/healthcare-market-research-reports-467678/healthcare-industry-healthcare-market-research-

reports-healthcare-industry-analysis-healthcare-sector1.html

Types & Symptoms of Eating Disorders | National Eating Disorders Association. (n.d). Retrieved June 21, 2016, from

http://www.nationaleatingdisorders.org/types-symptoms-eating-disorders

University of Southern California. "Video Game Minority Report: Lots Of Players, Few Characters." ScienceDaily. ScienceDaily, 30

July 2009. <www.sciencedaily.com/releases/2009/07/090729140931.htm>.

U.S. Department of Justice. Post Hearing Memorandum of Points and Authorities, at l, ACLU v. Reno, 929 F. Supp. 824, 1996.

Victoria L. Brescoll. (n.d.). Retrieved July 21, 2016, from http://som.yale.edu/victoria-l-brescoll

Violence against adults and children with disabilities. (n.d.). Retrieved June 10, 2016, from

http://www.who.int/disabilities/violence/en/

Walters, M.L., Chen J., & Breiding, M.J. (2013). The National Intimate Partner and Sexual Violence Survey (NISVS): 2010 Findings on

Victimization by Sexual Orientation. Retrieved from the Centers for Disease Control and Prevention, National Center for

Injury Prevention and Control: http://www.cdc.gov/ViolencePrevention/pdf/NISVS_SOfindings.pdf

Weisgram, E. S., Fulcher, M., & Dinella, L. M. (2014). Pink gives girls permission: Exploring the roles of explicit gender labels and

gender-typed colors on preschool children's toy preferences. *Journal of Applied Developmental Psychology, 35*(5), 401-409.

doi:10.1016/j.appdev.2014.06.004

What is Binge Eating Disorder? (2015, April 24). Retrieved June 21, 2016, from http://www.nedc.com.au/binge-eating-disorder

What the Research Says: Gender-Typed Toys | National Association for the Education of Young Children. (n.d.). Retrieved May 30,

2016, from http://www.naeyc.org/content/what-research-says-gender-typed-toys

Wilson, M. D. (2014, November 10). Pregnant woman slammed on the ground, stabbed after rejecting man's advances. Retrieved

June 11, 2016, from http://www.mysanantonio.com/news/local/article/Woman-eight-moths-pregnant-slammed-on-the-

5883072.php

Wiseman, R. (2002). *Queen bees & wannabes: Helping your daughter survive cliques, gossip, boyfriends, and other realities of

adolescence*. New York: Crown.

Wolf, N. (1991). *The beauty myth: How images of beauty are used against women*. New York: W. Morrow.

"Women's Health," June/July 2004, Family Violence Prevention Fund and Advocates for Youth,

http://www.med.umich.edu/whp/newsletters/summer04/p03-dating.html.

Yan, H., Almsay, S., & Sidner, S. (2014, May 27). California mass killer thought plan was over during April visit by deputies.

Retrieved June 11, 2016, from http://www.cnn.com/2014/05/25/justice/california-shooting-deaths/

8 Fifth & Pacific Companies, Inc. (Formerly: Liz Claiborne, Inc.), Conducted by Knowledge Networks, (December 2010).

"College Dating Violence and Abuse Poll," Available at: https://www.breakthecycle.org/surveys.

NOTES:

Introduction

1. **It is my thesis that the core of the problem:** Friedan, B. (1963). *The feminine mystique*. New York: W.W. Norton.
2. **If women do not put forth:** Friedan, B. (1963). *The feminine mystique*. New York: W.W. Norton.
3. **Maslow believed that:** Cherry, K. (2016, April 26). Maslow's Hierarchy of Needs: What Motivates Behavior? Retrieved May 28, 2016, from https://www.verywell.com/hierarchy-of-needs-2795947
4. **Essentially, self-actualization is:** McLeod, S. A. (2014). Maslow's Hierarchy of Needs. Retrieved from www.simplypsychology.org/maslow.html
5. **Self-actualization is awesome because:** McLeod, S. A. (2014). Maslow's Hierarchy of Needs. Retrieved from www.simplypsychology.org/maslow.html

Femininity

6. **To lose confidence in one's:** Beauvoir, S. ., Borde, C., & Malovany-Chevallier, S. (2010). *The second sex*. New York: Alfred A. Knopf.
7. **51% of 9 and 10 year-old:** LM, Irwin CE & Scully S: Disordered eating characteristics in girls: A survey of middle class children. Journal of the American Dietetic Association. 1992.
8. **One woman analyzed 46 meta-analyses:** Hyde, J. S. (2005). The Gender Similarities Hypothesis. *American Psychologist,60*(6), 581-592. doi:10.1037/0003-066x.60.6.581
9. **What I found, after an exhaustive:** Eliot, L. (2009). *Pink brain, blue brain: How small differences grow into troublesome gaps--and what we can do about it*. Boston: Houghton Mifflin Harcourt.
10. **A Kaiser Family Foundation Study:** Rideout, V. J., Foehr, U. G., & Roberts, D. F. (2010). *Generation M2: Media in the lives of 8- to 18-year-olds*. Menlo Park, CA: Henry J. Kaiser Family Foundation.
11. **And, the time spent on media:** Rideout, V. J., Foehr, U. G., & Roberts, D. F. (2010). *Generation M2: Media in the lives of 8- to 18-year-olds*. Menlo Park, CA: Henry J. Kaiser Family Foundation.
12. **Juliet Schor writes:** Schor, J. (2004). *Born to buy: The commercialized child and the new consumer culture*. New York: Scribner.
13. **Consequently creating culture:** Kilbourne, J. (2000). *Can't buy my love: How advertising changes the way we think and feel*. Free Press.
14. **Newer research:** Johnson, S. B., Blum, R. W., & Giedd, J. N. (2009). Adolescent Maturity and the Brain: The Promise and Pitfalls of Neuroscience Research in Adolescent Health Policy. *Journal of Adolescent Health, 45*(3), 216-221. doi:10.1016/j.jadohealth.2009.05.016
15. **A Newsweek article states:** Juskalian, R. (2010, December 16). HOW TEEN EXPERIENCES AFFECT YOUR BRAIN FOR LIFE. Retrieved January 09, 2016, from http://www.newsweek.com/how-teen-experiences-affect-your-brain-life-69099
16. **As one study writes:** C., U., & N. (2002, May). Adolescent Brain Development - ACT for Youth. Retrieved January 9, 2016, from http://www.actforyouth.net/resources/rf/rf_brain_0502.pdf
17. **Heartbreakingly, 78% of the:** Grant, Jaime M., Lisa A. Mottet, Justin Tanis, Jack Harrison, Jody L. Herman, and Mara Keisling. Injustice at Every Turn: A Report of the National Transgender Discrimination Survey. Washington: National Center for Transgender Equality and National Gay and Lesbian Task Force, 2011.
18. **Sadly, 1 in 5 members:** Grant, Jaime M., Lisa A. Mottet, Justin Tanis, Jack Harrison, Jody L. Herman, and Mara Keisling. Injustice at Every Turn: A Report of the National Transgender Discrimination Survey. Washington: National Center for Transgender Equality and National Gay and Lesbian Task Force, 2011.
19. **1 in 8 transgender people:** Grant, Jaime M., Lisa A. Mottet, Justin Tanis, Jack Harrison, Jody L. Herman, and Mara Keisling. Injustice at Every Turn: A Report of the National Transgender Discrimination Survey. Washington: National Center for Transgender Equality and National Gay and Lesbian Task Force, 2011.
20. **The community experiences unemployment:** Grant, Jaime M., Lisa A. Mottet, Justin Tanis, Jack Harrison, Jody L. Herman, and Mara Keisling. Injustice at Every Turn: A Report of the National

Transgender Discrimination Survey. Washington: National Center for Transgender Equality and National Gay and Lesbian Task Force, 2011.

21. **Horrifyingly 90% of the community:** Grant, Jaime M., Lisa A. Mottet, Justin Tanis, Jack Harrison, Jody L. Herman, and Mara Keisling. Injustice at Every Turn: A Report of the National Transgender Discrimination Survey. Washington: National Center for Transgender Equality and National Gay and Lesbian Task Force, 2011.

22. **The result is that girls are:** Weisgram, E. S., Fulcher, M., & Dinella, L. M. (2014). Pink gives girls permission: Exploring the roles of explicit gender labels and gender-typed colors on preschool children's toy preferences. *Journal of Applied Developmental Psychology, 35*(5), 401-409. doi:10.1016/j.appdev.2014.06.004

23. **Believe it or not, little girls aren't born loving pink:** Orenstein, P. (2011). *Cinderella ate my daughter: Dispatches from the front lines of the new girlie-girl culture.* New York, NY: HarperCollins.

24. **As Orenstein says on the color pink:** Orenstein, P. (2011). *Cinderella ate my daughter: Dispatches from the front lines of the new girlie-girl culture.* New York, NY: HarperCollins.

25. **The toys most associated with girls:** What the Research Says: Gender-Typed Toys | National Association for the Education of Young Children. (n.d.). Retrieved May 30, 2016, from http://www.naeyc.org/content/what-research-says-gender-typed-toys

26. **Girls aged 5 to 8 showed lower levels:** Dittmar, H., Halliwell, E., & Ive, S. (2006). "Does Barbie make girls want to be thin? The effect of experimental exposure to images of dolls on the body image of 5- to 8-year-old girls": Correction to Dittmar, Halliwell, and Ive (2006).*Developmental Psychology, 42*(6), 1258-1258. doi:10.1037/0012-1649.42.6.1258

27. **The boys seemed to be exploring the world:** Orenstein, P. (2011). *Cinderella ate my daughter: Dispatches from the front lines of the new girlie-girl culture.* New York, NY: HarperCollins.

28. **As Born to Buy puts it:** Schor, J. (2004). *Born to buy: The commercialized child and the new consumer culture.* New York: Scribner.

29. **Chimamanda Ngozi Adichie once said:** Adichie, C. N. (n.d.). *We Should All Be Feminists.* Speech presented at TEDxEuston. Retrieved May 31, 2016, from https://www.youtube.com/watch?v=hg3umXU_qWc

30. **It's important to note that the very concept:** Schor, J. (2004). *Born to buy: The commercialized child and the new consumer culture.* New York: Scribner.

31. **Juliet Schor, author of <u>Born to Buy</u> writes:** Schor, J. (2004). *Born to buy: The commercialized child and the new consumer culture.* New York: Scribner.

32. **As Lamb and Brown write: Lamb, S., & Brown, L. M. (2006).** *Packaging girlhood: Rescuing our daughters from marketers' schemes.* New York: St. Martin's Press.

33. **To expand on that point I'd like to quote Schor:** Schor, J. (2004). *Born to buy: The commercialized child and the new consumer culture.* New York: Scribner.

34. **"The commercials between:** Lamb, S., & Brown, L. M. (2006). *Packaging girlhood: Rescuing our daughters from marketers' schemes.* New York: St. Martin's Press.

35. **One of the easiest ways to segment:** Orenstein, P. (2011). *Cinderella ate my daughter: Dispatches from the front lines of the new girlie-girl culture.* New York, NY: HarperCollins.

36. **What's in this girl culture:** Lamb, S., & Brown, L. M. (2006). *Packaging girlhood: Rescuing our daughters from marketers' schemes.* New York: St. Martin's Press.

37. **The majority of games for girls:** Lamb, S., & Brown, L. M. (2006). *Packaging girlhood: Rescuing our daughters from marketers' schemes.* New York: St. Martin's Press.

38. **Girls learn that having a 'hot' body:** Karnasiewicz, S. (2005, November 03). Teens launch "girlcott" against Abercrombie. Retrieved June 03, 2016, from http://www.salon.com/2005/11/03/girlcott/

39. **Girls learn that they always have to look beautiful:** Lamb, S., & Brown, L. M. (2006). *Packaging girlhood: Rescuing our daughters from marketers' schemes.* New York: St. Martin's Press.

40. **Girls learn that they have nothing important:** Lamb, S., & Brown, L. M. (2006). *Packaging girlhood: Rescuing our daughters from marketers' schemes.* New York: St. Martin's Press.

41. **Will Americans want to watch a woman:** Does Our Looks-Obsessed Culture Want to Stare at an Aging Woman? - The Rush Limbaugh Show. (2007, December 17). Retrieved June 03, 2016, from http://www.rushlimbaugh.com/daily/2007/12/17/does_our_looks_obsessed_culture_want_to_stare_at_an_aging_woman6

42. **The fact that her dress size is:** Sciolino, E. (2000, December 18). THE 43rd PRESIDENT: WOMAN IN THE NEWS; Compulsion To Achieve -- Condoleezza Rice. Retrieved June 03, 2016, from

http://www.nytimes.com/2000/12/18/us/the-43rd-president-woman-in-the-news-compulsion-to-achieve-condoleezza-rice.html?pagewanted=all

43. **Fat Amy in Pitch Perfect:** Moore, J., Kendrick, A., Astin, S., Wilson, R., DeVine, A., Camp, A., Snow, B., ,.. Universal Studios Home Entertainment (Firm). (2012). *Pitch perfect*. Universal City, CA: Universal Studios.

44. **When radio host Bill Cooksey:** Heslam, J. (2010). Radio Producer on Hot Seat for Referring to GOP Candidate's 'Tight Little Butt' | Fox News. Retrieved June 03, 2016, from http://www.foxnews.com/politics/2010/09/21/radio-producer-hot-seat-referring-gop-candidates-tight-little-butt.html

45. **It's when former TV hosts say things like:** Frick, A. (2008, September 05). CNBC host praises Palin for 'putting a skirt on': 'I want her laying next to me in bed.'. Retrieved June 03, 2016, from http://thinkprogress.org/politics/2008/09/05/28702/cnbc-host-praises-palin-for-putting-a-skirt-on-i-want-her-laying-next-to-me-in-bed/

46. **Or when the Senate Majority Leader:** Haberman, M. (2010, September 20). Reid calls Gillibrand the 'hottest' member at fundraiser - Maggie Haberman. Retrieved June 03, 2016, from http://www.politico.com/blogs/maggiehaberman/0910/Reid_calls_Gillibrand_the_hottest_member_at_fundraiser_.html

47. **I've never received such positive:** Funk, L. (2009). *Supergirls speak out: Inside the secret crisis of overachieving girls*. New York: Simon & Schuster.

48. **Nope. Best breasts:** Jacobs, A. (2006, October 31). Scarlett Johansson Is the Sexiest Woman Alive, 2006. Retrieved June 03, 2016, from http://www.esquire.com/entertainment/interviews/a367/scarlett-johansson-pics/

49. **Lise Eliot writes:** Eliot, L. (2009). *Pink brain, blue brain: How small differences grow into troublesome gaps--and what we can do about it*. Boston: Houghton Mifflin Harcourt.

50. **Girls learn that all that:** Somarriba, M. R. (2014, March 17). Sexism and Sports Illustrated - Acculturated. Retrieved June 03, 2016, from http://acculturated.com/sexism-and-sports-illustrated/

51. **Lamb and Brown note:** Lamb, S., & Brown, L. M. (2006). *Packaging girlhood: Rescuing our daughters from marketers' schemes*. New York: St. Martin's Press.

52. **And speaking of sports, they write:** Lamb, S., & Brown, L. M. (2006). *Packaging girlhood: Rescuing our daughters from marketers' schemes*. New York: St. Martin's Press.

53. **There was also this gross comment, made by Gene Lyon:** Lyons, G. (2010, September 22). Forget the tea party, what about the crumpets? Retrieved June 03, 2016, from http://www.salon.com/2010/09/23/gene_lyons_tea_party/

54. **Sam, I want to ask a question:** Bennett, S. (2010, September 16). This just in: The measure of a female candidate isn't in her measurements. Retrieved June 03, 2016, from http://www.nameitchangeit.org/blog/entry/measure-of-a-female-candidate

55. **One of the most bizarre comments I found:** Lyons, G. (2010, September 22). Forget the tea party, what about the crumpets? Retrieved June 03, 2016, from http://www.salon.com/2010/09/23/gene_lyons_tea_party/

56. **Susan Douglas, author of <u>Where the Girls Are</u> wrote:** Douglas, S. J. (1994). *Where the girls are: Growing up female with the mass media*. New York: Times Books.

57. **In fact, I found that 71% of girls:** This is a statistic from a personal survey I conducted of over 1 thousand girls. It's important to note that the study was not a scientific one.

58. **In 2015 alone, the global:** Revenue of the cosmetic industry in the U.S. 2002-2016 | Forecast. (n.d.). Retrieved June 03, 2016, from http://www.statista.com/statistics/243742/revenue-of-the-cosmetic-industry-in-the-us/

59. **One example of a marketing campaign:** Petri, A. (2014, April 8). 'Don't risk dudeness'? Veet's new ad hair-removal is a throwback dud. Retrieved June 03, 2016, from https://www.washingtonpost.com/blogs/compost/wp/2014/04/08/dont-risk-dudeness-veets-new-ad-hair-removal-is-a-throwback-dud/

60. **One advertisement I saw while:** Morago, G. (2014, October 29). New creams go neck-and-neck to sculpt your neck, decolletage. Retrieved June 03, 2016, from http://www.houstonchronicle.com/news/article/New-creams-go-neck-and-neck-to-sculpt-your-neck-5856042.php#photo-7069135

61. **And, the APA writes:** American Psychological Association,Task Force on the Sexualization of Girls. (2007). Report of the APA Task Force on the Sexualization of Girls. Retrieved from http://www.apa.org/pi/women/programs/girls/report-full.pdf

62. **In 2013 alone, 63,538: 2014** Plastic Surgery Procedural Statistics. (2014). Retrieved June 03, 2016, from http://plasticsurgery.org/news/plastic-surgery-statistics/2014-statistics.html

63. **Marketers love anxiety:** Lamb, S., & Brown, L. M. (2006). *Packaging girlhood: Rescuing our daughters from marketers' schemes*. New York: St. Martin's Press.

64. **Jean Kilbourne states:** Kilbourne, J. (2000). *Can't buy my love: How advertising changes the way we think and feel*. Free Press.

65. **Perhaps that's why the weight loss:** The U.S. Weight Loss Market: 2015 Status Report & Forecast. (2015, January). Retrieved June 03, 2016, from https://www.bharatbook.com/healthcare-market-research-reports-467678/healthcare-industry-healthcare-market-research-reports-healthcare-industry-analysis-healthcare-sector1.html

66. **Giuliana Rancic, a host of E News!:** Part of Giuliana Rancic's Zendaya Joke Was Edited Out, Says Source. (2015, March 04). Retrieved June 03, 2016, from http://www.people.com/article/giuliana-rancic-fashion-police-comment-edited-zendaya-dreadlocks

67. **Rosalind Wiseman writes in her book:** Wiseman, R. (2002). *Queen bees & wannabes: Helping your daughter survive cliques, gossip, boyfriends, and other realities of adolescence*. New York: Crown.

68. **Did you know that 42%:** Collins M.E. (1991) Body figure and preferences among pre-adolescent children. International Journal of Eating Disorders, 199-208.

69. **A Common Sense Media report states:** Children, Teens, Media, and Body Image | Common Sense Media. (n.d.). Retrieved June 03, 2016, from https://www.commonsensemedia.org/research/children-teens-media-and-body-image

70. **80 percent of 10-year-old girls:** Mellin LM, Irwin CE & Scully S: Disordered eating characteristics in girls: A survey of middle class children. Journal of the American Dietetic Association. 1992; 92:851-53.

71. **In one study, 91 percent:** Kurth CL, Krahn DD, Nairn K & Drewnowski A: The severity of dieting and bingeing behaviors in college women: Interview validation of survey data. Journal of Psychiatric Research. 1995; 29(3):211-25.

72. **YoungWomensHealth.org defines self-esteem:** Center for Young Women's Health. (2014, June 2). Retrieved June 03, 2016, from http://youngwomenshealth.org/2012/05/30/self-esteem/

73. **Research shows that males' self-esteem:** Bleidorn, W., Arslan, R. C., Denissen, J. J. A., Rentfrow, P. J., Gebauer, J. E., Potter, J., & Gosling, S. D. (2015, December 21). Age and Gender Differences in Self-Esteem—A Cross-Cultural Window. Journal of Personality and Social Psychology. Advance online publication. http:// dx.doi.org/10.1037/pspp0000078

74. **Interestingly, Eliot notes that:** Eliot, L. (2009). *Pink brain, blue brain: How small differences grow into troublesome gaps--and what we can do about it*. Boston: Houghton Mifflin Harcourt.

75. **We know from research that the way:** Mann, M., Hosman, C. M., Schaalma, H. P., & De Vries, N. K. (2004). Self-esteem in a broad-spectrum approach for mental health promotion. *Health Education Research, 19*(4), 357-372. doi:10.1093/her/cyg041

76. **Self-esteem leads "to:** Mann, M., Hosman, C. M., Schaalma, H. P., & De Vries, N. K. (2004). Self-esteem in a broad-spectrum approach for mental health promotion. *Health Education Research, 19*(4), 357-372. doi:10.1093/her/cyg041

77. **One study wrote, "As part of:** Children, Teens, Media, and Body Image | Common Sense Media. (n.d.). Retrieved June 03, 2016, from https://www.commonsensemedia.org/research/children-teens-media-and-body-image

78. **It is important to know that body image:** Children, Teens, Media, and Body Image | Common Sense Media. (n.d.). Retrieved June 03, 2016, from https://www.commonsensemedia.org/research/children-teens-media-and-body-image

79. **Research shows that we learn:** Children, Teens, Media, and Body Image | Common Sense Media. (n.d.). Retrieved June 03, 2016, from https://www.commonsensemedia.org/research/children-teens-media-and-body-image

80. **Naomi Wolf writes:** Wolf, N. (1991). *The beauty myth: How images of beauty are used against women*. New York: W. Morrow.

81. **Research shows that visualization:** Coyle, D. (2009). *The talent code: Greatness isn't born: It's grown, here's how*. New York: Bantam Books.

82. **In The Talent Code, there is a scene:** Coyle, D. (2009). *The talent code: Greatness isn't born: It's grown, here's how*. New York: Bantam Books.

83. **The Geena Davis Institute tracked over five thousand:** Smith, S. L., & Choueiti, M. (2010). Gender Disparity On Screen and Behind the Camera in Family Films; The Executive Report. Retrieved June 4, 2016, from http://seejane.org/wp-content/uploads/full-study-gender-disparity-in-family-films-v2.pdf

84. **The Geena Davis Institute found that:** Smith, S. L., & Cook, C. A. (n.d.). Gender Stereotypes: An Analysis of Popular Films and TV. Retrieved June 4, 2016, from http://seejane.org/wp-content/uploads/GDIGM_Gender_Stereotypes.pdf

85. **Females are over five times more likely:** Smith, S. L., & Choueiti, M. (2010). Gender Disparity On Screen and Behind the Camera in Family Films; The Executive Report. Retrieved June 4, 2016, from http://seejane.org/wp-content/uploads/full-study-gender-disparity-in-family-films-v2.pdf

86. **Furthermore, right now, females are far more likely:** Smith, S. L., & Choueiti, M. (2010). Gender Disparity On Screen and Behind the Camera in Family Films; The Executive Report. Retrieved June 4, 2016, from http://seejane.org/wp-content/uploads/full-study-gender-disparity-in-family-films-v2.pdf

87. **In fact, a study of 134 episodes:** Northup, T., & Liebler, C. M. (2010). The Good, the Bad, and the Beautiful. *Journal of Children and Media, 4*(3), 265-282. doi:10.1080/17482798.2010.496917

88. **With such a devastating reality:** Ozer EM, Brindis CD, Millstein SG, et al. America's adolescents: Are they healthy? San Francisco: University of California, School of Medicine; 1998.

89. **In fact, the body type portrayed:** Jalees, T., & Majid, H. (2009). Impact of 'Ideal Models' Being Portrayed by Media on YoungFemales. Paradigm (Institute of Management Technology), 13 (1), 11-19.

90. **Gail Dines, author of Pornland:** Dines, G. (2010). *Pornland: How porn has hijacked our sexuality.* Boston: Beacon Press.

91. **Common Sense Media reports:** Children, Teens, Media, and Body Image | Common Sense Media. (n.d.). Retrieved June 03, 2016, from https://www.commonsensemedia.org/research/children-teens-media-and-body-image

92. **Exposure to a white ideal:** American Psychological Association,Task Force on the Sexualization of Girls. (2007). Report of the APA Task Force on the Sexualization of Girls. Retrieved from http://www.apa.org/pi/women/programs/girls/report-full.pdf

93. **Research shows that there is a negative:** American Psychological Association,Task Force on the Sexualization of Girls. (2007). Report of the APA Task Force on the Sexualization of Girls. Retrieved from http://www.apa.org/pi/women/programs/girls/report-full.pdf

94. **Currently, men hold 97% of clout, or key:** Slass, L., & Porter, N. (2001). *Progress or no room at the top?: The role of women in telecommunications, broadcast, cable and e-companies.* Philadelphia, PA: Annenberg Public Policy Center.

95. **Caroline Heldman, a Professor and media critic:** Schnall, M. (2013). *What will it take to make a woman president?: Conversations about women, leadership and power.* Berkeley, CA: Seal Press.

96. **Sadly, research shows that:** Salk, R. H., & Engeln-Maddox, R. (2011). "If You're Fat, Then I'm Humongous!": Frequency, Content, and Impact of Fat Talk Among College Women. *Psychology of Women Quarterly, 35*(1), 18-28. doi:10.1177/0361684310384107

97. **Courtney E. Martin writes:** Martin, C. E. (2007). *Perfect girls, starving daughters: The frightening new normalcy of hating your body.* New York: Free Press.

98. **I want to recount a part:** Martin, C. E. (2007). *Perfect girls, starving daughters: The frightening new normalcy of hating your body.* New York: Free Press.

99. **Martin continues to then say:** Martin, C. E. (2007). *Perfect girls, starving daughters: The frightening new normalcy of hating your body.* New York: Free Press.

100. **As Courtney E. Martin says:** Martin, C. E. (2007). *Perfect girls, starving daughters: The frightening new normalcy of hating your body.* New York: Free Press.

Popularity

101. **Naomi Wolf writes:** Wolf, N. (1991). *The beauty myth: How images of beauty are used against women.* New York: W. Morrow.

102. **Cindy Crawford, a famous model, once said:** Cindy Crawford quote. (n.d.). Retrieved June 04, 2016, from http://www.brainyquote.com/quotes/quotes/c/cindycrawf140664.html

103. **Taylor Swift smartly said:** Dickey, J. (2014, November 13). Taylor Swift on 1989, Spotify, Her Next Tour and Female Role Models. Retrieved June 04, 2016, from http://time.com/3578249/taylor-swift-interview/

104. **Juliet Schor of <u>Born to Buy</u> writes:** Schor, J. (2004). *Born to buy: The commercialized child and the new consumer culture*. New York: Scribner.

105. **Schor writes, "When cool:** Schor, J. (2004). *Born to buy: The commercialized child and the new consumer culture*. New York: Scribner.

106. **Stereotype threat is a well known phenomenon:** ReducingStereotypeThreat.org. (n.d.). Retrieved June 05, 2016, from http://www.reducingstereotypethreat.org/definition.html

107. **Several studies have been done:** Spencer, S. J., Steele, C. M., & Quinn, D. M. (n.d.). Stereotype Threat and Women's Math Performance. Retrieved June 5, 2016, from http://www.leedsbeckett.ac.uk/carnegie/learning_resources/LAW_PGCHE/SteeleandQuinnStereotypeThreat.pdf

108. **Chimamanda Ngozi Adichie put it best:** Adichie, C. N. (n.d.). *The danger of a single story*. Speech presented at TEDGlobal 2009. Retrieved June 05, 2016, from https://www.ted.com/talks/chimamanda_adichie_the_danger_of_a_single_story?language=en

109. **And research by Professor Carol:** Dweck, C. S. (2006). *Mindset: The new psychology of success*. **New York: Random House.**

110. **Wiseman discusses the fear of being called:** Wiseman, R. (2002). *Queen bees & wannabes: Helping your daughter survive cliques, gossip, boyfriends, and other realities of adolescence*. New York: Crown.

111. **Wiseman adds, "When:** Wiseman, R. (2002). *Queen bees & wannabes: Helping your daughter survive cliques, gossip, boyfriends, and other realities of adolescence*. New York: Crown.

112. **The author of <u>The Lolita Effect</u> writes:** Durham, M. G. (2008). *The Lolita effect: The media sexualization of young girls and what we can do about it*. Woodstock, NY: Overlook Press.

113. **The authors of <u>Difficult Conversations</u> state,:** Stone, D., Patton, B., & Heen, S. (1999). *Difficult conversations: How to discuss what matters most*. New York, NY: Viking.

114. **The authors of <u>Packaging Girlhood</u>:** Lamb, S., & Brown, L. M. (2006). *Packaging girlhood: Rescuing our daughters from marketers' schemes*. New York: St. Martin's Press.

115. **Naomi Wolf, author of <u>The Beauty Myth</u>:** Wolf, N. (1991). *The beauty myth: How images of beauty are used against women*. New York: W. Morrow.

Masculinity

116. **"The Act Like a Man box controls:** Wiseman, R. (2002). *Queen bees & wannabes: Helping your daughter survive cliques, gossip, boyfriends, and other realities of adolescence*. New York: Crown.

117. **Chu found that "the boys in:** Chu, J. Y., & Gilligan, C. (n.d.). *When boys become boys: Development, relationships, and masculinity*.

118. **She described the young boys as:** Chu, J. Y., & Gilligan, C. (n.d.). *When boys become boys: Development, relationships, and masculinity*.

119. **Began to show signs of becoming:** Chu, J. Y., & Gilligan, C. (n.d.). *When boys become boys: Development, relationships, and masculinity*.

120. **She wrote, "The boys:** Chu, J. Y., & Gilligan, C. (n.d.). *When boys become boys: Development, relationships, and masculinity*.

121. **Personas they had seen, by stating:** Chu, J. Y., & Gilligan, C. (n.d.). *When boys become boys: Development, relationships, and masculinity*.

122. **Michael Kimmel once said:** Mustich, E. (2013, July 16). 'The Mask You Live In': Jennifer Siebel Newsom Documentary Will Examine Masculinity (VIDEO). Retrieved June 06, 2016, from http://www.huffingtonpost.com/2013/07/16/the-mask-you-live-in-jennifer-siebel-newsom-masculinity_n_3599812.html

123. **In fact, nearly 18 percent:** Field, A. E. (2013, November 4). Prospective Associations of Male Physique Concerns. Retrieved June 06, 2016, from http://archpedi.jamanetwork.com/article.aspx?articleid=1766495

124. **As the study puts it:** Field, A. E. (2013, November 4). Prospective Associations of Male Physique Concerns. Retrieved June 06, 2016, from http://archpedi.jamanetwork.com/article.aspx?articleid=1766495

125. **Two meta-analyses found a:** Barlett, C. P., Vowels, C. L., & Saucier, D. A. (2008). META–ANALYSES OF THE EFFECTS OF MEDIA IMAGES ON MEN'S BODY–IMAGE CONCERNS. *Journal of Social and Clinical Psychology, 27*(3), 279-310. doi:10.1521/jscp.2007.26.issue-6

126. **And, we know from Schor that:** Schor, J. (2004). *Born to buy: The commercialized child and the new consumer culture.* New York: Scribner.

127. **For example, "Boys in:** Santa Cruz, J. (2014, March 10). Body-Image Pressure Increasingly Affects Boys. Retrieved June 06, 2016, from http://www.theatlantic.com/health/archive/2014/03/body-image-pressure-increasingly-affects-boys/283897/

128. **Gail Dines writes that in pornography:** Dines, G. (2010). *Pornland: How porn has hijacked our sexuality.* Boston: Beacon Press.

129. **Research shows that boys:** Eliot, L. (2009). *Pink brain, blue brain: How small differences grow into troublesome gaps--and what we can do about it.* Boston: Houghton Mifflin Harcourt.

130. **In some studies, "men:** Eliot, L. (2009). *Pink brain, blue brain: How small differences grow into troublesome gaps--and what we can do about it.* Boston: Houghton Mifflin Harcourt.

131. **In 2014 alone, white:** Suicide Statistics - AFSP. (n.d.). Retrieved June 06, 2016, from https://afsp.org/about-suicide/suicide-statistics/

132. **Furthermore, boys:** Eliot, L. (2009). *Pink brain, blue brain: How small differences grow into troublesome gaps--and what we can do about it.* Boston: Houghton Mifflin Harcourt.

133. **Eliot notes that the level of aggression:** Eliot, L. (2009). *Pink brain, blue brain: How small differences grow into troublesome gaps--and what we can do about it.* Boston: Houghton Mifflin Harcourt.

134. **Toys have to do with violence, stating:** What the Research Says: Gender-Typed Toys | National Association for the Education of Young Children. (n.d.). Retrieved May 30, 2016, from http://www.naeyc.org/content/what-research-says-gender-typed-toys

135. **One study contradicts past findings:** Escudero, P., Robbins, R. A., & Johnson, S. P. (2013). Sex-related preferences for real and doll faces versus real and toy objects in young infants and adults.*Journal of Experimental Child Psychology, 116*(2), 367-379. doi:10.1016/j.jecp.2013.07.001

136. **This challenges the notion:** Escudero, P., Robbins, R. A., & Johnson, S. P. (2013). Sex-related preferences for real and doll faces versus real and toy objects in young infants and adults.*Journal of Experimental Child Psychology, 116*(2), 367-379. doi:10.1016/j.jecp.2013.07.001

137. **One article reiterates, saying:** Fine, C. (2014, April 05). Science Doesn't Support a Gender Divide for Toys. Retrieved June 06, 2016, from http://www.slate.com/articles/health_and_science/new_scientist/2014/04/girl_and_boy_toys_childhood_preferences_for_gendered_toys_are_not_innate.html

138. **Schor got a President of an advertising:** Schor, J. (2004). *Born to buy: The commercialized child and the new consumer culture.* New York: Scribner.

139. **Eliot wrote, "In dozens:** Eliot, L. (2009). *Pink brain, blue brain: How small differences grow into troublesome gaps--and what we can do about it.* Boston: Houghton Mifflin Harcourt.

140. **As Wiseland puts it, "The:** Wiseman, R. (2002). *Queen bees & wannabes: Helping your daughter survive cliques, gossip, boyfriends, and other realities of adolescence.* New York: Crown.

141. **Wiseman puts it, they "normalize violence:** Wiseman, R. (2002). *Queen bees & wannabes: Helping your daughter survive cliques, gossip, boyfriends, and other realities of adolescence.* New York: Crown.

142. **United States Congress "issued:** Schor, J. (2004). *Born to buy: The commercialized child and the new consumer culture.* New York: Scribner.

143. **In fact, we know from Chu that:** Chu, J. Y., & Gilligan, C. (n.d.). *When boys become boys: Development, relationships, and masculinity.*

144. **One radio host, Mike Francesca, who:** Cliff Pinckard, Northeast Ohio Media Group. (2014, April 04). New York Mets' Dan Murphy criticized for missing games for child's birth; team backs decision (poll) (video). Retrieved June 06, 2016, from http://www.cleveland.com/tribe/index.ssf/2014/04/new_york_mets_dan_murphy_criti.html

145. **A radio host by the name of Esiason:** Cliff Pinckard, Northeast Ohio Media Group. (2014, April 04). New York Mets' Dan Murphy criticized for missing games for child's birth; team backs decision (poll) (video).

Retrieved June 06, 2016, from
http://www.cleveland.com/tribe/index.ssf/2014/04/new_york_mets_dan_murphy_criti.html

146. **About 1 out of every 6 custodial:** Custodial Mothers and Fathers and Their Child Support: 2009. (n.d.).
Retrieved June 6, 2016, from http://www.census.gov/prod/2011pubs/p60-240.pdf

147. **As one study said:** McCabe, J., Fairchild, E., Grauerholz, L., Pescosolido, B. A., & Tope, D. (n.d.). Gender
in Twentieth-Century Children's Books. Retrieved June 06, 2016, from
http://gas.sagepub.com/content/25/2/197.abstract

148. **One absolutely enormous study researched:** McCabe, J., Fairchild, E., Grauerholz, L., Pescosolido, B. A.,
& Tope, D. (n.d.). Gender in Twentieth-Century Children's Books. Retrieved June 06, 2016, from
http://gas.sagepub.com/content/25/2/197.abstract

149. **They concluded that:** McCabe, J., Fairchild, E., Grauerholz, L., Pescosolido, B. A., & Tope, D. (n.d.).
Gender in Twentieth-Century Children's Books. Retrieved June 06, 2016, from
http://gas.sagepub.com/content/25/2/197.abstract

150. **Here are some of the interesting things:** McCabe, J., Fairchild, E., Grauerholz, L., Pescosolido, B. A., &
Tope, D. (n.d.). Gender in Twentieth-Century Children's Books. Retrieved June 06, 2016, from
http://gas.sagepub.com/content/25/2/197.abstract

151. **As the study puts it:** McCabe, J., Fairchild, E., Grauerholz, L., Pescosolido, B. A., & Tope, D. (n.d.).
Gender in Twentieth-Century Children's Books. Retrieved June 06, 2016, from
http://gas.sagepub.com/content/25/2/197.abstract

152. **In fact, "As a whole:** McCabe, J., Fairchild, E., Grauerholz, L., Pescosolido, B. A., & Tope, D. (n.d.).
Gender in Twentieth-Century Children's Books. Retrieved June 06, 2016, from
http://gas.sagepub.com/content/25/2/197.abstract

153. **They concluded that:** McCabe, J., Fairchild, E., Grauerholz, L., Pescosolido, B. A., & Tope, D. (n.d.).
Gender in Twentieth-Century Children's Books. Retrieved June 06, 2016, from
http://gas.sagepub.com/content/25/2/197.abstract

154. **Second, females are less frequently:** McCabe, J., Fairchild, E., Grauerholz, L., Pescosolido, B. A., &
Tope, D. (n.d.). Gender in Twentieth-Century Children's Books. Retrieved June 06, 2016, from
http://gas.sagepub.com/content/25/2/197.abstract

155. **This huge difference has:** McCabe, J., Fairchild, E., Grauerholz, L., Pescosolido, B. A., & Tope, D. (n.d.).
Gender in Twentieth-Century Children's Books. Retrieved June 06, 2016, from
http://gas.sagepub.com/content/25/2/197.abstract

156. But books are a "key source: McCabe, J., Fairchild, E., Grauerholz, L., Pescosolido, B. A., & Tope, D.
(n.d.). Gender in Twentieth-Century Children's Books. Retrieved June 06, 2016, from
http://gas.sagepub.com/content/25/2/197.abstract

157. **The study suggested that:** Beasley, B., & Standley, T. C. (2002). Shirts vs. Skins: Clothing as an Indicator
of Gender Role Stereotyping in Video Games. *Mass Communication and Society,5*(3), 279-293.
doi:10.1207/s15327825mcs0503_3

158. **Research shows that there is a significant:** University of Southern California. "Video Game Minority
Report: Lots Of Players, Few Characters." ScienceDaily. ScienceDaily, 30 July 2009.
<www.sciencedaily.com/releases/2009/07/090729140931.htm>.

159. **Males outnumber females 3 to 1 in family:** Research Informs & Empowers - See Jane. (n.d.). Retrieved
June 07, 2016, from http://seejane.org/research-informs-empowers/

160. **One study from Packaging Girlhood found:** *Packaging girlhood: Rescuing our daughters from
marketers' schemes.* New York: St. Martin's Press.

161. **The study on board games also found that:** *Packaging girlhood: Rescuing our daughters from marketers'
schemes.* New York: St. Martin's Press.

162. **On the other hand, girls:** *Packaging girlhood: Rescuing our daughters from marketers' schemes.* New
York: St. Martin's Press.

163. **One study gave Yale freshmen an article:** Coyle, D. (2009). *The talent code: Greatness isn't born: It's
grown, here's how.* New York: Bantam Books.

Mental Health

164. **One in five youth aged 13 to 18:** Any Disorder Among Children. (n.d.) Retrieved June 21, 2016, from http://www.nimh.nih.gov/health/statistics/prevalence/any-disorder-among-children.shtml - See more at: https://www.nami.org/Learn-More/Mental-Health-By-the-Numbers#sthash.Du0ETCvH.dpuf

165. **"Women must claim anorexia:** Wolf, N. (1991). *The beauty myth: How images of beauty are used against women.* New York: W. Morrow.

166. **Serious emotional and physical: Types & Symptoms of Eating Disorders | National Eating Disorders Association. (n.d.). Retrieved June 21, 2016, from http://www.nationaleatingdisorders.org/types-symptoms-eating-disorders**

167. **And according to the National Institute of:** Eating Disorders: About More Than Food. (n.d.). Retrieved June 21, 2016, from https://www.nimh.nih.gov/health/publications/eating-disorders-new-trifold/index.shtml

168. **The average woman is:** Center of Excellence for Eating Disorders. (n.d.). Retrieved June 21, 2016, from https://www.med.unc.edu/psych/eatingdisorders/Learn More/about-eating-disorders/statistics

169. **Susie Orbach in Fat is a Feminist Issue writes:** Orbach, S. (1978). *Fat is a feminist issue: The anti-diet guide to permanent weight loss.* New York: Paddington Press.

170. **One study proclaims that eating:** The Renfrew Center Foundation for Eating Disorders, "Eating Disorders 101 Guide: A Summary of Issues, Statistics and Resources," published September 2002, revised October 2003, http://www.renfrew.org.

171. **An estimated 10 to 15% of:** Carlat, D.J. Camargo. Review of Bulimia in Males. American Journal of Psychiatry, 154, 1997

172. **According to the National Institute:** Eating Disorders: About More Than Food. (n.d.). Retrieved June 21, 2016, from https://www.nimh.nih.gov/health/publications/eating-disorders-new-trifold/index.shtml

173. **Here are some characteristics of anorexia:** Anorexia Nervosa | National Eating Disorders Association. (n.d.). Retrieved June 21, 2016, from http://www.nationaleatingdisorders.org/anorexia-nervosa

174. **Fat is a Feminist Issue states:** Orbach, S. (1978). *Fat is a feminist issue: The anti-diet guide to permanent weight loss.* New York: Paddington Press.

175. **Orbach writes, "They:** Orbach, S. (1978). *Fat is a feminist issue: The anti-diet guide to permanent weight loss.* New York: Paddington Press.

176. **Liz Funk, author of Supergirls Speak Out:** Funk, L. (2009). *Supergirls speak out: Inside the secret crisis of overachieving girls.* New York: Simon & Schuster.

177. **According to the NIMH, bulimics:** Eating Disorders: About More Than Food. (n.d.). Retrieved June 21, 2016, from https://www.nimh.nih.gov/health/publications/eating-disorders-new-trifold/index.shtml

178. **As Mary Pipher, author of:** Pipher, M. B. (1994). *Reviving Ophelia: Saving the selves of adolescent girls.* New York: Putnam.

179. **Which I referenced using the NEDA website:** Bulimia Nervosa | National Eating Disorders Association. (n.d.). Retrieved June 21, 2016, from http://www.nationaleatingdisorders.org/bulimia-nervosa

180. **Though, with Urban Outfitters selling shirts:** Odell, A. (2010, June 04). Urban Outfitters Stopped Selling Its 'Eat Less' Shirt Online. Retrieved June 21, 2016, from http://nymag.com/thecut/2010/06/urban_outfitters_stopped_selli.html

181. **Binge Eating Disorder is:** What is Binge Eating Disorder? (2015, April 24). Retrieved June 21, 2016, from http://www.nedc.com.au/binge-eating-disorder

182. **According to the NEDA:** Binge Eating Disorder | National Eating Disorders Association. (n.d.). Retrieved June 21, 2016, from http://www.nationaleatingdisorders.org/binge-eating-disorder

183. **Reviving Ophelia suggests:** Pipher, M. B. (1994). *Reviving Ophelia: Saving the selves of adolescent girls.* New York: Putnam.

184. **The book continues, saying:** Pipher, M. B. (1994). *Reviving Ophelia: Saving the selves of adolescent girls.* New York: Putnam.

185. **Jean Kilbourne writes:** Kilbourne, J. (2000). *Can't buy my love: How advertising changes the way we think and feel*. Free Press.

186. **As <u>Body Outlaws</u> puts it:** Edut, O. (2003). *Body outlaws: Rewriting the rules of beauty and body image*. Emeryville, CA: Seal Press.

187. **Clinical depression is:** Depression. (2016, April). Retrieved June 21, 2016, from http://www.who.int/mediacentre/factsheets/fs369/en/

188. **The National Alliance on Mental Illness:** Pomona Valley. (n.d.). Retrieved June 21, 2016, from http://namipv.org/depression/

189. **Kalman Heller, PhD from:** Heller, K., PhD. (2012, October 15). Depression in Teens and Children | Psych Central. Retrieved June 21, 2016, from http://psychcentral.com/lib/depression-in-teens-and-children/

190. **The World Health Organization states:** Depression. (2016, April). Retrieved June 21, 2016, from http://www.who.int/mediacentre/factsheets/fs369/en/

191. **Sadly, white males have:** Suicide Statistics - AFSP. (n.d.). Retrieved June 21, 2016, from https://afsp.org/about-suicide/suicide-statistics/

192. **46% of trans men have attempted:** Haas, A. P., Ph.D., Rodgers, P. L., Ph.D., & Herman, J. L., Ph.D. (2014, January). Suicide Attempts Among Transgender and Gender Non-Conforming Adults: FINDINGS OF THE NATIONAL TRANSGENDER DISCRIMINATION SURVEY. Retrieved June 21, 2016, from http://williamsinstitute.law.ucla.edu/wp-content/uploads/AFSP-Williams-Suicide-Report-Final.pdf

193. **Moreover, suicide affects multiracial:** Haas, A. P., Ph.D., Rodgers, P. L., Ph.D., & Herman, J. L., Ph.D. (2014, January). Suicide Attempts Among Transgender and Gender Non-Conforming Adults: FINDINGS OF THE NATIONAL TRANSGENDER DISCRIMINATION SURVEY. Retrieved June 21, 2016, from http://williamsinstitute.law.ucla.edu/wp-content/uploads/AFSP-Williams-Suicide-Report-Final.pdf

194. **The National Institute of Mental Health outlines:** Depression. (n.d.). Retrieved June 21, 2016, from https://www.nimh.nih.gov/health/topics/depression/index.shtml

195. **Leymah Gbowee summed up depression:** Gbowee, L., & Mithers, C. L. (2011). *Mighty be our powers: How sisterhood, prayer, and sex changed a nation at war: A memoir*. New York: Beast.

196. **The best description I have EVER:** Lenker, M. (2015, August 01). 5 Times J.K. Rowling Got Real About Depression. Retrieved July 08, 2016, from https://themighty.com/2015/08/5-times-j-k-rowling-got-real-about-depression/

197. **Depression can be traced back throughout:** NEMADE, R., Ph.D., STAATS REISS, N., Ph.D., & DOMBECK, M., Ph.D. (2007, September 19). Historical Understandings Of Depression. Retrieved July 08, 2016, from https://www.mentalhelp.net/articles/historical-understandings-of-depression/

198. **In <u>Reviving Ophelia:</u>** Pipher, M. B. (1994). *Reviving Ophelia: Saving the selves of adolescent girls*. New York: Putnam.

199. **I found that self-harm is growing in rates higher:** Magaldi, K. (2015, June 25). Why Do People Self-Harm? It's More Complicated Than You Think. Retrieved July 08, 2016, from http://www.medicaldaily.com/self-harm-rise-teens-and-needing-attention-has-nothing-do-it-339974

200. **Sexually repressive Victorian Era:** Spiegel, A. (2005, June 10). The History and Mentality of Self-Mutilation. Retrieved July 08, 2016, from http://www.npr.org/templates/story/story.php?storyId=4697319

201. **During the Victorian age:** Spiegel, A. (2005, June 10). The History and Mentality of Self-Mutilation. Retrieved July 08, 2016, from http://www.npr.org/templates/story/story.php?storyId=4697319

202. **The 'needle girls' were often:** Steggals, P. (2015). *Making sense of self-harm: The cultural meaning and social context of non-suicidal self-injury*.

203. **Before puberty, boys and girls are:** Mental Health, N. (2015). Child Depression and Adolescent Depression. *Psych Central*. Retrieved on July 8, 2016 from http://psychcentral.com/lib/child-depression-and-adolescent-depression/

204. **Pipher states:** Pipher, M. B. (1994). *Reviving Ophelia: Saving the selves of adolescent girls*. New York: Putnam.

205. **Addiction is defined by the:** American Society of Addiction Medicine. (n.d.). Retrieved July 13, 2016, from http://www.asam.org/quality-practice/definition-of-addiction

206. **Jarin Kasper, of the National Eating:** Jasper, K., Ph.D. (1989). Are Eating Disorders Addictions? Retrieved July 13, 2016, from http://nedic.ca/sites/default/files/files/Are Eating Disorders Addictions.pdf

207. **Jean Kilbourne, advertising:** Kilbourne, J. (2000). *Can't buy my love: How advertising changes the way we think and feel.* Free Press.

208. **2.05 billion dollars:** U.S. ad spend by medium 2013 | Statistic. (n.d.). Retrieved July 13, 2016, from http://www.statista.com/statistics/245318/advertising-spending-of-the-alcohol-industry-in-the-us-by-medium/

209. **Jean Kilbourne, they:** Kilbourne, J. (2000). *Can't buy my love: How advertising changes the way we think and feel.* Free Press.

210. **A National Survey from 2005:** Pratt, L. A., Ph.D., & Brody, D. J., M.P.H. (2010, January 19). Depression in the United States Household Population, 2005-2006. Retrieved July 13, 2016, from http://www.cdc.gov/nchs/products/databriefs/db07.htm

211. **Here's a VERY shortened:** All About Depression: Overview. (n.d.). Retrieved July 13, 2016, from http://www.allaboutdepression.com/gen_01.html

212. **Orbach writes:** Orbach, S. (1978). *Fat is a feminist issue: The anti-diet guide to permanent weight loss.* New York: Paddington Press.

213. **Here are a few of the problems:** Health Consequences of Eating Disorders | National Eating Disorders Association. (n.d.). Retrieved July 13, 2016, from https://www.nationaleatingdisorders.org/health-consequences-eating-disorders

214. **Kilbourne writes:** Kilbourne, J. (2000). *Can't buy my love: How advertising changes the way we think and feel.* Free Press.

215. **Kilbourne writes, "The:** Kilbourne, J. (2000). *Can't buy my love: How advertising changes the way we think and feel.* Free Press.

216. **Jean Kilbourne, advertising expert:** Kilbourne, J. (2000). *Can't buy my love: How advertising changes the way we think and feel.* Free Press.

217. **Naomi Wolf wrote in The Beauty Myth:** Wolf, N. (1991). *The beauty myth: How images of beauty are used against women.* New York: W. Morrow.

218. **Orbach writes:** Orbach, S. (1978). *Fat is a feminist issue: The anti-diet guide to permanent weight loss.* New York: Paddington Press.

219. **She "concluded that:** Victoria L. Brescoll. (n.d.). Retrieved July 21, 2016, from http://som.yale.edu/victoria-l-brescoll

220. **As Jean Kilbourne writes:** Kilbourne, J. (2000). *Can't buy my love: How advertising changes the way we think and feel.* Free Press.

221. **Orbach reiterates this statement:** Orbach, S. (1978). *Fat is a feminist issue: The anti-diet guide to permanent weight loss.* New York: Paddington Press.

222. **"Everyone thinks of changing:** A quote by Leo Tolstoy. (n.d.). Retrieved July 21, 2016, from https://www.goodreads.com/quotes/12841-everyone-thinks-of-changing-the-world-but-no-one-thinks

223. **"Yesterday I was clever, so:** A quote by Rumi. (n.d.). Retrieved July 21, 2016, from https://www.goodreads.com/quotes/551027

224. **Albert Einstein offers our solution:** A quote by Albert Einstein. (n.d.). Retrieved July 21, 2016, from https://www.goodreads.com/quotes/1799-the-world-as-we-have-created-it-is-a-process

225. **A study of college-age females:** Children, Teens, Media, and Body Image | Common Sense Media. (n.d.). Retrieved July 21, 2016, from https://www.commonsensemedia.org/research/children-teens-media-and-body-image

226. **Depression help service Samaritans:** Listen, Ask, Get Help - Helping the Suicidal. (n.d.). Retrieved July 21, 2016, from http://samaritanshope.org/get-help/helping-suicidal/

227. **The Samaritans have a list of things:** The Samaritans of Bristol County - About Suicide. (n.d.). Retrieved July 22, 2016, from http://www.samaritans-bristolcounty.org/suicide.html

228. **Anorexia has the highest:** Sullivan, P. (1995). American Journal of Psychiatry, 152 (7), 10731074.

229. **The World Health Organization:** Suicide data. (n.d.). Retrieved July 22, 2016, from http://www.who.int/mental_health/prevention/suicide/suicideprevent/en/

230. **Only 1 in 10 people suffering:** Hoek and van Hoeken, 2003. Review of the prevalence and incidence of eating disorders. International Journal of Eating Disorders, 386-396.

231. **Additionally, only about a third of:** Pratt LA, Brody DJ. Depression in the U.S. household population, 2009–2012. NCHS data brief, no 172. Hyattsville, MD: National Center for Health Statistics. 2014.

232. **62% of females have dreamed of:** This was taken from a personal survey I conducted on SurveyMonkey - this is not scientifically accurate, though it provides interesting insight.

233. **"Never doubt that a:** A quote by Margaret Mead. (n.d.). Retrieved July 22, 2016, from https://www.goodreads.com/quotes/1071-never-doubt-that-a-small-group-of-thoughtful-committed-citizens

Sexualization

234. **"Developing sense of oneself as:** American Psychological Association,Task Force on the Sexualization of Girls. (2007). Report of the APA Task Force on the Sexualization of Girls. Retrieved from http://www.apa.org/pi/women/programs/girls/report-full.pdf

235. **"Cross culturally, unequal nakedness:** Wolf, N. (1991). *The beauty myth: How images of beauty are used against women*. New York: W. Morrow.

236. **"Nobody's surprised that girls:** Schnall, M. (2013). *What will it take to make a woman president?: Conversations about women, leadership and power*. Berkeley, CA: Seal Press.

237. **The World Health Organization defines:** Sexual health. (n.d.). Retrieved June 07, 2016, from http://www.who.int/topics/sexual_health/en/

238. **Mary Pipher writes in Reviving Ophelia:** Pipher, M. B. (1994). *Reviving Ophelia: Saving the selves of adolescent girls*. New York: Putnam.

239. **According to a 2001 study, 63% of:** commissioned by the American Association of University Women ; researched by Harris/Scholastic Research. (1993). Hostile hallways : the AAUW survey on sexual harassment in America's schools. Washington, D.C. :AAUW Educational Foundation,

240. **Though research is limited, research:** RESULTS OF 2015 UNIVERSITY OF MICHIGAN CAMPUS CLIMATE SURVEY ON SEXUAL MISCONDUCT. (n.d.). Retrieved June 7, 2016, from https://publicaffairs.vpcomm.umich.edu/wp-content/uploads/sites/19/2015/04/Complete-survey-results.pdf

241. **To begin with, 1 in 4 girls and 1 in 6 boys:** Finkelhor, D., Hotaling, G., Lewis, I. A., & Smith, C. (1990). Sexual abuse in a national survey of adult men and women: Prevalence, characteristics and risk factors. Child Abuse & Neglect 14, 19-28. doi:10.1016/0145-2134(90)90077-7

242. **1 in 5 women and 1 in 71 men:** Black, M. C., Basile, K. C., Breiding, M. J., Smith, S .G., Walters, M. L., Merrick, M. T., ... Stevens, M. R. (2011). The National Intimate Partner and Sexual Violence Survey: 2010 summary report. Retrieved from the Centers for Disease Control and Prevention, National Center for Injury Prevention and Control: http://www.cdc.gov/ViolencePrevention/pdf/NISVS_Report2010-a.pdf

243. **American Indians are twice:** Department of Justice, Office of Justice Programs, Bureau of Justice Statistics, American Indians and Crime, 1992-2002 (2004).

244. **Rape rates are disproportionately high:** Department of Justice, Office of Justice Programs, Bureau of Justice Statistics, Sexual Victimization in Prisons and Jails Reported by Inmates, 2011-2012 (2013).

245. **46% lesbians and 75% bisexual women:** Walters, M.L., Chen J., & Breiding, M.J. (2013). The National Intimate Partner and Sexual Violence Survey (NISVS): 2010 Findings on Victimization by Sexual Orientation. Retrieved from the Centers for Disease Control and Prevention, National Center for Injury Prevention and Control: http://www.cdc.gov/ViolencePrevention/pdf/NISVS_SOfindings.pdf

246. **Nearly 1.5 million:** Centers for Disease Control and Prevention, "Physical Dating Violence Among High School Students—United States, 2003," Morbidity and Mortality Weekly Report, May 19, 2006, Vol. 55, No. 19.

247. **One in ten high school students:** Grunbaum JA, Kann L, Kinchen S, et al. 2004. Youth Risk Behavior Surveillance—United States, 2003. Morbidity and Mortality Weekly Report. 53(SS02); 1-96. Available at http://www.cdc.gov/mmwr/preview/mmwrhtml/ss5302a1.htm.

248. **One in three adolescent girls in the U.S. is:** Davis, Antoinette, MPH. 2008. Interpersonal and Physical Dating Violence among Teens. The National Council on Crime and Delinquency Focus. Available at http://www.nccd-crc.org/nccd/pubs/2008_focus_teen_dating_violence.pdf

249. **Nearly half of dating college women report:** 8 Fifth & Pacific Companies, Inc. (Formerly: Liz Claiborne, Inc.), Conducted by Knowledge Networks, (December 2010). "College Dating Violence and Abuse Poll," Available at: https://www.breakthecycle.org/surveys.

250. **Females between the ages of 16 and 24:** Department of Justice, Bureau of Justice and Statistics, Intimate Partner Violence in the United States, 1993-2004. Dec. 2006.

251. **Disabled individuals face abuse at much higher:** Violence against adults and children with disabilities. (n.d.). Retrieved June 10, 2016, from http://www.who.int/disabilities/violence/en/

252. **Seventeen Magazine and the Henry J. Kaiser Family Foundation:** *Communication: A Series of National Surveys of Teens about Sex.* Menlo Park, CA: Henry J. Kaiser Family Foundation, 2002.

253. **One study found that parents :** Eisenberg ME et al., Parents' beliefs about condoms and oral contraceptives: Are they medically accurate? *Perspectives on Sexual and Reproductive Health,* 2004, 36(2):50–57.

254. **Only 24 states and the District of Columbia:** Sex and HIV Education. (2016). Retrieved June 10, 2016, from https://www.guttmacher.org/state-policy/explore/sex-and-hiv-education

255. **Only 13 states require that:** Sex and HIV Education. (2016). Retrieved June 10, 2016, from https://www.guttmacher.org/state-policy/explore/sex-and-hiv-education

256. **81% of parents believe teen:** "Women's Health," June/July 2004, Family Violence Prevention Fund and Advocates for Youth, http://www.med.umich.edu/whp/newsletters/summer04/p03-dating.html.

257. **Half of teenagers have had sex by age 17:** Finer LB and Philbin JM, Sexual initiation, contraceptive use, and pregnancy among young adolescents, *Pediatrics,* 2013, 131(5):886–891.

258. **Nearly a quarter of teens have posted nude:** Teenage Sexting Statistics | GuardChild. (n.d.). Retrieved June 10, 2016, from http://www.guardchild.com/teenage-sexting-statistics/

259. **The harsh reality is the largest group:** Internet Statistics | GuardChild. (n.d.). Retrieved June 10, 2016, from http://www.guardchild.com/statistics/

260. **51% of boys have viewed porn:** Michael Leahy, Porn University: What College Students Are Really Saying About Sex on Campus (Chicago: Northfield

261. **Average exposure of males to pornography:** Elizabeth M. Morgan, "Association between young adults' use of sexually explicit materials and their sexual preferences, behaviors, and satisfaction," Journal of Sex Research 48 (2011): 520–530.

262. **32% of females have viewed porn:** Michael Leahy, Porn University: What College Students Are Really Saying About Sex on Campus (Chicago: Northfield

263. **88% of top rated porn :** Ana Bridges, Robert Wosnitzer, Chyng Sun, and Rachael Liberman, "Aggression and sexual behavior in best-selling pornography videos: A content analysis update," Violence Against Women 16 (Oct. 2010): 1065-1085.

264. **Here are some of the things that kids:** Chiara Sabina, Janis Wolak, and David Finkelhor, "The nature and dynamics of Internet pornography exposure for youth," *CyberPsychology and Behavior* 11 (2008): 691-693.

265. **She writes that:** Dines, G. (2010). *Pornland: How porn has hijacked our sexuality.* Boston: Beacon Press.

266. **"vaginal, anal, and oral:** Dines, G. (2010). *Pornland: How porn has hijacked our sexuality.* Boston: Beacon Press.

267. **The US Department of Justice has even stated:** U.S. Department of Justice. Post Hearing Memorandum of Points and Authorities, at l, ACLU v. Reno, 929 F. Supp. 824, 1996.

268. **64% of college men and 18%:** Michael Leahy, *Porn University: What College Students Are Really Saying About Sex on Campus* (Chicago: Northfield Publishing, 2009).

269. **The Kaiser Family Foundation reports:** Kaiser Family Foundation, H. J. (2005). *Sex on TV 4* (Rep.). Retrieved June 11, 2016, from Kaiser Family Foundation website: https://kaiserfamilyfoundation.files.wordpress.com/2013/01/sex-on-tv-4-executive-summary.pdf

270. **In 2009, 92% of the 174 songs:** Grandoni, D. (2011, September 30). 92% of Top Ten Billboard Songs Are About Sex. Retrieved June 11, 2016, from http://www.thewire.com/entertainment/2011/09/92-top-ten-billboard-songs-are-about-sex/43182/

271. **The APA reports that 44:** American Psychological Association,Task Force on the Sexualization of Girls. (2007). Report of the APA Task Force on the Sexualization of Girls. Retrieved from http://www.apa.org/pi/women/programs/girls/report-full.pdf

272. **The American Psychological Association states that:** American Psychological Association,Task Force on the Sexualization of Girls. (2007). Report of the APA Task Force on the Sexualization of Girls. Retrieved from http://www.apa.org/pi/women/programs/girls/report-full.pdf

273. **Disgustingly, the APA reports that studies find:** American Psychological Association,Task Force on the Sexualization of Girls. (2007). Report of the APA Task Force on the Sexualization of Girls. Retrieved from http://www.apa.org/pi/women/programs/girls/report-full.pdf

274. **One study concluded, "Together:** Smith, S. L., & Choueiti, M. (2010). Gender Disparity On Screen and Behind the Camera in Family Films; The Executive Report. Retrieved June 4, 2016, from http://seejane.org/wp-content/uploads/full-study-gender-disparity-in-family-films-v2.pdf

275. **Studies have found that female artists:** American Psychological Association,Task Force on the Sexualization of Girls. (2007). Report of the APA Task Force on the Sexualization of Girls. Retrieved from http://www.apa.org/pi/women/programs/girls/report-full.pdf

276. **Furthermore, females are frequently portrayed:** American Psychological Association,Task Force on the Sexualization of Girls. (2007). Report of the APA Task Force on the Sexualization of Girls. Retrieved from http://www.apa.org/pi/women/programs/girls/report-full.pdf

277. **Ample evidence of the sexualization:** American Psychological Association,Task Force on the Sexualization of Girls. (2007). Report of the APA Task Force on the Sexualization of Girls. Retrieved from http://www.apa.org/pi/women/programs/girls/report-full.pdf

278. **In 2014, a 22 year old man named:** Yan, H., Almsay, S., & Sidner, S. (2014, May 27). California mass killer thought plan was over during April visit by deputies. Retrieved June 11, 2016, from http://www.cnn.com/2014/05/25/justice/california-shooting-deaths/

279. **According to him:** Rodger, E. (2014, April 23). Life is so unfair because girls dont want me. Retrieved June 11, 2016, from https://www.youtube.com/watch?v=7KP62TE1prs

280. **A 16 year old girl was killed:** Katersky, A., & Newcomb, A. (2014, April 25). Conn. High School Student Stabbed to Death Over Apparent Prom Date Rejection. Retrieved June 11, 2016, from http://abcnews.go.com/US/conn-high-school-student-stabbed-death-apparent-prom/story?id=23470009

281. **A woman was shot and killed:** Abbey-Lambertz, K. (2014, October 07). Woman Shot, Killed After Saying No To A Man's Advances, Detroit Police Say. Retrieved June 11, 2016, from http://www.huffingtonpost.com/2014/10/07/mary-spears-killed-detroit_n_5945518.html

282. **A pregnant woman was slammed:** Wilson, M. D. (2014, November 10). Pregnant woman slammed on the ground, stabbed after rejecting man's advances. Retrieved June 11, 2016, from http://www.mysanantonio.com/news/local/article/Woman-eight-moths-pregnant-slammed-on-the-5883072.php

283. **Dines writes how porn:** Dines, G. (2010). *Pornland: How porn has hijacked our sexuality.* Boston: Beacon Press.

284. **Fight the New Drug, a company dedicated:** Porn Kills Love. (2014, August 8). Retrieved June 11, 2016, from http://fightthenewdrug.org/porn-kills-love/

285. **One study found that about 84%one study found that about 84%:** American Psychological Association,Task Force on the Sexualization of Girls. (2007). Report of the APA Task Force on the Sexualization of Girls. Retrieved from

286. **Statistics show that the:** Grant, Jaime M., Lisa A. Mottet, Justin Tanis, Jack Harrison, Jody L. Herman, and Mara Keisling. Injustice at Every Turn: A Report of the National Transgender Discrimination Survey. Washington: National Center for Transgender Equality and National Gay and Lesbian Task Force, 2011.

287. **"It isn't really sex that's a problem:** Durham, M. G. (2008). *The Lolita effect: The media sexualization of young girls and what we can do about it.* Woodstock, NY: Overlook Press.

288. **Jean Kilbourne writes:** Kilbourne, J. (2000). *Can't buy my love: How advertising changes the way we think and feel.* Free Press.

289. **Male participants who heard:** Fischer, P., & Greitemeyer, T. (2006). Music and Aggression: The Impact of Sexual-Aggressive Song Lyrics on Aggression-Related Thoughts, Emotions, and Behavior Toward the Same and the Opposite Sex. *Personality and Social Psychology Bulletin, 32*(9), 1165-1176. doi:10.1177/0146167206288670

290. **One study notes how rap:** Adams, T., & Fuller, D. (2006). The Words Have Changed But the Ideology Remains the Same: Misogynistic Lyrics in Rap Music. *Journal of Black Studies, 36*(6), 938-957. Retrieved from http://www.jstor.org/stable/40034353

291. **The study described how:** Adams, T., & Fuller, D. (2006). The Words Have Changed But the Ideology Remains the Same: Misogynistic Lyrics in Rap Music. *Journal of Black Studies, 36*(6), 938-957. Retrieved from http://www.jstor.org/stable/40034353

292. **Durham eloquently writes:** Durham, M. G. (2008). *The Lolita effect: The media sexualization of young girls and what we can do about it.* Woodstock, NY: Overlook Press.

293. **In 70% of occurrences:** Facts and Figures. (2013). Retrieved June 12, 2016, from
http://stoppornculture.org/about/about-the-issue/facts-and-figures-2/

294. **One study found that 95%:** Porn Leads to Violence. (n.d.). Retrieved June 12, 2016, from
http://fightthenewdrug.org/porn-leads-to-violence/

295. **In other words, _in porn:_** Porn Leads to Violence. (n.d.). Retrieved June 12, 2016, from
http://fightthenewdrug.org/porn-leads-to-violence/

296. **In a majority of pornography:** Dines, G. (2010). _Pornland: How porn has hijacked our sexuality._ Boston:
Beacon Press.

297. **Unfortunately, a majority of our media depicts sex:** Dines, G. (2010). _Pornland: How porn has hijacked
our sexuality._ Boston: Beacon Press.

298. **We also know that when people start:** Zillmann, D., and Bryant, J. (1984). Effects of Massive Exposure to
Pornography. In N. M. Malamuth and E. Donnerstein (Eds.) Pornography and Sexual Aggression. New
York: Academic Press.

299. **And, we know that people are more:** Layden, M. A. (2004). Committee on Commerce, Science, and
Transportation, Subcommittee on Science and Space, U.S. Senate, Hearing on the Brain Science Behind
Pornography Addiction, November 18; Cline, V. B. (2001). Pornography's Effect on Adults and Children.
New York: Morality in Media; Zillmann, D., and Bryant, J. (1984). Effects of Massive Exposure to
Pornography. In N. M. Malamuth and E. Donnerstein (Eds.) Pornography and Sexual Aggression. New
York: Academic Press.

300. **Moreover, one analysis of 33 studies:** Allen, M., Emmers, T., Gebhardt, L., and Giery, M. A. (1995).
Exposure to Pornography and Acceptance of the Rape Myth. Journal of Communication 45, 1: 5–26.

301. **Scarily, studies show that after viewing pornography men are more likely to:** Facts and Figures. (2013).
Retrieved June 14, 2016, from http://stoppornculture.org/about/about-the-issue/facts-and-figures-2/

302. **Several recent studies have found:** Facts and Figures. (2013). Retrieved June 14, 2016, from
http://stoppornculture.org/about/about-the-issue/facts-and-figures-2/

303. **The Lolita Effect puts it best saying:** Durham, M. G. (2008). _The Lolita effect: The media sexualization of
young girls and what we can do about it._ Woodstock, NY: Overlook Press.

304. **In Yes Means Yes!:** Friedman, J., & Valenti, J. (n.d.). _Yes means yes!: Visions of female sexual power & a
world without rape._

305. **The book noted, "Nowhere:** Friedman, J., & Valenti, J. (n.d.). _Yes means yes!: Visions of female sexual
power & a world without rape._

306. **Studies report that sex depicted:** Facts and Figures. (2013). Retrieved June 14, 2016, from
http://stoppornculture.org/about/about-the-issue/facts-and-figures-2/

307. **Moreover, an APA report states that:** American Psychological Association, Task Force on the
Sexualization of Girls. (2007). Report of the APA Task Force on the Sexualization of Girls. Retrieved from
http://www.apa.org/pi/women/programs/girls/report-full.pdf

308. **The Lolita Effect included:** Durham, M. G. (2008). _The Lolita effect: The media sexualization of young
girls and what we can do about it._ Woodstock, NY: Overlook Press.

309. **As The Lolita Effect puts it:** Durham, M. G. (2008). _The Lolita effect: The media sexualization of young
girls and what we can do about it._ Woodstock, NY: Overlook Press.

310. **The APA report says:** American Psychological Association, Task Force on the Sexualization of Girls.
(2007). Report of the APA Task Force on the Sexualization of Girls. Retrieved from
http://www.apa.org/pi/women/programs/girls/report-full.pdf

311. **Sadly, the simple truth is:** American Psychological Association, Task Force on the Sexualization of Girls.
(2007). Report of the APA Task Force on the Sexualization of Girls. Retrieved from
http://www.apa.org/pi/women/programs/girls/report-full.pdf

312. **That being stated, the APA reports that:** American Psychological Association, Task Force on the
Sexualization of Girls. (2007). Report of the APA Task Force on the Sexualization of Girls. Retrieved from
http://www.apa.org/pi/women/programs/girls/report-full.pdf

313. **John Berger famously once wrote:** Berger, J. (n.d.). A quote from Ways of Seeing. Retrieved June 14,
2016, from https://www.goodreads.com/quotes/380575-a-woman-must-continually-watch-herself-she-is-
almost-continually

314. **And, it's a fact that near constant:** American Psychological Association, Task Force on the Sexualization
of Girls. (2007). Report of the APA Task Force on the Sexualization of Girls. Retrieved from
http://www.apa.org/pi/women/programs/girls/report-full.pdf

315. **Sexualization is linked to:** American Psychological Association,Task Force on the Sexualization of Girls. (2007). Report of the APA Task Force on the Sexualization of Girls. Retrieved from http://www.apa.org/pi/women/programs/girls/report-full.pdf

316. **Globally, teen is the:** Facts and Figures. (2013). Retrieved June 14, 2016, from http://stoppornculture.org/about/about-the-issue/facts-and-figures-2/

317. **Men are more than 543%:** Steven Stack, Ira Wasserman, and Roger Kern, "Adult social bonds and use of Internet pornography." *Social Science Quarterly.* 85 (March 2004): 75-88.

318. **'Fight the New Drug' comments:** Porn Ruins Your Sex Life. (2014, August 8). Retrieved June 16, 2016, from http://fightthenewdrug.org/porn-ruins-your-sex-life/

319. **In fact, one study found that:** Kunkel D, Eyal K, Donnerstein E, Farrar KM, Biely E, Rideout V. Sexual socialization messages on entertainment television: comparing content trends 1997–2002. *Media Psychol.* 2007;9(3):595–622

320. **Dines notes that different colors:** Dines, G. (2010). *Pornland: How porn has hijacked our sexuality.* Boston: Beacon Press.

321. **Asian women are depicted:** Dines, G. (2010). *Pornland: How porn has hijacked our sexuality.* Boston: Beacon Press.

322. **As Dines puts it:** Dines, G. (2010). *Pornland: How porn has hijacked our sexuality.* Boston: Beacon Press.

323. **Yes Means Yes notes:** Friedman, J., & Valenti, J. (n.d.). *Yes means yes!: Visions of female sexual power & a world without rape.*

324. **Durham puts it clearly:** Durham, M. G. (2008). *The Lolita effect: The media sexualization of young girls and what we can do about it.* Woodstock, NY: Overlook Press.

325. **The United States has one:** About Teen Pregnancy. (2016, April 26). Retrieved June 16, 2016, from http://www.cdc.gov/teenpregnancy/about/

326. **More than half of all people:** Koutsky L. (1997). Epidemiology of genital human papillomavirus infection. American Journal of Medicine, 102(5A), 3-8.

327. **Because once again, Durham states:** Durham, M. G. (2008). *The Lolita effect: The media sexualization of young girls and what we can do about it.* Woodstock, NY: Overlook Press.

328. **One study found that teens who:** Kohler et al. "Abstinence-only and Comprehensive Sex Education and the Initiation of Sexual Activity and Teen Pregnancy." *Journal of Adolescent Health*, 42(4): 344-351.

329. **There are many studies like this:** Comprehensive Sex Education: Research and Results. (2009, September). Retrieved June 16, 2016, from http://www.advocatesforyouth.org/publications/1487#ref

330. **In the words of Yes Means Yes!:** Friedman, J., & Valenti, J. (n.d.). *Yes means yes!: Visions of female sexual power & a world without rape.*

331. **Durham wrote, "For girls:** Durham, M. G. (2008). *The Lolita effect: The media sexualization of young girls and what we can do about it.* Woodstock, NY: Overlook Press.

332. **In Female Chauvinist Pigs, Levy:** Levy, A. (2005). *Female chauvinist pigs: Women and the rise of raunch culture.* New York: Free Press.

333. **She continues to say:** Levy, A. (2005). *Female chauvinist pigs: Women and the rise of raunch culture.* New York: Free Press.

334. **The dictionary definition of rape is:** Rape. (n.d.). Retrieved June 17, 2016, from http://www.dictionary.com/browse/rape

335. **Sally Armstrong, author of Uprising:** Haddix, M. P. (2007). *Uprising.* New York: Simon & Schuster Books for Young Readers.

336. **From Queen Bees and Wannabe's:** Wiseman, R. (2002). *Queen bees & wannabes: Helping your daughter survive cliques, gossip, boyfriends, and other realities of adolescence.* New York: Crown.

337. **Queen Bee's and Wannabe's lists:** Wiseman, R. (2002). *Queen bees & wannabes: Helping your daughter survive cliques, gossip, boyfriends, and other realities of adolescence.* New York: Crown.

338. **Kilbourne notes that one of:** Schor, J. (2004). *Born to buy: The commercialized child and the new consumer culture.* New York: Scribner.

339. **According to The United States Department of Justice:** Sexual Assault. (2016, April 1). Retrieved June 17, 2016, from https://www.justice.gov/ovw/sexual-assault

340. **Levy questioned, "We:** Levy, A. (2005). *Female chauvinist pigs: Women and the rise of raunch culture.* New York: Free Press.

Empowerment

341. **"Your voice matters:** Lazo, K. (2016, June 17). *Feminism Isn't Dead, Its Gone Viral.* Speech presented at TEDxNavesink, Monmouth County, NJ.

342. **The word 'selfie' is now:** Selfie. (n.d.). Retrieved June 17, 2016, from http://www.oxforddictionaries.com/us/definition/american_english/selfie

343. **The President of the United:** https://twitter.com/potus

344. **Book Backlash, Faludi states:** Faludi, S. (1991). *Backlash: The undeclared war against American women.* New York: Crown.

345. **You've gained weight' was a compliment:** Goode, E. (1999, May 20). Study Finds TV Alters Fiji Girls' View of Body. Retrieved June 17, 2016, from http://www.nytimes.com/1999/05/20/world/study-finds-tv-alters-fiji-girls-view-of-body.html

346. **Nonexistent at 3%:** Goode, E. (1999, May 20). Study Finds TV Alters Fiji Girls' View of Body. Retrieved June 17, 2016, from http://www.nytimes.com/1999/05/20/world/study-finds-tv-alters-fiji-girls-view-of-body.html

347. **But within three years:** Goode, E. (1999, May 20). Study Finds TV Alters Fiji Girls' View of Body. Retrieved June 17, 2016, from http://www.nytimes.com/1999/05/20/world/study-finds-tv-alters-fiji-girls-view-of-body.html

348. **64% of online teens ages 12-17:** Lenhart, A., Madden, M., Smith, A., & Macgill, A. (2007, December 19). Teens and Social Media. Retrieved June 17, 2016, from http://www.pewinternet.org/2007/12/19/teens-and-social-media/

349. **Courtney E. Martin described an:** Martin, C. E. (2007). *Perfect girls, starving daughters: The frightening new normalcy of hating your body.* New York: Free Press.

350. **Courtney's story "began:** Martin, C. E. (2007). *Perfect girls, starving daughters: The frightening new normalcy of hating your body.* New York: Free Press.

351. **In 1963, Betty Friedan questioned:** Friedan, B. (1963). *The feminine mystique.* New York: W.W. Norton.

352. **In 1990, Naomi Wolf questioned:** Wolf, N. (1991). *The beauty myth: How images of beauty are used against women.* New York: W. Morrow.

353. **Nancy Pelosi once wrote:** Pelosi, N., & Hearth, A. H. (2008). *Know your power: A message to America's daughters.* New York: Doubleday.

Acknowledgements

"Alone we can do so little, together we can do so much." - Helen Keller

Wow. I am sort of in awe right now that I'm writing acknowledgements. I literally cannot believe that I am finally done with this big project and that it actually, somehow got finished.

I am one hundred percent confident that I could NOT have written a book without the incredible help I got from so many people...I am seriously SO blessed to have such helpful, supportive, and generous people in my life.

So here we go:

Mom - You are the most selfless individual I have ever known. Thank you for giving up everything to raise me...I owe so much of my success to you. I'm so glad you're my mom, and can't imagine being raised any other way. And thank you especially for paying attention to detail during the final edit. This book would have turned out VERY differently without your guidance and assistance. I love you!

Dad - Dad, thank you for everything. Thank you for things like driving me to speeches, for helping me when I'm stuck on something, and for your sage business advice. But more importantly, thank you for loving me and letting me reach my full potential. I love you so much and you really are a 'warrior dad'.

Mrs. Grady - You were the first person to believe in me. You could have easily shut me down...I was a 15 year old with a vague big idea who was asking for a lot, but instead you believed in me. And not only that, but you have supported me and helped me throughout this entire journey. I cannot thank you enough for your kindness; I truly would not have accomplished any of this if it weren't for you. Thank you so so SO much for your endless love and support.

Mrs. Worrell - Thank you for giving up so much of your time to help me...I can't even believe how lucky I am to have a mentor like you, who always treats my work so seriously. Thank you for vouching for me always, and especially for helping me think through my setbacks. Whenever I walk out of a meeting of ours I feel a million times better, reenergized, and ready to tackle the next thing.

Mr. Franchock - Thank you thank you THANK YOU for teaching me that I have an 'equal voice within the discourse'. I am so grateful you taught me how to think critically - before your class, I simply accepted nearly everything I was given. I so appreciate the tireless effort and dedication you put into critiquing my writing and making it stronger. My writing has strengthened so much since your class, and I owe it all to you...you are the best teacher I've ever had.

Ms. Murray - You are the best guidance counselor, friend, and mentor that I could have ever asked for. Thank you for always supporting me and helping me carry out my work - even if that means giving up part of your weekend to come supervise a workshop. Thank you for always giving me critical advice - both personally and for my work.

Barbara - Thank you so much for editing my book and giving me important feedback! You are such an amazing editor and person and I know that God made us meet for a good reason. This book would have been VERY different if it weren't for your help, and not a good different.

Hopkinton Public Schools - Honestly, I am so endlessly grateful that I got to experience such high quality education. Thank you for becoming a second home to me and giving me opportunities to grow from and lead from. I feel very blessed to have received such a great education, and I do not underestimate what a role that has played in my success. Because of HPS, I want to work (eventually) in the education field.

Ms. Gifford, Valerie, and Tommy - You three have created safe, comfortable, happy environments for me to grow up in, and for that I am forever grateful. Each of you have supported me much more than you realize, and each of you has helped me grow into the person I am today. You are all incredible leaders and I have learned from each of you...thank you for theater.

Mr. Simoes - While writing this book, I thought a lot about your teaching style. You took difficult concepts and broke them down into simple, easy to understand points. You also made learning fun and enjoyable, through storytelling and humor. I tried to mimic some of your teaching strategies in this book, so thank you for being such an effective and awesome teacher!!

Maddie - Maddie. I don't even know how to *begin* to sum up what you mean to me. But I do know that I would not have even CONSIDERED dreaming this big without you. Thank you for relentlessly chasing your passions and being yourself always...you have showed me firsthand that young girls CAN make a difference.

Emily - You are the most generous, selfless person I have ever met. Thank you for not only designing my cover art, but also for tirelessly editing my work. Don't know where I would be without our adventures full of coffee, friendship, and car rides.

Lexie - Thanks for being brave enough to create a MOVEment with me. You're an exceptional person and friend and I am so grateful we've been on this journey together. Very happy to call you my best friend and business buddy :)

Everyone who wrote for this book - Honestly cannot thank you kind people enough. I am so glad that each of you contributed your own beautiful voice and filled in a few of my many gaps. You all made this book possible, and I am forever grateful.

To the parents who signed up their kids for a 5 day summer program run by teenagers - Thank you for believing in Lexie and I. Though I usually have a lot of words, you leave me speechless for one of the first times probably ever.

To the MOVE girls and supporters of MOVE + my various other work – Thank you. You allow me to do what I am so passionate about, and for that I am forever grateful. None of this would be possible without you believing in me and giving me a chance...I am constantly humbled by your continual support, encouragement, and love. Your words mean so much more to me than you realize, and I love spending time with you and watching you all grow into the capable, driven, game changers I know you all are. Proud of you people.